COLLECT BRITISH STAMPS

A STANLEY GIBBONS CHECKLIST OF
THE STAMPS OF GREAT BRITAIN

1993 (Forty-fifth) Edition

STANLEY GIBBONS LTD
By Appointment to H. M. the Queen
Stanley Gibbons Ltd, London Philatelists.

London and Ringwood

COLLECT BRITISH STAMPS

The 1993 Edition

From the famous Penny Black of 1840 to the absorbing issues of today, the stamps of Great Britain are highly popular with collectors. *Collect British Stamps* has been our message since very early days – but particularly since the First Edition of this checklist in September 1967. This 45th edition includes all the recent issues. Prices have been carefully revised to reflect today's market. Total sales of *Collect British Stamps* are now over 3½ million copies.

Collect British Stamps appears in the autumn of each year. A more detailed Great Britain catalogue, the *Concise*, is published each spring. The *Great Britain Concise* incorporates many additional listings covering watermark varieties, phosphor omitted errors, missing colour errors, stamp booklets and special commemorative First Day Cover postmarks. It is ideally suited for the collector who wishes to discover more about GB stamps.

Listings in this edition of *Collect British Stamps* include all 1993 issues which have appeared up to the publication date.

Scope. *Collect British Stamps* comprises:

- All stamps with different watermark (*wmk*) or perforation (*perf*).
- Visible plate numbers on the Victorian issues.
- Graphite-lined and phosphor issues, including variations in the number of phosphor bands.
- First Day Covers for all Special Issues.
- Special Sections for Definitive and Regional First Day Covers of the present reign.
- Presentation, Gift and Souvenir Packs.
- Post Office Yearbooks.
- Regional issues and War Occupation stamps of Guernsey and Jersey.
- Postage Due and Official Stamps.
- Post Office Picture Cards (PHQ cards).
- Commemorative gutter pairs and "Traffic Light" gutter pairs listed as mint sets.
- Royal Mail Postage Labels priced as sets and on P.O. First Day Cover.

Stamps of the independent postal administrations of Guernsey, Isle of Man and Jersey are contained in *Collect Channel Islands and Isle of Man Stamps*.

Layout. Stamps are set out chronologically by date of issue. In the catalogue lists the first numeral is the Stanley Gibbons catalogue number; the black (boldface) numeral alongside is the type number referring to the respective illustration. A blank in this column implies that the number immediately above is repeated. The denomination and colour of the stamp are then shown. Before February 1971 British currency was:

£1 = 20s   One pound = twenty shillings *and*
1s = 12d   One shilling = twelve pence.

Upon decimalisation this became:

£1 = 100p   One pound = one hundred (new) pence.

The catalogue list then shows two price columns. The left-hand is for unused stamps and the right-hand for used. Corresponding small boxes are provided in which collectors may wish to check off the items in their collection.

Our method of indicating prices is:
Numerals for pence, e.g. 10 denotes 10p (10 pence). Numerals for pounds and pence, e.g. 4·25 denotes £4·25 (4 pounds and 25 pence). For £100 and above, prices are in whole pounds and so include the £ sign and omit the zeros for pence.

Colour illustrations. The colour illustrations of stamps are intended as a guide only; they may differ in shade from the originals.

Size of illustrations. To comply with Post Office regulations stamp illustrations are three-quarters linear size. Separate illustrations of surcharges, overprints and watermarks are actual size.

Prices. Prices quoted in this catalogue are our selling prices at the time the book went to press. They are for stamps in fine condition; in issues where condition varies we may ask more for the superb and less for the sub-standard. The unused prices for stamps of Queen Victoria to King Edward VIII are for lightly hinged examples. Unused prices for King George VI and Queen Elizabeth II are for unmounted mint (though when not available unmounted, mounted stamps are often supplied at a lower price). Prices for used stamps refer to postally used copies. All prices are subject to change without prior notice and we give no guarantee to supply all stamps priced, since it is not possible to keep every catalogued item in stock. Individual low value stamps sold at 399, Strand are liable to an additional handling charge.

In the price columns:

† = Does not exist.

(—) or blank = Exists, or may exist, but price cannot be quoted.

* = Not normally issued (the so-called 'Abnormals' of 1862–80).

Perforations. The 'perforation' is the number of holes in a length of 2 cm, as measured by the Gibbons *Instanta* gauge. The stamp is viewed against a dark background with the transparent gauge put on top of it. Perforations are quoted to the nearest half. Stamps without perforation are termed 'imperforate'.

From 1992 certain stamps occur with a large elliptical (oval) hole inserted in each line of vertical perforations. The £10 definitive, No. 1658, is unique in having two such holes in the horizontal perforations.

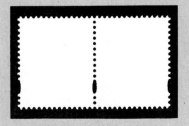

Elliptical perforations

Se-tenant combinations. *Se-tenant* means 'joined together'. Some sets include stamps of different design arranged *se-tenant* as blocks or strips and these are often collected unsevered as issued. Where such combinations exist the stamps are priced both mint and used, as singles or complete combinations. The set price for mint refers to the unsevered combination plus singles of any other values in the set. The used set price is for single stamps of all values.

First day covers. Prices for first day covers are for complete sets used on plain covers (1924, 1925, 1929) or on special covers (1935 onwards), the stamps of which are cancelled with ordinary operational postmarks (1924–1962) or by the *standard* "First Day of Issue" postmarks (1963 onwards). Where the stamps in a set were issued on different days, prices are for a cover from each day.

PHQ cards. Since 1973 the Post Office has produced a series of picture cards, which can be sent through the post as postcards. Each card shows an enlarged colour reproduction of a current British stamp, either of one or more values from a set or of all values. Cards are priced here in fine mint condition for sets complete as issued. The Post Office gives each card a 'PHQ' serial number, hence the term. The cards are usually on sale shortly before the date of issue of the stamps, but there is no officially designated 'first day'.

Used prices are for cards franked with the stamp depicted, on the obverse or reverse; the stamp being cancelled with an official postmark for first day of issue.

Gutter pairs. All modern Great Britain commemoratives are produced in sheets containing two panes of stamps separated by a blank horizontal or vertical margin known as a gutter. This feature first made its appearance on some supplies of the 1972 Royal Silver Wedding 3p, and marked the introduction of Harrison & Sons' new "Jumelle" stamp-printing press. There are advantages for both the printer and the Post

Office in such a layout which has now been used for all commemorative issues since 1974.

The term "gutter pair" is used for a pair of stamps separated by part of the blank gutter margin.

Gutter pair

Most printers include some form of colour check device on the sheet margins, in addition to the cylinder or plate numbers. Harrison & Sons use round "dabs", or spots of colour, resembling traffic lights. For the period from the 1972 Royal Silver Wedding until the end of 1979 these colour dabs appeared in the gutter margin. Gutter pairs showing these "traffic lights" are worth considerably more than the normal version.

Traffic light gutter pair

Catalogue numbers used. The checklist uses the same catalogue numbers as the Stanley Gibbons *British Commonwealth* Catalogue (Part 1), 1993 edition.

Latest issue date for stamps recorded in this edition is 9 November 1993.

STANLEY GIBBONS LTD

Head Office: 399 Strand, London WC2R 0LX
Auction Room and Specialist Stamp Departments—Open Monday-Friday 9.30 a.m to 5 p.m.
Shop—Open Monday to Friday 8.30 a.m. to 6 p.m. and Saturday 10.00 a.m. to 4 p.m.

Telephone 071-836 8444 for all departments

Stanley Gibbons Publications:
Editorial, Sales Offices and
  Distribution Centre,
5, Parkside, Christchurch Road,
Ringwood, Hants BH24 3SH.
Telephone 0425 472363

ISBN: 0-85259-359-7
© Stanley Gibbons Ltd 1993

Printed in Great Britain by BPCC Paulton Books Ltd, Bristol, Avon.

WIN A PUC £1

IN OUR FREE TO ENTER COMPETITION.

Imagine the satisfaction of being able to add a 1929 PUC £1. to your collection now you have your chance.

This mint PUC £1. valued at £500. is the prize in our *'free to enter'* Collect British Stamps competition. To become the proud owner, all you need to do is study the five questions shown overleaf, select the correct answers and complete the tie breaker question.

VALUE £500!

TEN RUNNER UP PRIZES

£10.00 Britannia

Even if you don't win the PUC £1. you will still have the chance of being one of ten collectors to receive a £10. Britannia presentation pack.

COMPETITION ENTRY FORM OVERLEAF

STUDY THE FOLLOWING QUESTIONS AND MARK YOUR ANSWERS BELOW.

The answers to the following questions can all be found in this edition of COLLECT BRITISH STAMPS:

1. The first £5 postage stamp appeared in the reign of:
   (A) *King George V*   (B) *Queen Elizabeth II*   (C) *Queen Victoria*

2. Which famous ship is featured on a 2s. 6d. stamp issued before 1952?
   (A) *Liner Queen Elizabeth*   (B) *Golden Hind*   (C) *H.M.S. Victory*

3. Which character from Shakespeare appears on a 2s. 6d. stamp of 1964?
   (A) *Hamlet*   (B) *King Lear*   (C) *Bottom*

4. Which of the King George V high values was not issued in a re-engraved version during 1934?
   (A) *10s.*   (B) *£1*   (C) *2s. 6d.*

5. Which watermark was used for the very first 5s., 10s. and £1 stamps?
   (A) *Orb*   (B) *Crown*   (C) *Maltese Cross*

OFFICIAL ENTRY FORM ···· CUT OUT & RETURN ····

COLLECT BRITISH STAMPS
— *PUC £1 Competition* —

The correct answers are:
PLEASE CIRCLE

Question 1	A	B	C	Name
Question 2	A	B	C	Address
Question 3	A	B	C	
Question 4	A	B	C	
Question 5	A	B	C	...........................Postcode...............

NOW COMPLETE THE TIE BREAK (No more than 25 words)

'I buy the Collect British Stamp catalogue because ....

....

....

Please return your completed entries to: ➡
DAVID AGGERSBERG (Catalogue Editor), STANLEY GIBBONS LIMITED., 5 PARKSIDE, CHRISTCHURCH ROAD, RINGWOOD, HANTS BH24 3SH

If you do not wish to be placed on our customer mailing list, to receive information regarding our range of quality philatelic products and special offers – tick this box ☐

CUT OUT & RETURN ···· OFFICIAL ENTRY FORM ···· CUT OUT & RETURN

QUEEN VICTORIA

1837 (20 June)–1901 (22 Jan.)

IDENTIFICATION. In this checklist ,Victorian stamps are classified firstly according to which printing method was used – line-engraving, embossing or surface-printing.

Corner letters. Numerous stamps also have letters in all four, or just the lower, corners. These were an anti-forgery device and the letters differ from stamp to stamp. If present in all four corners the upper pair are the reverse of the lower. Note the importance of these corner letters in the way the checklist is arranged.

Watermarks. Further classification depends on watermarks: these are illustrated in normal position, with stamps priced accordingly.

1 Line-engraved Issues

1

POSTAGE

1a

2

2a White lines added above and below head

3 Small Crown watermark

4 Large Crown watermark

Letters in lower corners

1840 *Wmk Small Crown Type 3* *Imperforate*

Cat. No.	Type			Unused	Used		
2	1	1d black	.. ..	£3000	£150	☐	☐
5	2	2d blue	.. ..	£5500	£300	☐	☐

1841

8	1a	1d red-brown	..	£130	3·50	☐	☐
14	2a	2d blue	.. ..	£1000	35·00	☐	☐

1854–57 (*i*) *Wmk Small Crown Type 3*   *Perf* 16

17	1a	1d red-brown	..	£150	3·50	☐	☐
19	2a	2d blue	.. ..	£1300	35·00	☐	☐

(*ii*) *Wmk Small Crown Type 3*   *Perf* 14

24	1a	1d red-brown	..	£250	16·00	☐	☐
23	2a	2d blue	.. ..	£1800	£120	☐	☐

(*iii*) *Wmk Large Crown Type 4*   *Perf* 16

26	1a	1d red ..	..	£500	35·00	☐	☐
27	2a	2d blue	.. ..	£2000	£130	☐	☐

(*iv*) *Wmk Large Crown Type 4*   *Perf* 14

40	1a	1d red ..	.. ..	25·00	1·00	☐	☐
34	2a	2d blue	.. ..	£1000	25·00	☐	☐

5

6 Watermark extending over three stamps

7

8

9

Letters in all four corners

Plate numbers. Stamps included a 'plate number' in their design and this affects valuation. The cheapest plates are priced here; see complete list of plate numbers overleaf.

1858–70 (*i*) *Wmk Type 6*   *Perf* 14

48	5	½d red	.. .. ..	45·00	6·00	☐	☐

(*ii*) *Wmk Large Crown Type 4*   *Perf* 14

43	7	1d red	.. .. ..	4·50	50	☐	☐
51	8	1½d red	.. .. ..	£150	18·00	☐	☐
45	9	2d blue	.. .. ..	£160	4·00	☐	☐

PLATE NUMBERS
on stamps of 1858–70 having letters in all four corners

Positions of Plate Numbers

Shows Plate 9 (½d)   Shows Plate 170 (1d, 2d)   Shows Plate 3 (1½d)

HALFPENNY VALUE (S.G. 48)

Plate	Un.	Used			Plate	Un.	Used		
1	95·00	40·00	□	□	11	45·00	6·00	□	□
3	60·00	14·00	□	□	12	45·00	6·00	□	□
4	75·00	8·00	□	□	13	45·00	6·00	□	□
5	55·00	6·00	□	□	14	45·00	6·00	□	□
6	45·00	6·00	□	□	15	60·00	9·00	□	□
8	85·00	40·00	□	□	19	90·00	18·00	□	□
9	£2250	£300	□	□	20	95·00	30·00	□	□
10	75·00	6·00	□	□					

Plates 2, 7, 16, 17 and 18 were not completed, while Plates 21 and 22, though made, were not used. Plate 9 was a reserve plate, not greatly used

PENNY VALUE (S.G. 43)

Plate	Un.	Used			Plate	Un.	Used			Plate	Un.	Used			Plate	Un.	Used		
71	12·00	2·00	□	□	112	30·00	1·00	□	□	154	7·50	50	□	□	190	7·00	3·50	□	□
72	18·00	2·50	□	□	113	8·00	7·50	□	□	155	8·00	75	□	□	191	4·50	4·00	□	□
73	12·00	2·00	□	□	114	£175	8·00	□	□	156	7·50	50	□	□	192	13·00	50	□	□
74	10·00	50	□	□	115	50·00	1·00	□	□	157	7·50	50	□	□	193	4·50	50	□	□
76	20·00	50	□	□	116	38·00	6·00	□	□	158	4·50	50	□	□	194	7·50	5·00	□	□
77	£50000	£30000	□	□	117	8·00	50	□	□	159	4·50	50	□	□	195	7·50	5·00	□	□
78	50·00	50	□	□	118	12·00	50	□	□	160	4·50	50	□	□	196	5·00	3·00	□	□
79	15·00	50	□	□	119	5·00	75	□	□	161	15·00	4·00	□	□	197	8·00	6·00	□	□
80	10·00	75	□	□	120	4·50	50	□	□	162	8·00	4·00	□	□	198	4·50	3·50	□	□
81	30·00	1·00	□	□	121	20·00	6·00	□	□	163	7·50	1·50	□	□	199	10·00	3·50	□	□
82	60·00	2·50	□	□	122	4·50	50	□	□	164	7·50	2·00	□	□	200	10·00	50	□	□
83	70·00	4·00	□	□	123	6·00	75	□	□	165	10·00	50	□	□	201	4·50	3·00	□	□
84	30·00	1·00	□	□	124	6·00	50	□	□	166	7·50	3·50	□	□	202	7·50	5·00	□	□
85	12·00	1·00	□	□	125	8·00	1·00	□	□	167	5·00	50	□	□	203	4·50	10·00	□	□
86	15·00	2·50	□	□	127	17·00	1·00	□	□	168	6·00	5·50	□	□	204	6·00	75	□	□
87	4·50	50	□	□	129	6·00	5·00	□	□	169	15·00	4·00	□	□	205	6·00	2·00	□	□
88	80·00	5·50	□	□	130	9·00	1·00	□	□	170	6·00	50	□	□	206	6·00	6·00	□	□
89	20·00	50	□	□	131	38·00	11·00	□	□	171	4·50	50	□	□	207	6·00	6·00	□	□
90	14·00	50	□	□	132	50·00	16·00	□	□	172	4·50	90	□	□	208	6·00	10·00	□	□
91	20·00	3·50	□	□	133	45·00	6·00	□	□	173	25·00	6·00	□	□	209	7·50	6·00	□	□
92	7·00	50	□	□	134	4·50	50	□	□	174	4·50	40	□	□	210	10·00	8·00	□	□
93	20·00	50	□	□	135	50·00	20·00	□	□	175	18·00	1·75	□	□	211	22·00	15·00	□	□
94	20·00	3·00	□	□	136	50·00	15·00	□	□	176	13·00	90	□	□	212	7·50	7·50	□	□
95	12·00	50	□	□	137	8·00	90	□	□	177	5·00	50	□	□	213	7·50	7·50	□	□
96	14·00	50	□	□	138	6·00	50	□	□	178	7·50	2·00	□	□	214	13·00	13·00	□	□
97	8·00	1·75	□	□	139	16·00	11·00	□	□	179	8·00	1·00	□	□	215	13·00	13·00	□	□
98	8·00	3·50	□	□	140	6·00	50	□	□	180	8·00	3·00	□	□	216	13·00	13·00	□	□
99	12·00	50	□	□	141	75·00	6·00	□	□	181	7·50	50	□	□	217	10·00	4·00	□	□
100	18·00	1·25	□	□	142	25·00	18·00	□	□	182	50·00	3·00	□	□	218	6·00	5·00	□	□
101	25·00	6·00	□	□	143	15·00	10·00	□	□	183	13·00	1·50	□	□	219	30·00	50·00	□	□
102	10·00	55	□	□	144	50·00	15·00	□	□	184	4·50	75	□	□	220	4·50	3·50	□	□
103	10·00	1·50	□	□	145	4·50	1·00	□	□	185	7·50	1·50	□	□	221	15·00	10·00	□	□
104	14·00	3·00	□	□	146	5·00	3·50	□	□	186	15·00	1·00	□	□	222	25·00	25·00	□	□
105	35·00	4·00	□	□	147	9·00	2·00	□	□	187	6·00	50	□	□	223	30·00	40·00	□	□
106	15·00	55	□	□	148	10·00	1·50	□	□	188	10·00	7·00	□	□	224	35·00	35·00	□	□
107	20·00	3·75	□	□	149	7·50	3·50	□	□	189	18·00	4·00	□	□	225	£1000	£300	□	□
108	15·00	1·00	□	□	150	4·50	50	□	□										
109	38·00	1·75	□	□	151	13·00	6·00	□	□										
110	10·00	6·00	□	□	152	9·00	3·25	□	□										
111	18·00	1·00	□	□	153	35·00	6·00	□	□										

Plates 69, 70, 75, 77, 126 and 128 were prepared but rejected. No stamps therefore exist, except for a very few from Plate 77 which somehow reached the public. Plate 177 stamps, by accident or design, are sometimes passed off as the rare Plate 77.

THREE-HALFPENNY VALUE (S.G. 51)

Plate	Un.	Used			Plate	Un.	Used		
(1)	£350	20·00	□	□	3	£150	18·00	□	□

Plate 1 did *not* have the plate number in the design. Plate 2 was not completed and no stamps exist.

TWOPENNY VALUE (S.G. 45)

Plate	Un.	Used			Plate	Un.	Used		
7	£400	18·00	□	□	13	£180	6·00	□	□
8	£450	14·00	□	□	14	£200	8·00	□	□
9	£160	4·00	□	□	15	£160	8·00	□	□
12	£700	40·00	□	□					

Plates 10 and 11 were prepared but rejected.

2 Embossed Issues

Prices are for stamps cut square and with average to fine embossing. Stamps with exceptionally clear embossing are worth more.

10

11

12

13

1847–54 *Wmk* **13** (6d), *no wmk* (*others*)   *Imperforate*

59	10	6d lilac ..	..	..	£2500	£400	□	□
57	11	10d brown	..	..	£2250	£575	□	□
54	12	1s green	..	..	£2750	£350	□	□

3 Surface-printed Issues

IDENTIFICATION. Check first whether the design includes corner letters or not, as mentioned for 'Line-engraved Issues'. The checklist is divided up according to whether any letters are small or large, also whether they are white (uncoloured) or printed in the colour of the stamp. Further identification then depends on watermark.

PERFORATION. Except for Nos. 126/9 all the following issues of Queen Victoria are perf 14.

14

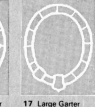

15 Small Garter   **16** Medium Garter   **17** Large Garter

18

19

20 Emblems

No corner letters

1855–57 (*i*) *Wmk Small Garter Type* **15**

62	14	4d red ..	..	..	£2250	£170	□	□

(*ii*) *Wmk Medium Garter Type* **16**

64	14	4d red ..	..	..	£1800	£150	□	□

(*iii*) *Wmk Large Garter Type* **17**

66a	14	4d red ..	..	..	£600	40·00	□	□

(*iv*) *Wmk Emblems Type* **20**

70	18	6d lilac ..	..	..	£500	40·00	□	□
72	19	1s green	..	..	£650	£140	□	□

Plate numbers. Stamps Nos. 90/163 should be checked for the 'plate numbers' indicated, as this affects valuation (the cheapest plates are priced here). The mark '*Pl.*' shows that several numbers exist, priced in a separate list overleaf.

Plate numbers are the small numerals appearing in duplicate in some part of the frame design or adjacent to the lower corner letters (in the 5s value a single numeral above the lower inscription).

21

22

23

24

25

Small white corner letters

1862–64 *Wmk Emblems Type* **20**, *except 4d* (*Large Garter Type* **17**)

77	21	3d red ..	..	..	£700	£100	□	□
80	22	4d red ..	..	..	£500	35·00	□	□
84	23	6d lilac ..	..	..	£650	30·00	□	□
87	24	9d bistre	..	..	£1100	£130	□	□
90	25	1s green *Pl.*	..	..	£700	65·00	□	□

26

27

28 (hyphen in SIX-PENCE)

32

33 Spray of Rose

34

29

30

31

Large white corner letters

1865–67 *Wmk Emblems Type* **20**, *except 4d* (*Large Garter Type* **17**)

92	**26**	3d red (Plate 4)	..	£375	40·00	☐	☐
94	**27**	4d vermilion *Pl.*		£225	15·00	☐	☐
97	**28**	6d lilac *Pl.*	..	£350	28·00	☐	☐
98	**29**	9d straw *Pl.* ..	..	£700	£200	☐	☐
99	**30**	10d brown (Plate 1)		†	£12000		☐
101	**31**	1s green (Plate 4)		£650	65·00	☐	☐

1867–80 *Wmk Spray of Rose Type* **33**

103	**26**	3d red *Pl.*	..	..	£200	12·00	☐	☐
105	**28**	6d lilac (with hyphen) (Plate 6)			£550	30·00	☐	☐
109		6d mauve (without hyphen) *Pl.*		..	£275	25·00	☐	☐
111	**29**	9d straw (Plate 4)			£600	£100	☐	☐
112	**30**	10d brown *Pl.*			£1000	£130	☐	☐
117	**31**	1s green *Pl.*	..	..	£350	10·00	☐	☐
119	**32**	2s blue *Pl.*	..	..	£950	60·00	☐	☐
121		2s brown (Plate 1)			£6000	£1000	☐	☐

1872–73 *Wmk Spray of Rose Type* **33**

123	**34**	6d brown *Pl.*	..	£350	18·00	☐	☐
125		6d grey (Plate 12)		£600	80·00	☐	☐

PLATE NUMBERS
on stamps
of 1862–83

Cat. No.		Plate No.	Un.	Used		

Small White Corner Letters (1862–64)

90	1s green	2	£700	65·00	☐	☐
		3	£11000		☐	☐

Plate 2 is actually numbered as '1' and Plate 3 as '2' on the stamps.

Large White Corner Letters (1865–83)

103	3d red	4	£300	50·00	☐	☐
		5	£200	14·00	☐	☐
		6	£225	12·00	☐	☐
		7	£275	15·00	☐	☐
		8	£250	14·00	☐	☐
		9	£250	20·00	☐	☐
		10	£275	42·00	☐	☐
94	4d verm	7	£300	19·00	☐	☐
		8	£250	19·00	☐	☐
		9	£250	15·00	☐	☐
		10	£300	30·00	☐	☐
		11	£250	15·00	☐	☐
		12	£225	15·00	☐	☐
		13	£250	17·00	☐	☐
		14	£300	35·00	☐	☐
97	6d lilac	5	£350	28·00	☐	☐
		6	£1000	55·00	☐	☐
109	6d mauve	8	£275	25·00	☐	☐
		9	£275	25·00	☐	☐
		10	*	£12000	☐	☐
123	6d brown	11	£350	18·00	☐	☐
		12	£750	55·00	☐	☐

98	9d straw	4	£700	£200	☐	☐
		5	£10000	*	☐	☐
112	10d brown	1	£1000	£130	☐	☐
		2	£12000	£2500	☐	☐
117	1s green	4	£350	15·00	☐	☐
		5	£400	12·00	☐	☐
		6	£550	10·00	☐	☐
		7	£550	30·00	☐	☐
119	2s blue	1	£950	60·00	☐	☐
		3	*	£3000	☐	☐
126	5s red	1	£2500	£250	☐	☐
		2	£3500	£325	☐	☐

Large Coloured Corner Letters (1873–83)

139	2½d mauve	1	£225	25·00	☐	☐
		2	£225	25·00	☐	☐
		3	£400	30·00	☐	☐
141	2½d mauve	3	£500	30·00	☐	☐
		4	£225	14·00	☐	☐
		5	£225	18·00	☐	☐
		6	£225	14·00	☐	☐
		7	£225	14·00	☐	☐
		8	£225	18·00	☐	☐
		9	£225	14·00	☐	☐
		10	£250	20·00	☐	☐
		11	£225	14·00	☐	☐
		12	£225	18·00	☐	☐
		13	£225	18·00	☐	☐
		14	£225	14·00	☐	☐
		15	£225	14·00	☐	☐
		16	£225	14·00	☐	☐
		17	£550	90·00	☐	☐
142	2½d blue	17	£180	20·00	☐	☐
		18	£200	12·00	☐	☐
		19	£180	10·00	☐	☐
		20	£180	10·00	☐	☐

157	2½d blue	21	£225	9·00	☐	☐
		22	£180	8·00	☐	☐
		23	£180	8·00	☐	☐
143	3d red	11	£200	12·00	☐	☐
		12	£225	14·00	☐	☐
		14	£250	15·00	☐	☐
		15	£200	14·00	☐	☐
		16	£200	14·00	☐	☐
		17	£225	14·00	☐	☐
		18	£225	14·00	☐	☐
		19	£200	14·00	☐	☐
		20	£200	30·00	☐	☐
158	3d red	20	£250	45·00	☐	☐
		21	£200	30·00	☐	☐
152	4d verm	15	£600	£140	☐	☐
		16	*	£10000	☐	☐
153	4d green	15	£450	95·00	☐	☐
		16	£400	90·00	☐	☐
		17	*	£6000	☐	☐
160	4d brown	17	£180	25·00	☐	☐
		18	£180	25·00	☐	☐
147	6d grey	13	£225	22·00	☐	☐
		14	£225	22·00	☐	☐
		15	£225	20·00	☐	☐
		16	£225	20·00	☐	☐
		17	£300	38·00	☐	☐
161	6d grey	17	£180	25·00	☐	☐
		18	£150	25·00	☐	☐
150	1s green	8	£325	35·00	☐	☐
		9	£325	35·00	☐	☐
		10	£300	35·00	☐	☐
		11	£300	35·00	☐	☐
		12	£250	28·00	☐	☐
		13	£250	28·00	☐	☐
		14	*	£10000	☐	☐
163	1s brown	13	£275	45·00	☐	☐
		14	£225	45·00	☐	☐

35

36

37

38

44

45

46

47 Small Anchor

48 Orb

Large coloured corner letters

1873–80 (*i*) *Wmk Small Anchor Type* **47**

139	41	2½d	mauve *Pl.*	..	£225	25·00	□ □

(*ii*) *Wmk Orb Type* **48**

141	41	2½d	mauve *Pl.*	..	£225	14·00	□ □
142		2½d	blue *Pl.*	..	£180	10·00	□ □

(*iii*) *Wmk Spray of Rose Type* **33**

143	42	3d	red *Pl.*	..	£200	12·00	□ □
145	43	6d	pale buff				
			(Plate 13)	..	*	£4500	□ □
147		6d	grey *Pl.*	..	£225	20·00	□ □
150	44	1s	green *Pl.*	..	£250	28·00	□ □
151		1s	brown (Plate 13)	£1100	£190		□ □

(*iv*) *Wmk Large Garter Type* **17**

152	45	4d	vermilion *Pl.*	..	£600	£140	□ □
153		4d	green *Pl.*	..	£400	90·00	□ □
154		4d	brown (Plate 17)	£600	£150		□ □
156	46	8d	orange (Plate 1)	£550	£110		□ □

49 Imperial Crown   **(50)** Surcharges in red **(51)**

1880–83 *Wmk Imperial Crown Type* **49**

157	41	2½d	blue *Pl.*	..	£180	8·00	□ □
158	42	3d	red *Pl.*	..	£200	30·00	□ □
159		3d	on 3d lilac				
			(surch Type 50)		£225	70·00	□ □
160	45	4d	brown *Pl.*	..	£180	25·00	□ □
161	43	6d	grey *Pl.*	..	£150	25·00	□ □
162		6d	on 6d lilac				
			(surch Type 51)		£200	70·00	□ □
163	44	1s	brown *Pl.*	..	£225	45·00	□ □

39 Maltese Cross   **40** Large Anchor

1867–83 (*i*) *Wmk Maltese Cross Type* **39**   *Perf* 15½ × 15

126	35	5s	red *Pl.*	.. ..	£2500	£250	□ □
128	36	10s	grey (Plate 1)	..	£18000	£850	□ □
129	37	£1	brown (Plate 1)		£22000	£1200	□ □

(*ii*) *Wmk Large Anchor Type* **40**   *Perf* 14

134	35	5s	red (Plate 4)	..	£4500	£850	□ □
131	36	10s	grey (Plate 1)		£20000	£1200	□ □
132	37	£1	brown (Plate 1)		£27000	£2250	□ □
137	38	£5	orange (Plate 1)		£4250	£1200	□ □

41

42

43

52

53

54

55

56

1880–81 *Wmk Imperial Crown Type* **49**

164	52	½d	green	..	..	15·00	3·00	☐ ☐
166	53	1d	brown	..	..	5·00	2·00	☐ ☐
167	54	1½d	brown	..	..	80·00	14·00	☐ ☐
168	55	2d	red ..		..	95·00	30·00	☐ ☐
169	56	5d	indigo	..	..	£350	45·00	☐ ☐

57

Die I

Die II

1881 *Wmk Imperial Crown Type* **49**

(*a*) **14** *dots in each corner, Die* I

171	57		1d lilac	..		75·00	12·00	☐ ☐

(*b*) **16** *dots in each corner, Die* II

173	57		1d lilac	..	..	1·00	30	☐ ☐

58

59

60

1883-84 *Wmk Anchor Type* **40**

179	58	2s 6d	deep lilac	..	..	£200	60·00	☐ ☐
181	59	5s	red	..	..	£400	75·00	☐ ☐
183	60	10s	blue ..	..	..	£750	£225	☐ ☐

61

1884 *Wmk 3 Imperial Crowns Type* **49**

185	61	£1	brown	..	..	£10000	£850	☐ ☐

1888 *Wmk 3 Orbs Type* **48**

186	61	£1	brown	..	..	£16000	£1300	☐ ☐

1891 *Wmk 3 Imperial Crowns Type* **49**

212	61	£1	green	..	..	£2000	£350	☐ ☐

62

63

64

65

66

1883–84 *Wmk Imperial Crown Type* **49** (*sideways on horiz. designs*)

187	52	½d	blue	..	..	8·00	1·50	☐ ☐
188	62	1½d	lilac	..	..	55·00	18·00	☐ ☐
189	63	2d	lilac	..	..	70·00	30·00	☐ ☐
190	64	2½d	lilac	..	..	40·00	5·00	☐ ☐
191	65	3d	lilac	..	..	90·00	40·00	☐ ☐
192	66	4d	dull green	..	..	£225	90·00	☐ ☐
193	62	5d	dull green	..	..	£225	90·00	☐ ☐
194	63	6d	dull green	..	..	£250	95·00	☐ ☐
195	64	9d	dull green	..	..	£475	£225	☐ ☐
196	65	1s	dull green	..	..	£350	£130	☐ ☐

The above prices are for stamps in the true dull green colour. Stamps which have been soaked, causing the colour to run, are virtually worthless.

67

68

69

70

71

72

73

74

75

76

77

78

KING EDWARD VII
1901 (22 Jan.)–1910 (6 May)

79

80

81

82

83

84

85

86

87

88

89

90

91

92

93

'Jubilee' issue
1887–1900 *The bicoloured stamps have the value tablets, or the frames including the value tablets, in the second colour.*
Wmk Imperial Crown Type **49**

197	**67**	½d vermilion ..	1·00	50	☐	☐
213		½d green*	1·00	60	☐	☐
198	**68**	1½d purple and green	10·00	4·00	☐	☐
200	**69**	2d green and red ..	15·00	6·00	☐	☐
201	**70**	2½d purple on blue	10·00	75	☐	☐
203	**71**	3d purple on yellow	15·00	1·50	☐	☐
205a	**72**	4d green and brown	18·00	7·25	☐	☐
206	**73**	4½d green and red ..	5·00	20·00	☐	☐
207a	**74**	5d purple and blue	18·00	6·00	☐	☐
208	**75**	6d purple on red ..	18·00	7·50	☐	☐
209	**76**	9d purple and blue	40·00	25·00	☐	☐
210	**77**	10d purple and red	35·00	22·00	☐	☐
211	**78**	1s green	£130	30·00	☐	☐
214		1s green and red ..	45·00	80·00	☐	☐
	Set of 14	.. ..	£325	£190	☐	☐

* The ½d, No. 213, in blue, has had the colour changed due to exposure to moisture.

7

1902–13 *Wmks Imperial Crown Type* **49** (½d to 1s); *Anchor Type* **40** (2s 6d to 10s); *Three Crowns Type* **49** (£1)

(a) *Perf* 14

215	**79**	½d blue-green ..	50	30 □ □
217		½d yellow-green ..	40	30 □ □
219		1d red	40	30 □ □
288	**80**	1½d purple and green	10·00	10·00 □ □
291	**81**	2d green and red ..	10·00	5·00 □ □
231	**82**	2½d blue	4·00	2·50 □ □
232	**83**	3d purple on yellow	15·00	2·50 □ □
236a	**84**	4d green and brown	15·00	7·00 □ □
240		4d orange ..	7·50	6·50 □ □
294	**85**	5d purple and blue	10·00	4·75 □ □
245	**79**	6d purple	12·00	4·00 □ □
249	**86**	7d grey	3·00	6·00 □ □
307	**87**	9d purple and blue	30·00	22·00 □ □
311	**88**	10d purple and red ..	30·00	20·00 □ □
314	**89**	1s green and red ..	25·00	8·00 □ □
260	**90**	2s 6d lilac	90·00	45·00 □ □
263	**91**	5s red	£100	55·00 □ □
319	**92**	10s blue	£275	£200 □ □
320	**93**	£1 green	£750	£300 □ □
		Set of 15 (*to* 1s)	£160	90·00 □ □

(b) *Perf* 15 × 14

279a	**79**	½d green	20·00	20·00 □ □
282		1d red	8·00	3·00 □ □
283	**82**	2½d blue	10·00	5·00 □ □
285	**83**	3d purple on yellow	15·00	4·00 □ □
286	**84**	4d orange	10·00	6·00 □ □
		Set of 5	55·00	40·00 □ □

KING GEORGE V
1910 (6 May)–1936 (20 Jan.)

PERFORATION. All the following issues are Perf 15 × 14 except vertical commemorative stamps which are 14 × 15, unless otherwise stated.

94 (Hair dark)   **95** (Lion unshaded)   **96**

1911–12 *Wmk Imperial Crown Type* **49**

322	**94**	½d green	2·50	1·00 □ □
327	**95**	1d red	2·25	1·00 □ □

1912 *Wmk Royal Cypher* ('*Simple*') *Type* **96**

335	**94**	½d green	20·00	22·00 □ □
336	**95**	1d red	12·00	12·00 □ □

97 (Hair light)   **98** (Lion shaded)   **99**

1912 *Wmk Imperial Crown Type* **49**

339	**97**	½d green	3·00	50 □ □
341	**98**	1d red	1·25	50 □ □

1912 *Wmk Royal Cypher* ('*Simple*') *Type* **96**

344	**97**	½d green	2·50	70 □ □
345	**98**	1d red	2·00	50 · □ □

1912 *Wmk Royal Cypher* ('*Multiple*') *Type* **99**

348 –	**97**	½d green	6·00	4·00 □ □
350	**98**	1d red	5·00	4·50 □ □

100   **101**   **102**

103   **104**

1912–24 *Wmk Royal Cypher Type* **96**

351	**101**	½d green	30	25 □ □
357	**100**	1d red	30	25 □ □
362	**101**	1½d brown	1·00	25 □ □
368	**102**	2d orange	1·00	25 □ □
372	**100**	2½d blue	4·50	1·00 □ □
375	**102**	3d violet	2·00	75 □ □
379		4d grey-green ..	4·00	75 □ □
381	**103**	5d brown	3·50	3·00 □ □
385		6d purple	6·00	1·50 □ □
		a. Perf 14	60·00	85·00 □ □
387		7d olive-green ..	6·00	3·75 □ □
390		8d black on yellow	15·00	6·50 □ □
392	**104**	9d black	5·00	2·50 □ □
393a		9d olive-green ..	65·00	15·00 □ □
394		10d blue	9·00	12·00 □ □
395		1s brown	7·50	1·00 □ □
		Set of 15	£120	45·00 □ □

1913 *Wmk Royal Cypher ('Multiple') Type* **99**

397	**101**	½d green	..	..	50·00	95·00	☐ ☐
398	**100**	1d red ..	..	..	£110	£130	☐ ☐

See also Nos. 418/29.

105

106

T **105.** *Background around portrait consists of horizontal lines*

1913–18 *Wmk Single Cypher Type* **106**   *Perf* 11 × 12

413a	**105**	2s 6d brown	..	..	55·00	25·00	☐ ☐
416		5s red ..	..	..	£125	45·00	☐ ☐
417		10s blue	..	..	£175	80·00	☐ ☐
403		£1 green	..	..	£950	£600	☐ ☐
	Set of 4	..	..	..	£1200	£700	☐ ☐

See also Nos. 450/2.

108

109

British Empire Exhibition

1924–25 *Wmk* **107**   *Perf* 14

(a) 23.4.24.   *Dated* '1924'

430	**108**	1d red ..	..	..	5·00	6·00	☐ ☐
431	**109**	1½d brown	..	..	7·50	11·00	☐ ☐
	First Day Cover	..	..		£350		☐

(b) 9.5.25.   *Dated* '1925'

432	**108**	1d red ..	..	..	8·00	17·00	☐ ☐
433	**109**	1½d brown	..	..	25·00	50·00	☐ ☐
	First Day Cover	..	..		£1200		☐

110

111

112

113 St George and the Dragon

107

1924–26 *Wmk Block Cypher Type* **107**

418	**101**	½d green	..	..	15	25	☐ ☐
419	**100**	1d red ..	..	..	15	25	☐ ☐
420	**101**	1½d brown	..	..	15	25	☐ ☐
421	**102**	2d orange	..	..	75	80	☐ ☐
422	**100**	2½d blue	..	..	3·00	1·25	☐ ☐
423	**102**	3d violet	..	..	4·00	1·00	☐ ☐
424		4d grey-green	..	..	6·00	1·00	☐ ☐
425	**103**	5d brown	..	..	10·00	1·60	☐ ☐
426a		6d purple	..	..	1·50	50	☐ ☐
427	**104**	9d olive-green	..	..	5·00	2·25	☐ ☐
428		10d blue	..	..	15·00	16·00	☐ ☐
429		1s brown	..	..	10·00	1·00	☐ ☐
	Set of 12	..	..	..	50·00	23·00	☐ ☐

For full information on all future British issues, collectors should write to the British Post Office Philatelic Bureau, 20 Brandon Street, Edinburgh EH3 5TT

114

Ninth Universal Postal Union Congress

1929 (10 MAY) (*a*) *Wmk* **107**

434	110	½d green	..	..	1·50	1·50	☐	☐
435	111	1d red	..	..	1·50	1·50	☐	☐
436		1½d brown	..	..	1·00	1·00	☐	☐
437	112	2½d blue	..	..	7·50	9·00	☐	☐

(*b*) *Wmk* **114** *Perf* 12

438	113	£1 black	..	..	£500	£400	☐	☐
434/7	*Set of 4*		..	..	10·00	11·50	☐	☐
434/7	*First Day Cover* (4 *vals.*)			..		£500	☐	
434/8	*First Day Cover* (5 *vals.*)			..		£2500	☐	

120

121

122

123

115

116

117

118

119

Silver Jubilee

1935 (7 MAY) *Wmk* **107**

453	120	½d green	..	..	25	20	☐	☐
454	121	1d red	..	..	1·00	1·00	☐	☐
455	122	1½d brown	..	..	25	20	☐	☐
456	123	2½d blue	..	..	3·00	5·50	☐	☐
	Set of 4				4·00	6·00	☐	☐
	First Day Cover	..	..			£400	☐	

1934–36 *Wmk* **107**

439	115	½d green	..	..	10	25	☐	☐
440	116	1d red	..	..	10	25	☐	☐
441	115	1½d brown	..	..	10	25	☐	☐
442	117	2d orange	..	..	25	25	☐	☐
443	116	2½d blue	..	..	75	60	☐	☐
444	117	3d violet	..	..	75	50	☐	☐
445		4d grey-green	..	..	1·00	55	☐	☐
446	118	5d brown	..	..	3·50	1·50	☐	☐
447	119	9d olive-green	..	..	8·00	1·60	☐	☐
448		10d blue	..	..	10·00	8·00	☐	☐
449		1s brown	..	..	10·00	50	☐	☐
	Set of 11		..	..	30·00	11·00	☐	☐

T 105 (*re-engraved*). *Background around portrait consists of horizontal and diagonal lines*

1934 *Wmk* **106** *Perf* 11 × 12

450	105	2s 6d brown	..	..	40·00	15·00	☐	☐
451		5s red	..	..	85·00	50·00	☐	☐
452		10s blue	..	..	£200	50·00	☐	☐
	Set of 3		..	..	£275	£100	☐	☐

KING EDWARD VIII
1936 (20 Jan.–10 Dec.)

124

125

1936 *Wmk* **125**

457	124	½d green	..	..	20	15	☐	☐
458		1d red	..	..	50	20	☐	☐
459		1½d brown	..	..	25	15	☐	☐
460		2½d blue	..	..	25	60	☐	☐
	Set of 4		..	..	1·00	1·00	☐	☐

KING GEORGE VI
1936 (11 Dec.)–1952 (6 Feb.)

126 King George VI
and Queen Elizabeth

 (127 watermark image)

127

Coronation

1937 (13 MAY) *Wmk* 127

461	**126**	1½d brown	40	25	□	□
		First Day Cover		24·00		□

 (128)

128   **129**   **130**

King George VI and National Emblems

1937–47 *Wmk* 127

462	**128**	½d	green	.. ..	10	15	□ □
463		1d	scarlet	.. ..	10	15	□ □
464		1½d	brown	.. ..	20	15	□ □
465		2d	orange	.. ..	1·25	45	□ □
466		2½d	blue	.. ..	25	15	□ □
467		3d	violet	.. ..	4·50	60	□ □
468	**129**	4d	green	.. ..	35	40	□ □
469		5d	brown	.. ..	3·00	35	□ □
470		6d	purple	.. ..	1·75	40	□ □
471	**130**	7d	green	.. ..	4·00	50	□ □
472		8d	red ..	.. ..	5·00	50	□ □
473		9d	deep green	..	6·50	50	□ □
474		10d	blue	.. ..	6·00	60	□ □
474a		11d	plum	.. ..	3·00	1·50	□ □
475		1s	brown	.. ..	7·00	40	□ □
		Set of 15	.. ..	..	39·00	6·00	□ □

For later printings of the lower values in apparently lighter
shades and different colours, see Nos. 485/90 and 503/8.

For full information on all future British issues, collectors
should write to the British Post Office Philatelic Bureau, 20
Brandon Street, Edinburgh EH3 5TT

131 King George VI   **131a**

132   **132a**

 (133 watermark image)

133

1939–48 *Wmk* 133   *Perf* 14

476	**131**	2s 6d	brown	.. ..	40·00	7·00	□ □
476a		2s 6d	green		9·00	1·00	□ □
477	**131a**	5s	red ..		18·00	1·50	□ □
478	**132**	10s	dark blue	..	£130	18·00	□ □
478a		10s	bright blue		40·00	4·50	□ □
478b	**132a**	£1	brown	..	15·00	19·00	□ □
		Set of 6	..	..	£225	45·00	□ □

134 Queen Victoria and King George VI

Centenary of First Adhesive Postage Stamps

1940 (6 MAY) *Wmk* 127   *Perf* 14½ × 14

479	**134**	½d	green	.. ..	30	20	□ □
480		1d	red ..	..	90	40	□ □
481		1½d	brown	.. ..	30	30	□ □
482		2d	orange	.. ..	50	40	□ □
483		2½d	blue	.. ..	1·90	80	□ □
484		3d	violet	.. ..	4·00	4·00	□ □
		Set of 6	.. ..	..	7·00	5·50	□ □
		First Day Cover ..	.. ..		35·00		□

11

Head as Nos. 462/7, but lighter background
1941–42 *Wmk* **127**

485	**128**	½d pale green		15	10	☐	☐
486		1d pale red	..	15	10	☐	☐
487		1½d pale brown		75	45	☐	☐
488		2d pale orange	..	50	40	☐	☐
489		2½d light blue		15	10	☐	☐
490		3d pale violet		1·50	50	☐	☐
	Set of 6	.. .. ..	..	2·75	1·50	☐	☐

135 Symbols of Peace and Reconstruction

136 Symbols of Peace and Reconstruction

Victory
1946 (11 JUNE) *Wmk* **127**

491	**135**	2½d blue	.. ..	25	15	☐	☐
492	**136**	3d violet	.. ..	25	15	☐	☐
	First Day Cover	.. ..		42·00		☐	

137 King George VI and Queen Elizabeth

138 King George VI and Queen Elizabeth

Royal Silver Wedding
1948 (26 APR.) *Wmk* **127**

493	**137**	2½d blue	.. ..	30	30	☐	☐
494	**138**	£1 blue	.. ..	32·00	32·00	☐	☐
	First Day Cover	.. .. ..		£375		☐	

1948 (10 MAY)

Stamps of 1d and 2½d showing seaweed-gathering were on sale at eight Head Post Offices elsewhere in Great Britain, but were primarily for use in the Channel Islands and are listed there (see after Regional Issues).

139 Globe and Laurel Wreath

140 'Speed'

141 Olympic Symbol

142 Winged Victory

Olympic Games
1948 (29 JULY) *Wmk* **127**

495	**139**	2½d blue	.. ..	10	10	☐	☐
496	**140**	3d violet	.. ..	30	30	☐	☐
497	**141**	6d purple	.. ..	60	30	☐	☐
498	**142**	1s brown	.. ..	1·25	1·50	☐	☐
	Set of 4	.. ..		2·00	2·00	☐	☐
	First Day Cover	.. ..		28·00			☐

143 Two Hemispheres

144 U.P.U. Monument, Berne

145 Goddess Concordia, Globe and Points of Compass

146 Posthorn and Globe

75th Anniversary of Universal Postal Union
1949 (10 OCT.) *Wmk* **127**

499	**143**	2½d blue	.. ..	10	10	☐	☐
500	**144**	3d violet	.. ..	30	40	☐	☐
501	**145**	6d purple	.. ..	60	75	☐	☐
502	**146**	1s brown	.. ..	1·25	1·50	☐	☐
	Set of 4	.. ..		2·00	2·75	☐	☐
	First Day Cover			50·00		☐	☐

4d as No. 468 and others as Nos. 485/9, but colours changed

1950–52 *Wmk* **127**

503	**128**	½d	pale orange	..	10	15	□ □
504		1d	light blue		15	15	□ □
505		1½d	pale green		25	30	□ □
506		2d	pale brown		25	20	□ □
507		2½d	pale red	..	20	15	□ □
508	**129**	4d	light blue		1·50	1·10	□ □
		Set of 6		..	2·25	1·75	□ □

147 HMS *Victory*

148 White Cliffs of Dover

149 St George and the Dragon

150 Royal Coat of Arms

1951 (3 MAY) *Wmk* **133** *Perf* 11 × 12

509	**147**	2s 6d	green	..	..	8·00	75	□ □
510	**148**	5s	red ..		..	30·00	1·50	□ □
511	**149**	10s	blue	..	..	18·00	10·00	□ □
512	**150**	£1	brown	..	..	40·00	14·00	□ □
		Set of 4		..	..	85·00	22·00	□ □

151 Commerce and Prosperity

152 Festival Symbol

Festival of Britain

1951 (3 MAY) *Wmk* **127**

513	**151**	2½d	red ..	..	..	25	15	□ □
514	**152**	4d	blue	..	..	50	45	□ □
		First Day Cover	..	..	..	16·00		□

QUEEN ELIZABETH II
6 February, 1952

153 Tudor Crown

154

155

156

157

158

159

160

Queen Elizabeth II and National Emblems

1952–54 *Wmk* **153**

515	**154**	½d	orange	..	..	10	15	□ □
516		1d	blue	..	..	20	20	□ □
517		1½d	green	..	..	10	15	□ □
518		2d	brown	..	..	20	15	□ □
519	**155**	2½d	red ..	..	..	10	15	□ □
520		3d	lilac	..	..	1·00	30	□ □
521	**156**	4d	blue	..	..	3·00	80	□ □
		4½d	*(See Nos.* 577, 594, 609 *and* 616*b)*					
522	**157**	5d	brown	..	..	90	2·00	□ □
523		6d	purple	..	..	3·00	60	□ □
524		7d	green	..	..	9·00	3·50	□ □
525	**158**	8d	magenta	..	..	1·00	60	□ □
526		9d	bronze-green	..	22·00	3·00	□ □
527		10d	blue	..	..	18·00	3·00	□ □
528		11d	plum	..	..	30·00	16·00	□ □
529	**159**	1s	bistre	..	..	1·00	40	□ □
530	**160**	1s 3d	green	..	..	4·50	2·00	□ □
531	**159**	1s 6d	indigo	..	..	11·00	2·75	□ □
		Set of 17	..	..	..	95·00	28·00	□ □

See also Nos. 540/56, 561/6, 570/94 and 599/618*a*.
For First Day Cover prices see page 37.

161

162

163

164

Coronation

1953 (3 JUNE) *Wmk* 153

532	**161**	2½d red ..	..	..	10	25	☐	☐
533	**162**	4d blue	..	..	40	1·50	☐	☐
534	**163**	1s 3d green	..	..	3·50	2·50	☐	☐
535	**164**	1s 6d blue	..	..	6·00	3·50	☐	☐
		Set of 4	..	..	9·00	7·00	☐	☐
		First Day Cover	..	..		40·00	☐	

165 St Edward's Crown

166 Carrickfergus Castle

167 Caernarvon Castle

168 Edinburgh Castle

169 Windsor Castle

1955–58 *Wmk* 165 *Perf* 11 × 12

536	**166**	2s 6d brown	..	..	10·00	2·00	☐	☐
537	**167**	5s red ..	..	..	40·00	3·50	☐	☐
538	**168**	10s blue	..	..	95·00	11·00	☐	☐
539	**169**	£1 black	..	..	£160	28·00	☐	☐
		Set of 4	..	..	£275	40·00	☐	☐

See also Nos. 595*a*/8*a*, 759/62 and F.D.C's on page 37.

1955–58 *Wmk* 165

540	**154**	½d orange	..	..	10	15	☐	☐
541		1d blue	..	..	25	15	☐	☐
542		1½d green		..	10	15	☐	☐
543		2d red-brown	..		20	20	☐	☐
543*b*		2d light red-brown			20	15	☐	☐
544	**155**	2½d red ..	..	..	20	15	☐	☐
545		3d lilac	..	..	20	15	☐	☐
546	**156**	4d blue	..	..	1·40	40	☐	☐
547	**157**	5d brown	..	..	5·00	3·50	☐	☐
548*a*		6d purple	..	..	3·50	80	☐	☐
549		7d green	..	..	48·00	7·50	☐	☐
550	**158**	8d magenta ..		..	5·50	1·00	☐	☐
551		9d bronze-green		..	17·00	2·25	☐	☐
552		10d blue	..	..	12·00	2·25	☐	☐
553		11d plum	..	..	40	1·50	☐	☐
554	**159**	1s bistre	..	..	15·00	40	☐	☐
555	**160**	1s 3d green	..	..	17·00	1·50	☐	☐
556	**159**	1s 6d indigo	..	..	16·00	1·25	☐	☐
		Set of 18	..	..	£120	22·00	☐	☐

170 Scout Badge and 'Rolling Hitch'

171 'Scouts coming to Britain'

172 Globe within a Compass

173

World Scout Jubilee Jamboree

1957 (1 AUG.) *Wmk* 165

557	**170**	2½d red ..	..	..	15	10	☐	☐
558	**171**	4d blue	..	..	50	1·00	☐	☐
559	**172**	1s 3d green	..	..	4·50	4·50	☐	☐
		Set of 3	..	..	4·50	4·50	☐	☐
		First Day Cover	..	..		12·00	☐	

46th Inter Parliamentary Union Conference

1957 (12 SEPT.) *Wmk* 165

560	**173**	4d blue	..	..	1·00	1·00	☐	☐
		First Day Cover	..	..		90·00	☐	

Graphite-lined and Phosphor Issues

These are used in connection with automatic sorting machinery, originally experimentally at Southampton but now also operating elsewhere. In such areas these stamps were the normal issue, but from mid 1967 *all* low-value stamps bear phosphor markings.

The graphite lines were printed in black on the back, beneath the gum; two lines per stamp except for the 2d (*see below*).

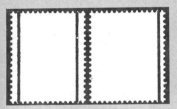

174   **175**   (2d only)
(Stamps viewed from back)

In November 1959, phosphor bands, printed on the front, replaced the graphite. They are wider than the graphite, not easy to see, but show as broad vertical bands at certain angles to the light.

Values representing the rate for printed papers (and second class mail from 1968) have one band and others have two, three or four bands according to size and format. From 1972 onwards some commemorative stamps were printed with 'all-over' phosphor.

In the small stamps the bands are on each side with the single band at left (except where otherwise stated). In the large-size commemorative stamps the single band may be at left, centre or right varying in different issues. The bands are vertical on both horizontal and vertical designs except where otherwise stated.

See also notes on page 35.

Graphite-lined issue

1957 (19 Nov.) *Two graphite lines on the back, except 2d value, which has one line.* Wmk **165**

561	**154**	½d orange	..	..	20	20	☐	☐
562		1d blue	..	..	20	35	☐	☐
563		1½d green	..	..	30	1·25	☐	☐
564		2d light red-brown			2·50	1·50	☐	☐
565	**155**	2½d red	..	..	6·00	6·25	☐	☐
566		3d lilac	..	..	30	50	☐	☐
	Set of 6	..	..	..	8·50	9·00	☐	☐

See also Nos. 587/94.

For First Day Cover price see page 37.

176 Welsh Dragon

177 Flag and Games Emblem

178 Welsh Dragon

Sixth British Empire and Commonwealth Games, Cardiff

1958 (18 JULY) Wmk **165**

567	**176**	3d lilac	..	..	15	10	☐	☐
568	**177**	6d mauve	..	..	25	45	☐	☐
569	**178**	1s 3d green	..	..	2·25	2·25	☐	☐
	Set of 3	..	..	..	2·25	2·25	☐	☐
	First Day Cover	..	..	..		55·00		☐

179 Multiple Crowns

WATERMARK. All the following issues to No. 755 are Watermark **179** (sideways on the vertical commemorative stamps) unless otherwise stated.

1958–65 *Wmk* **179**

570	**154**	½d orange	..	..	10	10	☐ ☐
571		1d blue	..	..	10	10	☐ ☐
572		1½d green	..	..	10	15	☐ ☐
573		2d light red-brown		10	10	☐ ☐
574	**155**	2½d red	..	..	10	10	☐ ☐
575		3d lilac	..	..	10	10	☐ ☐
576*a*	**156**	4d blue	..	..	15	10	☐ ☐
577		4½d brown	..	..	10	15	☐ ☐
578	**157**	5d brown	..	..	25	20	☐ ☐
579		6d purple	..	..	25	15	☐ ☐
580		7d green	..	..	40	20	☐ ☐
581	**158**	8d magenta	..	..	40	15	☐ ☐
582		9d bronze-green	..	40	15	☐ ☐
583		10d blue	..	..	1·00	15	☐ ☐
584	**159**	1s bistre	..	..	40	15	☐ ☐
585	**160**	1s 3d green	..	..	25	15	☐ ☐
586	**159**	1s 6d indigo	..	..	5·00	40	☐ ☐
	Set of 17	..	..	..	8·00	2·10	☐ ☐

For 4½d on First Day Cover see page 37.

For full information on all future British issues, collectors should write to the British Post Office Philatelic Bureau, 20 Brandon Street, Edinburgh EH3 5TT

Graphite-lined issue

1958–61 *Two graphite lines on the back, except 2d value, which has one line.* Wmk **179**

587	154	½d	orange	.. ..	6·00	6·00	□ □
588		1d	blue	.. ..	1·00	1·50	□ □
589		1½d	green	.. ..	40·00	40·00	□ □
590		2d	light red-brown		7·00	3·25	□ □
591	155	2½d	red	.. ..	12·00	10·00	□ □
592		3d	lilac	.. ..	50	50	□ □
593	156	4d	blue	.. ..	4·00	4·50	□ □
594		4½d	brown	.. ..	5·00	4·50	□ □
		Set of 8		.. ..	65·00	60·00	□ □

The prices quoted for No. 589 are for examples with inverted watermark. Stamps with upright watermark are *priced at £85 mint, £60 used.*

1959–63 *Wmk* **179**   *Perf* 11×12

595a	166	2s 6d	brown	.. /	50	30	□ □
596a	167	5s	red ..	.. ..	1·00	60	□ □
597a	168	10s	blue ..	.. ..	2·50	3·00	□ □
598a	169	£1	black ..	.. ..	10·00	5·00	□ □
		Set of 4	..	.. ..	13·00	8·00	□ □

Phosphor-Graphite issue

1959 (18 Nov.) *Two phosphor bands on front and two graphite lines on back, except 2d value, which has one band on front and one line on back*

    (*a*) Wmk **165**

599	154	½d	orange	.. ..	4·00	6·00	□ □
600		1d	blue	.. ..	6·00	6·00	□ □
601		1½d	green	.. ..	2·50	5·00	□ □

    (*b*) Wmk **179**

605	154	2d	light red-brown (1 band) ..		5·00	3·75	□ □
606	155	2½d	red ..	.. ..	22·00	11·00	□ □
607		3d	lilac	.. ..	11·00	8·00	□ □
608	156	4d	blue	.. ..	12·00	25·00	□ □
609		4½d	brown	.. ..	28·00	15·00	□ □
		Set of 8	..	.. ..	80·00	70·00	□ □

Phosphor issue

1960–67 *Two phosphor bands on front, except where otherwise stated.* Wmk **179**

610	154	½d	orange	.. ..	10	15	□ □
611		1d	blue	.. ..	10	10	□ □
612		1½d	green	.. ..	10	20	□ □
613		2d	light red-brown (1 band) ..		20·00	20·00	□ □
613a		2d	light red-brown (2 bands)		10	10	□ □
614	155	2½d	red (2 bands) ..		10	40	□ □
614a		2½d	red (1 band) ..		40	75	□ □
615		3d	lilac (2 bands)		60	45	□ □
615c		3d	lilac (1 side band) ..		35	60	□ □
615e		3d	lilac (1 centre band) ..		25	40	□ □

616a	156	4d	blue	.. ..	15	15	□ □
616b		4½d	brown	.. ..	15	25	□ □
616c	157	5d	brown	.. ..	20	25	□ □
617		6d	purple	.. ..	40	20	□ □
617a		7d	green	.. ..	60	25	□ □
617b	158	8d	magenta	.. ..	20	25	□ □
617c		9d	bronze-green	..	60	25	□ □
617d		10d	blue	.. ..	80	35	□ □
617e	159	1s	bistre	.. ..	40	20	□ □
618	160	1s 3d	green	.. ..	1·75	2·50	□ □
618a	159	1s 6d	indigo	.. ..	2·00	1·00	□ □
		Set of 17 (one of each value)			7·00	6·00	□ □

No. 615c exists with the phosphor band at the left or right of the stamp.

180 Postboy of 1660   **181** Posthorn of 1660

Tercentenary of Establishment of 'General Letter Office'

1960 (7 July)

619	180	3d lilac	..	..	20	10	□ □
620	181	1s 3d green	..	..	3·50	3·50	□ □
		Set of 2	..	..	3·50	3·50	□ □
		First Day Cover ..	.. ..		40·00		□

182 Conference Emblem

First Anniversary of European Postal and Telecommunications Conference

1960 (19 Sept.)

621	182	6d	green and purple	40	60	□ □
622		1s 6d	brown and blue	5·00	4·50	□ □
		Set of 2	.. .. ..	5·00	4·50	□ □
		First Day Cover ..	.. ..		28·00	□

183 Thrift Plant   **184** 'Growth of Savings'

185 Thrift Plant

Centenary of Post Office Savings Bank

1961 (28 Aug.)

623	**183**	2½d black and red ..	10	10	☐	☐
624	**184**	3d orange-brown and violet	10	10	☐	☐
625	**185**	1s 6d red and blue	2·25	2·00	☐	☐
		Set of 3	2·25	2·00	☐	
		First Day Cover		60·00	☐	

186 C.E.P.T. Emblem

187 Doves and Emblem

188 Doves and Emblem

European Postal and Telecommunications (C.E.P.T.) Conference, Torquay

1961 (18 Sept.)

626	**186**	2d orange, pink and brown ..	10	10	☐	☐
627	**187**	4d buff, mauve and ultramarine ..	20	10	☐	☐
628	**188**	10d turquoise, green and blue ..	40	35	☐	☐
		Set of 3	60	50	☐	☐
		First Day Cover		2·50	☐	

189 Hammer Beam Roof, Westminster Hall

190 Palace of Westminster

Seventh Commonwealth Parliamentary Conference

1961 (25 Sept.)

629	**189**	6d purple and gold	25	25	☐	☐
630	**190**	1s 3d green and blue	2·50	2·00	☐	☐
		Set of 2	2·50	2·00	☐	
		First Day Cover		26·00	☐	

191 'Units of Productivity'

192 'National Productivity'

193 'Unified Productivity'

National Productivity Year

1962 (14 Nov.) Wmk **179** (inverted on 2½d and 3d)

631	**191**	2½d green and red ..	20	10	☐	☐
		p. Phosphor ..	1·00	40	☐	☐
632	**192**	3d blue and violet	25	10	☐	☐
		p. Phosphor ..	1·00	50	☐	☐
633	**193**	1s 3d red, blue and green	1·75	1·60	☐	☐
		p. Phosphor ..	21·00	18·00	☐	☐
		Set of 3 (Ordinary) ..	2·00	1·60	☐	
		Set of 3 (Phosphor) ..	21·00	18·00	☐	
		First Day Cover (Ordinary) ..		30·00	☐	
		First Day Cover (Phosphor)		95·00	☐	

194 Campaign Emblem and Family

195 Children of Three Races

Freedom from Hunger

1963 (21 Mar.) Wmk **179** (inverted)

634	**194**	2½d crimson and pink	10	10	☐	☐
		p. Phosphor ..	1·00	1·00	☐	☐
635	**195**	1s 3d brown and yellow	2·00	1·75	☐	☐
		p. Phosphor ..	21·00	18·00	☐	☐
		Set of 2 (Ordinary)	2·00	1·75	☐	
		Set of 2 (Phosphor)	21·00	18·00	☐	
		First Day Cover (Ordinary) ..		28·00	☐	
		First Day Cover (Phosphor)..		30·00	☐	

196 'Paris Conference'

Paris Postal Conference Centenary

1963 (7 MAY) *Wmk* **179** *(inverted)*

636	**196**	6d green and mauve	50	40	☐	☐
		p. Phosphor ..	6·00	5·00	☐	☐
		First Day Cover (Ordinary) ..		12·00		☐
		First Day Cover (Phosphor) ..		20·00		☐

197 Posy of Flowers

198 Woodland Life

National Nature Week

1963 (16 MAY)

637	**197**	3d multicoloured ..	25	20	☐	☐
		p. Phosphor ..	50	50	☐	☐
638	**198**	4½d multicoloured ..	40	40	☐	☐
		p. Phosphor ..	2·50	2·50	☐	☐
		Set of 2 (Ordinary) ..	60	60	☐	☐
		Set of 2 (Phosphor) ..	3·00	3·00	☐	☐
		First Day Cover (Ordinary) ..		14·00		☐
		First Day Cover (Phosphor)		28·00		☐

199 Rescue at Sea

200 19th-century Lifeboat

201 Lifeboatmen

Ninth International Lifeboat Conference, Edinburgh

1963 (31 MAY)

639	**199**	2½d blue, black and red	10	10	☐	☐
		p. Phosphor ..	40	50	☐	☐
640	**200**	4d multicoloured ..	40	30	☐	☐
		p. Phosphor ..	20	50	☐	☐
641	**201**	1s 6d sepia, yellow and blue ..	2·50	2·50	☐	☐
		p. Phosphor ..	25·00	24·00	☐	☐
		Set of 3 (Ordinary) ..		2·75	2·50	☐	☐
		Set of 3 (Phosphor) ..		26·00	24·00	☐	☐
		First Day Cover (Ordinary)			26·00		☐
		First Day Cover (Phosphor)			38·00		☐

202 Red Cross

203

204

205 'Commonwealth Cable'

Red Cross Centenary Congress

1963 (15 AUG.)

642	**202**	3d red and lilac ..	10	10	☐	☐
		p. Phosphor ..	60	60	☐	☐
643	**203**	1s 3d red, blue and grey	2·75	2·50	☐	☐
		p. Phosphor ..	32·00	30·00	☐	☐
644	**204**	1s 6d red, blue and bistre ..	2·50	2·50	☐	☐
		p. Phosphor ..	23·00	20·00	☐	☐
		Set of 3 (Ordinary) ..	5·00	4·50	☐	☐
		Set of 3 (Phosphor) ..	50·00	45·00	☐	☐
		First Day Cover (Ordinary) ..		28·00		☐
		First Day Cover (Phosphor)		60·00		☐

Opening of COMPAC (Trans-Pacific Telephone Cable)

1963 (3 DEC.)

645	**205**	1s 6d blue and black	2·50	2·25	☐	☐
		p. Phosphor ..	15·00	13·50	☐	☐
		First Day Cover (Ordinary) ..		22·00		☐
		First Day Cover (Phosphor) ..		24·00		☐

206 Puck and Bottom
(*A Midsummer
Night's Dream*)

207 Feste (*Twelfth Night*)

208 Balcony Scene
(*Romeo and Juliet*)

209 'Eve of Agincourt'
(*Henry V*)

210 Hamlet contemplating
Yorick's skull (*Hamlet*)
and Queen Elizabeth II

Shakespeare Festival

1964 (23 APR.) *Perf* 11 × 12 (2s 6d) *or* 15 × 14 (*others*).

646	**206**	3d bis, blk & vio-bl	10	10	☐	☐
		p. Phosphor ..	20	30	☐	☐
647	**207**	6d multicoloured	20	30	☐	☐
		p. Phosphor ..	60	70	☐	☐
648	**208**	1s 3d multicoloured	90	1·00	☐	☐
		p. Phosphor ..	5·75	5·50	☐	☐
649	**209**	1s 6d multicoloured	1·25	1·00	☐	☐
		p. Phosphor ..	9·00	5·75	☐	☐
650	**210**	2s 6d deep slate-purple	2·00	2·00	☐	☐
		Set of 5 (Ordinary)	4·00	4·00	☐	☐
		Set of 4 (Phosphor)	13·00	11·00	☐	☐
		First Day Cover (Ordinary)		11·00		☐
		First Day Cover (Phosphor)		11·00		☐
		Presentation Pack (Ordinary)	10·00			☐

PRESENTATION PACKS were first introduced by the G.P.O. for the Shakespeare Festival issue. The packs include one set of stamps and details of the designs, the designer and the stamp printer. They were issued for almost all later definitive and special issues.

For note about Presentation Packs in foreign languages, see page 25.

211 Flats near Richmond Park
('Urban Development')

212 Shipbuilding Yards, Belfast
('Industrial Activity')

213 Beddgelert Forest Park,
Snowdonia ('Forestry')

214 Nuclear Reactor, Dounreay
('Technological Development')

20th International Geographical Congress, London

1964 (1 JULY)

651	**211**	2½d multicoloured ..	10	10	☐	☐
		p. Phosphor	50	40	☐	☐
652	**212**	4d multicoloured	25	·25	☐	☐
		p. Phosphor	75	70	☐	☐
653	**213**	8d multicoloured	60	50	☐	☐
		p. Phosphor	1·75	1·50	☐	☐
654	**214**	1s 6d multicoloured	3·25	3·25	☐	☐
		p. Phosphor	20·00	18·00	☐	☐
		Set of 4 (Ordinary)	4·00	4·00	☐	☐
		Set of 4 (Phosphor) ..	20·00	18·00	☐	☐
		First Day Cover (Ordinary) ..		18·00		☐
		First Day Cover (Phosphor)		27·00		☐
		Presentation Pack (Ordinary)	80·00			☐

215 Spring Gentian

216 Dog Rose

217 Honeysuckle

218 Fringed Water Lily

Tenth International Botanical Congress, Edinburgh

1964 (5 AUG.)

655	**215**	3d vio. blue & green	10	10	☐	☐
		p. Phosphor ..	20	20	☐	☐
656	**216**	6d multicoloured ..	20	20	☐	☐
		p. Phosphor ..	1·25	1·00	☐	☐
657	**217**	9d multicoloured ..	1·60	2·00	☐	☐
		p. Phosphor ..	3·75	3·00	☐	☐
658	**218**	1s 3d multicoloured ..	2·50	1·90	☐	☐
		p. Phosphor ..	20·00	16·00	☐	☐
		Set of 4 (Ordinary)	4·00	4·00	☐	☐
		Set of 4 (Phosphor) ..	22·00	18·00	☐	☐
		First Day Cover (Ordinary) ..		18·00		☐
		First Day Cover (Phosphor)		28·00		☐
		Presentation Pack (Ordinary)	80·00			☐

219 Forth Road Bridge

220 Forth Road and Railway Bridges

Opening of Forth Road Bridge

1964 (4 Sept.)

659	**219**	3d black, blue and violet	..	..	15	10	☐ ☐
		p. Phosphor			50	50	☐ ☐
660	**220**	6d black, blue and red	..	..	45	40	☐ ☐
		p. Phosphor			4·50	4·50	☐ ☐
		Set of 2 (Ordinary)			60	50	☐ ☐
		Set of 2 (Phosphor)	..	..	5·00	5·00	☐ ☐
		First Day Cover (Ordinary)				5·00	☐
		First Day Cover (Phosphor)				10·00	☐
		Presentation Pack (Ordinary)	£180				☐

221 Sir Winston Churchill

222 Sir Winston Churchill

Churchill Commemoration

1965 (8 July)

661	**221**	4d black and drab			15	10	☐ ☐
		p. Phosphor			30	30	☐ ☐
662	**222**	1s 3d black and grey			45	30	☐ ☐
		p. Phosphor			3·00	3·25	☐ ☐
		Set of 2 (Ordinary)	..	..	60	40	☐ ☐
		Set of 2 (Phosphor)	..	..	3·00	3·25	☐ ☐
		First Day Cover (Ordinary)	..			2·00	☐
		First Day Cover (Phosphor)				4·50	☐
		Presentation Pack (Ordinary)	13·00				☐

223 Simon de Montfort's Seal

224 Parliament Buildings (after engraving by Hollar, 1647)

700th Anniversary of Simon de Montfort's Parliament

1965 (19 July)

663	**223**	6d green	10	10	☐ ☐
		p. Phosphor	40	40	☐ ☐
664	**224**	2s 6d black, grey and drab	1·25	1·25	☐ ☐
		Set of 2 (Ordinary)	1·25	1·25	☐ ☐
		First Day Cover (Ordinary)		12·00	☐
		First Day Cover (Phosphor)		16·00	☐
		Presentation Pack (Ordinary) 35·00			☐

225 Bandsmen and Banner

226 Three Salvationists

Salvation Army Centenary

1965 (9 Aug.)

665	**225**	3d multicoloured ..	10	10	☐ ☐
		p. Phosphor ..	40	40	☐ ☐
666	**226**	1s 6d multicoloured	1·00	1·00	☐ ☐
		p. Phosphor ..	2·75	3·25	☐ ☐
		Set of 2 (Ordinary)	1·10	1·10	☐ ☐
		Set of 2 (Phosphor)	3·00	3·50	☐ ☐
		First Day Cover (Ordinary) ..		20·00	☐
		First Day Cover (Phosphor)		22·00	☐

227 Lister's Carbolic Spray

228 Lister and Chemical Symbols

Centenary of Joseph Lister's Discovery of Antiseptic Surgery

1965 (1 Sept.)

667	**227**	4d indigo, chestnut and grey ..	10	10	☐ ☐
		p. Phosphor ..	15	20	☐ ☐
668	**228**	1s black, purple and blue	1·00	1·25	☐ ☐
		p. Phosphor ..	1·60	1·60	☐ ☐
		Set of 2 (Ordinary)	1·10	1·25	☐ ☐
		Set of 2 (Phosphor)	1·75	1·75	☐ ☐
		First Day Cover (Ordinary) ..		9·50	☐
		First Day Cover (Phosphor)		8·50	☐

229 Trinidad Carnival Dancers   **230** Canadian Folk-dancers

Commonwealth Arts Festival

1965 (1 Sept.)

669	**229**	6d black and orange	10	10	☐	☐
		p. Phosphor	30	30	☐	☐
670	**230**	1s 6d black and violet	1·25	1·50	☐	☐
		p. Phosphor	2·25	2·25	☐	☐
		Set of 2 (Ordinary)	1·25	1·50	☐	☐
		Set of 2 (Phosphor)	2·50	2·50	☐	☐
		First Day Cover (Ordinary)		10·00		☐
		First Day Cover (Phosphor)		10·00		☐

231 Flight of Spitfires   **232** Pilot in Hurricane

233 Wing-tips of Spitfire and Messerschmitt 'ME-109'   **234** Spitfires attacking Heinkel 'HE-111' Bomber

235 Spitfire attacking Stuka Dive-bomber   **236** Hurricanes over Wreck of Dornier 'DO-17z2' Bomber

The above were issued together *se-tenant* in blocks of six (3 × 2) within the sheet.

237 Anti-aircraft Artillery in Action   **238** Air-battle over St Paul's Cathedral

25th Anniversary of Battle of Britain

1965 (13 Sept.)

671	**231**	4d olive and black	30	35	☐	☐
	a.	Block of 6			☐	☐
		Nos. 671/6	5·50	5·50	☐	☐
	p.	Phosphor	40	50	☐	☐
	pa.	Block of 6			☐	☐
		Nos. 671p/6p	10·50	9·00	☐	☐
672	**232**	4d olive, blackish olive and black	30	35	☐	☐
		p. Phosphor	40	50	☐	☐
673	**233**	4d multicoloured	30	35	☐	☐
		p. Phosphor	40	50	☐	☐
674	**234**	4d olive and black	30	35	☐	☐
		p. Phosphor	40	50	☐	☐
675	**235**	4d olive and black	30	35	☐	☐
		p. Phosphor	40	50	☐	☐
676	**236**	4d multicoloured	30	35	☐	☐
		p. Phosphor	40	50	☐	☐
677	**237**	9d violet, orange and purple	1·25	1·25	☐	☐
		p. Phosphor	1·25	80	☐	☐
678	**238**	1s 3d multicoloured	1·25	1·25	☐	☐
		p. Phosphor	1·25	80	☐	☐
		Set of 8 (Ordinary)	7·00	4·25	☐	☐
		Set of 8 (Phosphor)	12·00	4·25	☐	☐
		First Day Cover (Ordinary)		18·00		☐
		First Day Cover (Phosphor)		18·00		☐
		Presentation Pack (Ordinary)	48·00			☐

239 Tower and Georgian Buildings   **240** Tower and 'Nash' Terrace, Regent's Park

Opening of Post Office Tower

1965 (8 Oct.)

679	**239**	3d yellow, blue and green	10	10	☐	☐
		p. Phosphor	10	10	☐	☐
680	**240**	1s 3d green and blue	65	75	☐	☐
		p. Phosphor	50	50	☐	☐
		Set of 2 (Ordinary)	75	85	☐	☐
		Set of 2 (Phosphor)	60	60	☐	☐
		First Day Cover (Ordinary)		6·00		☐
		First Day Cover (Phosphor)		8·00		☐
		Presentation Pack (Ordinary)	2·50			☐
		Presentation Pack (Phosphor)	2·50			☐

241 U.N. Emblem **242** I.C.Y. Emblem

20th Anniversary of UNO and International Co-operation Year

1965 (25 Oct.)

681	**241**	3d	blk, orge & bl ..		15	20	□	□
		p.	Phosphor	..	25	25	□	□
682	**242**	1s 6d	blk, pur & bl ..		1·10	90	□	□
		p.	Phosphor	..	2·50	2·50	□	□
	Set of 2 (Ordinary)		..	..	1·25	1·10	□	□
	Set of 2 (Phosphor)		..	..	2·75	2·75	□	□
	First Day Cover (Ordinary) ..				11·00		□	
	First Day Cover (Phosphor)				9·50		□	

243 Telecommunications Network **244** Radio Waves and Switchboard

I.T.U. Centenary

1965 (15 Nov.)

683	**243**	9d	multicoloured ..		20	20	□	□
		p.	Phosphor	..	60	50	□	□
684	**244**	1s 6d	multicoloured ..		1·40	1·10	□	□
		p.	Phosphor	..	4·50	4·50	□	□
	Set of 2 (Ordinary)		..	..	1·50	1·25	□	□
	Set of 2 (Phosphor)		..	..	5·00	5·00	□	□
	First Day Cover (Ordinary) ..				11·00		□	
	First Day Cover (Phosphor)				11·50		□	

245 Robert Burns (after Skirving chalk drawing) **246** Robert Burns (after Nasmyth portrait)

Burns Commemoration

1966 (25 Jan.)

685	**245**	4d	blk, indigo & bl ..		15	15	□	□
		p.	Phosphor	..	25	25	□	□
686	**246**	1s 3d	blk, bl & orge	..	70	70	□	□
		p.	Phosphor	..	1·00	1·00	□	□
	Set of 2 (Ordinary)		..	..	85	85	□	□
	Set of 2 (Phosphor)		..	..	1·25	1·25	□	□
	First Day Cover (Ordinary) ..				2·50		□	
	First Day Cover (Phosphor)				3·50		□	
	Presentation Pack (Ordinary)			34·00			□	

247 Westminster Abbey **248** Fan Vaulting, Henry VII Chapel

900th Anniversary of Westminster Abbey

1966 (28 Feb.)   *Perf* 15×14 (3d) *or* 11×12 (2s 6d)

687	**247**	3d	black, brown and blue ..		15	10	□	□
		p.	Phosphor		30	30	□	□
688	**248**	2s 6d	black	..	85	90	□	□
	Set of 2		..	..	1·00	1·00	□	□
	First Day Cover (Ordinary) ..				4·50		□	
	First Day Cover (Phosphor)				7·50		□	
	Presentation Pack (Ordinary)			17·00			□	

249 View near Hassocks, Sussex **250** Antrim, Northern Ireland

251 Harlech Castle, Wales **252** Cairngorm Mountains, Scotland

Landscapes

1966 (2 May)

689	**249**	4d	black, yellow-green and blue		15	15	□	□
		p.	Phosphor	..	15	15	□	□
690	**250**	6d	black, green and blue ..	..	15	15	□	□
		p.	Phosphor	..	25	25	□	□
691	**251**	1s 3d	black, yellow and blue ..		35	35	□	□
		p.	Phosphor	..	35	35	□	□
692	**252**	1s 6d	black, orange and blue ..		50	50	□	□
		p.	Phosphor	..	50	50	□	□
	Set of 4 (Ordinary)		..	..	1·00	1·00	□	□
	Set of 4 (Phosphor)		..	..	1·00	1·00	□	□
	First Day Cover (Ordinary)				6·00		□	
	First Day Cover (Phosphor)				6·00		□	

253 Players with Ball

260 Cup Winners

254 Goalmouth Mêlée

255 Goalkeeper saving Goal

World Cup Football Competition

1966 (1 June)

693	**253**	4d multicoloured ..	15	10	☐	☐
		p. Phosphor ..	15	10	☐	☐
694	**254**	6d multicoloured ..	20	20	☐	☐
		p. Phosphor ..	20	20	☐	☐
695	**255**	1s 3d multicoloured ..	50	50	☐	☐
		p. Phosphor ..	50	50	☐	☐
		Set of 3 (Ordinary)	75	75	☐	☐
		Set of 3 (Phosphor)	75	75	☐	☐
		First Day Cover (Ordinary) ..		6·50		☐
		First Day Cover (Phosphor)		6·50		☐
		Presentation Pack (Ordinary)	14·00			☐

256 Black-headed Gull

257 Blue Tit

258 Robin

259 Blackbird

The above were issued *se-tenant* in blocks of four within the sheet.

British Birds

1966 (8 Aug.)

696	**256**	4d multicoloured ..	10	15	☐	☐
	a.	Block of 4				
		Nos. 696/9 ..	1·00	1·00	☐	☐
	p.	Phosphor ..	10	15	☐	☐
	pa.	Block of 4				
		Nos. 696p/9p ..	1·00	1·00	☐	☐
697	**257**	4d multicoloured ..	10	15	☐	☐
		p. Phosphor ..	10	15	☐	☐
698	**258**	4d multicoloured ..	10	15	☐	☐
		p. Phosphor ..	10	15	☐	☐
699	**259**	4d multicoloured ..	10	15	☐	☐
		p. Phosphor ..	10	15	☐	☐
		Set of 4 (Ordinary)	1·00	50	☐	☐
		Set of 4 (Phosphor)	1·00	50	☐	☐
		First Day Cover (Ordinary) ..		6·50		☐
		First Day Cover (Phosphor)		6·50		☐
		Presentation Pack (Ordinary)	7·00			☐

England's World Cup Football Victory

1966 (18 Aug.)

700	**260**	4d multicoloured ..	20	20	☐	☐
		First Day Cover		2·00		☐

261 Jodrell Bank Radio Telescope

262 British Motor-cars

263 SR N6 Hovercraft

264 Windscale Reactor

British Technology

1966 (19 Sept.)

701	**261**	4d black and lemon	15	15	☐	☐
		p. Phosphor ..	15	15	☐	☐
702	**262**	6d red, blue and				
		orange	15	15	☐	☐
		p. Phosphor ..	15	15	☐	☐
703	**263**	1s 3d multicoloured ..	30	40	☐	☐
		p. Phosphor ..	45	50	☐	☐
704	**264**	1s 6d multicoloured ..	50	45	☐	☐
		p. Phosphor ..	65	60	☐	☐
		Set of 4 (Ordinary)	1·00	1·00	☐	☐
		Set of 4 (Phosphor)	1·25	1·25	☐	☐
		First Day Cover (Ordinary) ..		3·00		☐
		First Day Cover (Phosphor)		3·00		☐
		Presentation Pack (Ordinary)	7·00			☐

265 / 266

267 / 268

269 / 270

The above show battle scenes, they were issued together *se-tenant* in horizontal strips of six within the sheet.

271 Norman Ship

272 Norman Horsemen attacking Harold's Troops

900th Anniversary of Battle of Hastings

1966 (14 Oct.) *Designs show scenes from Bayeux Tapestry.* **Wmk 179** (*sideways on* 1s 3d)

705	265	4d multicoloured ..	10	15	☐	☐
	a.	Strip of 6				
		Nos. 705/10 ..	2·00	2·00	☐	☐
		p. Phosphor ..	10	25	☐	☐
	pa.	Strip of 6				
		Nos. 705p/10p	2·00	2·00	☐	☐
706	266	4d multicoloured ..	10	15	☐	☐
		p. Phosphor ..	10	25	☐	☐
707	267	4d multicoloured ..	10	15	☐	☐
		p. Phosphor ..	10	25	☐	☐

708	268	4d multicoloured ..	10	15	☐	☐
		p. Phosphor ..	10	25	☐	☐
709	269	4d multicoloured ..	10	15	☐	☐
		p. Phosphor ..	10	25	☐	☐
710	270	4d multicoloured ..	10	15	☐	☐
		p. Phosphor ..	10	25	☐	☐
711	271	6d multicoloured ..	10	10	☐	☐
		p. Phosphor ..	10	10	☐	☐
712	272	1s 3d multicoloured ..	20	20	☐	☐
		p. Phosphor ..	20	20	☐	☐
		Set of 8 (Ordinary) ..	2·25	1·50	☐	☐
		Set of 8 (Phosphor)	2·25	1·90	☐	☐
		First Day Cover (Ordinary)		3·00		☐
		First Day Cover (Phosphor)		3·00		☐
		Presentation Pack (Ordinary)	7·00		☐	

273 King of the Orient / 274 Snowman

Christmas

1966 (1 Dec.) **Wmk 179** (*upright on* 1s 6d)

713	273	3d multicoloured ..	10	10	☐	☐
		p. Phosphor ..	10	10	☐	☐
714	274	1s 6d multicoloured ..	35	35	☐	☐
		p. Phosphor ..	35	35	☐	☐
		Set of 2 (Ordinary) ..	45	45	☐	☐
		Set of 2 (Phosphor)	45	45	☐	☐
		First Day Cover (Ordinary)		1·50		☐
		First Day Cover (Phosphor)		1·50		☐
		Presentation Pack (Ordinary)	7·00		☐	

275 Sea Freight / 276 Air Freight

European Free Trade Association (EFTA)

1967 (20 Feb.)

715	275	9d multicoloured ..	15	15	☐	☐
		p. Phosphor ..	15	15	☐	☐
716	276	1s 6d multicoloured ..	30	30	☐	☐
		p. Phosphor ..	30	30	☐	☐
		Set of 2 (Ordinary)	40	40	☐	☐
		Set of 2 (Phosphor)	40	40	☐	☐
		First Day Cover (Ordinary)		1·50		☐
		First Day Cover (Phosphor)		1·50		☐
		Presentation Pack (Ordinary)	1·50		☐	

277 Hawthorn and Bramble

278 Larger Bindweed and Viper's Bugloss

279 Ox-eye Daisy, Coltsfoot and Buttercup

280 Bluebell, Red Campion and Wood Anemone

The above were issued together *se-tenant* in blocks of four within the sheet.

281 Dog Violet

282 Primroses

British Wild Flowers

1967 (24 APR.)

717	**277**	4d multicoloured ..	15	10	□	□
		a. *Block of 4*				
		Nos. 717/20 ..	1·25	1·25	□	□
		p. *Phosphor*	10	10	□	□
		pa. *Block of 4*				
		Nos. 717p/20p	1·00	1·00	□	□
718	**278**	4d multicoloured ..	15	10	□	□
		p. *Phosphor*	10	10	□	□
719	**279**	4d multicoloured ..	15	10	□	□
		p. *Phosphor*	10	10	□	□
720	**280**	4d multicoloured ..	15	10	□	□
		p. *Phosphor*	10	10	□	□
721	**281**	9d multicoloured ..	15	10	□	□
		p. *Phosphor*	10	10	□	□
722	**282**	1s 9d multicoloured ..	20	20	□	□
		p. *Phosphor*	30	20	□	□
		Set of 6 (Ordinary)	1·40	65	□	□
		Set of 6 (Phosphor) ..	1·25	65	□	□
		First Day Cover (Ordinary)		2·50		□
		First Day Cover (Phosphor)		2·50		□
		Presentation Pack (Ordinary)	3·00		□	
		Presentation Pack (Phosphor)	3·00		□	

PRESENTATION PACKS IN FOREIGN LANGUAGES

German Presentation Packs are similar to the English versions but have the text printed in German. From the 1969 Collectors Pack until the end of 1974 they were replaced by separately printed insert cards in German. Similar cards in Japanese and Dutch were available from 1969 British Ships issue until end of 1974. A pack printed in Japanese was, however, issued for the 1972 Royal Silver Wedding set.

283 (value at left)

284 (value at right)

I

II

Two types of the 2d.
I. Value spaced away from left side of stamp.
II. Value close to left side from new multi-positive. This results in the portrait appearing in the centre, thus conforming with the other values.

1967–69 *Two phosphor bands, except where otherwise stated. No wmk*

723	**283**	½d orange-brown	10	20	□	□
724		1d olive (2 bands)	10	10	□	□
725		1d olive (1 centre band)	25	30	□	□
726		2d lake-brown (Type I) (2 bands)	10	15	□	□
727		2d lake-brown (Type II) (2 bands)	15	15	□	□
728		2d lake-brown (Type II) (1 centre band) ..	40	50	□	□
729		3d violet (1 centre band)	10	10	□	□
730		3d violet (2 bands)	30	30	□	□
731		4d sepia (2 bands)	10	10	□	□
732		4d olive-brown (1 centre band) ..	10	10	□	□
733		4d vermilion (1 centre band) ..	10	10	□	□
734		4d vermilion (1 side band) ..	1·40	1·60	□	□
735		5d blue	10	10	□	□
736.		6d purple	20	20	□	□
737	**284**	7d emerald	40	30	□	□
738		8d vermilion ..	15	30	□	□
739		8d turquoise-blue	45	50	□	□
740		9d green	50	30	□	□
741	**283**	10d drab	45	50	□	□
742		1s violet	40	30	□	□
743		1s 6d blue & dp blue ..	50	30	□	□
		c. *Phosphorised paper*	75	90	□	□
744		1s 9d orange & black	40	30	□	□
		Set of 16 (one of each value and colour)	3·00	3·25	□	□
		Presentation Pack (one of each value)	6·00		□	
		Presentation Pack (German)	45·00		□	

No 734 exists with the phosphor band at the left or right. For prices of First Day Covers and for listing of decimal issue, Nos. X841/X1058, see pages 32/7.

285 'Master Lambton'
(Sir Thomas Lawrence)

286 'Mares and Foals in a
Landscape' (George Stubbs)

287 'Children Coming Out
of School' (L. S. Lowry)

288 Gipsy Moth IV

British Paintings

1967 (10 July) *Two phosphor bands. No wmk*

748	**285**	4d multicoloured ..	10	10	□	□
749	**286**	9d multicoloured ..	20	20	□	□
750	**287**	1s 6d multicoloured ..	35	25	□	□
		Set of 3	50	50	□	□
		First Day Cover		1·50		□
		Presentation Pack ..	5·50		□	

Sir Francis Chichester's World Voyage

1967 (24 July) *Three phosphor bands. No wmk*

751	**288**	1s 9d multicoloured ..	25	25	□	□
		First Day Cover		1·00		□

289 Radar Screen

290 *Penicillium notatum*

291 'VC-10' Jet Engines

292 Television Equipment

British Discovery and Invention

1967 (19 Sept.) *Two phosphor bands (except 4d, three
bands). Wmk 179 (sideways on 1s 9d)*

752	**289**	4d yell, blk & verm..	10	10	□	□
753	**290**	1s multicoloured ..	10	10	□	□
754	**291**	1s 6d multicoloured ..	25	15	□	□
755	**292**	1s 9d multicoloured ..	30	20	□	□
		Set of 4	60	50	□	□
		First Day Cover		1·00		□
		Presentation Pack	2·00		□	

NO WATERMARK. All the following issues are on un-
watermarked paper unless stated.

293 'The Adoration of
the Shepherds'
(School of Seville)

294 'Madonna and
Child' (Murillo)

295 'The Adoration of the Shepherds'
(Louis Le Nain)

Christmas

1967 *Two phosphor bands (except 3d, one phosphor band)*

756	**293**	3d multicoloured (27 Nov.) ..	10	10	□	□
757	**294**	4d multicoloured (18 Oct.) ..	10	10	□	□
758	**295**	1s 6d multicoloured (27 Nov.) ..	35	35	□	□
		Set of 3	50	50	□	□
		First Day Covers (2)		1·00		□

Gift Pack 1967

1967 (27 Nov.) *Comprises Nos. 715p/22p and 748/58*

	Gift Pack	2·50		□

1967–68 *No wmk   Perf 11 × 12*

759	**166**	2s 6d brown	40	50	□	□
760	**167**	5s red	1·00	1·00	□	□
761	**168**	10s blue	5·00	5·50	□	□
762	**169**	£1 black	4·00	4·00	□	□
		Set of 4	9·00	10·00	□	□

296 Tarr Steps, Exmoor

297 Aberfeldy Bridge

298 Menai Bridge

299 M4 Viaduct

British Bridges

1968 (29 APR.) *Two phosphor bands*

763	296	4d multicoloured ..	10	10	□	□
764	297	9d multicoloured ..	10	10	□	□
765	298	1s 6d multicoloured ..	20	15	□	□
766	299	1s 9d multicoloured ..	25	30	□	□
		Set of 4	60	60	□	□
		First Day Cover		1·10	□	
		Presentation Pack	2·00		□	

300 'TUC' and Trades Unionists

301 Mrs Emmeline Pankhurst (statue)

302 Sopwith 'Camel' and 'Lightning' Fighters

303 Captain Cook's *Endeavour* and Signature

British Anniversaries. Events described on stamps

1968 (29 MAY) *Two phosphor bands*

767	300	4d multicoloured ..	10	10	□	□
768	301	9d violet, grey and black	10	10	□	□
769	302	1s multicoloured ..	20	20	□	□
770	303	1s 9d ochre and brown	25	25	□	□
		Set of 4	60	60	□	□
		First Day Cover		3·25	□	
		Presentation Pack	3·00		□	

304 'Queen Elizabeth I' (Unknown Artist)

305 'Pinkie' (Lawrence)

306 'Ruins of St Mary Le Port' (Piper)

307 'The Hay Wain' (Constable)

British Paintings

1968 (12 AUG.) *Two phosphor bands*

771	304	4d multicoloured ..	10	10	□	□
772	305	1s multicoloured ..	15	15	□	□
773	306	1s 6d multicoloured ..	20	20	□	□
774	307	1s 9d multicoloured ..	25	25	□	□
		Set of 4	60	60	□	□
		First Day Cover		1·00	□	
		Presentation Pack	2·00		□	
		Presentation Pack (German)	6·00		□	

Gift Pack 1968

1968 (16 SEPT.) *Comprises Nos. 763/74*

	Gift Pack	6·00	□
	Gift Pack (German)	24·00	□

Collectors Pack 1968

1968 (16 SEPT.) *Comprises Nos. 752/8 and 763/74*

	Collectors Pack	6·00	□

308 Girl and Boy with Rocking Horse

309 Girl with Doll's House

310 Boy with Train Set

Christmas

1968 (25 Nov.) *Two phosphor bands (except 4d, one centre phosphor band)*

775	**308**	4d multicoloured ..	10	10	☐	☐
776	**309**	9d multicoloured ..	15	15	☐	☐
777	**310**	1s 6d multicoloured ..	25	25	☐	☐
		Set of 3	50	50	☐	☐
		First Day Cover ..		1·00		☐
		Presentation Pack	2·00		☐	
		Presentation Pack (German)	5·00		☐	

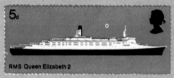

311 RMS *Queen Elizabeth 2*

312 Elizabethan Galleon

313 East Indiaman

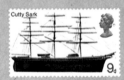

314 *Cutty Sark*

315 SS *Great Britain*

The 9d and 1s values were arranged in horizontal strips of three and pairs respectively throughout the sheet.

316 RMS *Mauretania*

British Ships

1969 (15 Jan.) *Two phosphor bands (except 5d, one horiz. phosphor band, 1s, two vert phosphor bands at right)*

778	**311**	5d multicoloured ..	10	10	☐	☐
779	**312**	9d multicoloured ..	10	15	☐	☐
		a. Strip of 3				
		Nos. 779/81	1·00	1·00	☐	☐
780	**313**	9d multicoloured ..	10	15	☐	☐
781	**314**	9d multicoloured ..	10	15	☐	☐
782	**315**	1s multicoloured ..	25	25	☐	☐
		a. Pair. Nos. 782/3	90	85	☐	☐
783	**316**	1s multicoloured ..	25	25	☐	☐
		Set of 6	1·75	90	☐	☐
		First Day Cover		3·25		☐
		Presentation Pack	3·00		☐	
		Presentation Pack (German)	22·00		☐	

317 'Concorde' in Flight

318 Plan and Elevation Views

319 'Concorde's' Nose and Tail

320 (See also Type 359a)

First Flight of 'Concorde'

1969 (3 Mar.) *Two phosphor bands*

784	**317**	4d multicoloured ..	10	10	☐	☐
785	**318**	9d multicoloured ..	20	20	☐	☐
786	**319**	1s 6d deep blue, grey and light blue ..	30	30	☐	☐
		Set of 3	50	50	☐	☐
		First Day Cover		1·25		☐
		Presentation Pack	2·50		☐	
		Presentation Pack (German)	18·00		☐	

1969 (5 Mar.) *P 12*

787	**320**	2s 6d brown	50	30	☐	☐
788		5s lake	2·25	60	☐	☐
789		10s ultramarine ..	7·00	7·50	☐	☐
790		£1 black	3·00	1·60	☐	☐
		Set of 4	11·50	9·00	☐	☐
		Presentation Pack	18·00		☐	
		Presentation Pack (German)	45·00		☐	

321 Page from the *Daily Mail*, and Vickers 'Vimy' Aircraft

322 Europa and C.E.P.T. Emblems

323 I.L.O. Emblem

324 Flags of N.A.T.O. Countries

325 Vickers 'Vimy' Aircraft and Globe showing Flight

Anniversaries. Events described on stamps

1969 (2 APR.) Two phosphor bands

791	321	5d multicoloured ..	10	10	☐	☐
792	322	9d multicoloured ..	20	20	☐	☐
793	323	1s claret, red and blue	20	20	☐	☐
794	324	1s 6d multicoloured ..	20	20	☐	☐
795	325	1s 9d olive, yellow and turquoise-green	25	25	☐	☐
		Set of 5	85	85	☐	☐
		First Day Cover		1·50		☐
		Presentation Pack	2·50		☐	
		Presentation Pack (German)	40·00		☐	

326 Durham Cathedral

327 York Minster

328 St Giles' Cathedral, Edinburgh

329 Canterbury Cathedral

The above were issued together *se-tenant* in blocks of four within the sheet.

330 St Paul's Cathedral

331 Liverpool Metropolitan Cathedral

British Architecture (Cathedrals)

1969 (28 MAY) Two phosphor bands

796	326	5d multicoloured ..	10	10	☐	☐
	a	Block of 4 Nos. 796/9 ..	85	1·00	☐	☐
797	327	5d multicoloured ..	10	10	☐	☐
798	328	5d multicoloured ..	10	10	☐	☐
799	329	5d multicoloured ..	10	10	☐	☐
800	330	9d multicoloured ..	15	15	☐	☐
801	331	1s 6d multicoloured ..	15	15	☐	☐
		Set of 6	1·00	55	☐	☐
		First Day Cover		2·00		☐
		Presentation Pack	3·00		☐	
		Presentation Pack (German)	22·00		☐	

332 The King's Gate, Caernarvon Castle

333 The Eagle Tower, Caernarvon Castle

334 Queen Eleanor's Gate, Caernarvon Castle

335 Celtic Cross, Margam Abbey

The 5d values were printed *se-tenant* in strips of three throughout the sheet.

336 Prince Charles

337 Mahatma Gandhi

Investiture of H.R.H. The Prince of Wales

1969 (1 July) *Two phosphor bands*

802	**332**	5d multicoloured ..	10	10	☐	☐
		a. Strip of 3				
		Nos. 802/4 ..	70	75	☐	☐
803	**333**	5d multicoloured ..	10	10	☐	☐
804	**334**	5d multicoloured ..	10	10	☐	☐
805	**335**	9d multicoloured ..	20	10	☐	☐
806	**336**	1s black and gold	20	10	☐	☐
		Set of 5	1·00	45	☐	☐
		First Day Cover		1·25		☐
		Presentation Pack	1·40			☐
		Presentation Pack (German)	16·00			☐

Gandhi Centenary Year

1969 (13 Aug.) *Two phosphor bands*

807	**337**	1s 6d multicoloured ..	30	30	☐	☐
		First Day Cover		1·00		☐

Collectors Pack 1969

1969 (15 Sept.) *Comprises Nos. 775/86 and 791/807*

	Collectors Pack	20·00	☐

338 National Giro

339 Telecommunications

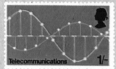

340 Telecommunications

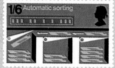

341 Automatic Sorting

British Post Office Technology

1969 (1 Oct.) *Two phosphor bands* Perf 13½ × 14

808	**338**	5d multicoloured ..	10	10	☐	☐
809	**339**	9d green, bl & blk ..	15	15	☐	☐
810	**340**	1s green, lav & blk..	15	15	☐	☐
811	**341**	1s 6d multicoloured ..	40	40	☐	☐
		Set of 4	70	70	☐	☐
		First Day Cover		1·00		☐
		Presentation Pack	2·25			☐

342 Herald Angel

343 The Three Shepherds

344 The Three Kings

Christmas

1969 (26 Nov.) *Two phosphor bands (5d, 1s 6d) or one centre band (4d)*

812	**342**	4d multicoloured ..	10	10	☐	☐
813	**343**	5d multicoloured ..	10	10	☐	☐
814	**344**	1s 6d multicoloured ..	30	30	☐	☐
		Set of 3	45	45	☐	☐
		First Day Cover		1·00		☐
		Presentation Pack	2·25			☐

345 Fife Harling

346 Cotswold Limestone

347 Welsh Stucco

348 Ulster Thatch

British Rural Architecture

1970 (11 Feb.) *Two phosphor bands*

815	**345**	5d multicoloured ..	10	10	☐	☐
816	**346**	9d multicoloured ..	20	20	☐	☐
817	**347**	1s multicoloured ..	20	20	☐	☐
818	**348**	1s 6d multicoloured ..	35	35	☐	☐
		Set of 4	75	75	☐	☐
		First Day Cover		1·25		☐
		Presentation Pack	3·00			☐

349 Signing the Declaration of Arbroath

350 Florence Nightingale attending Patients

351 Signing of International Co-operative Alliance

352 Pilgrims and *Mayflower*

353 Sir William Herschel, Francis Baily, Sir John Herschel and Telescope

Anniversaries. Events described on stamps

1970 (1 APR.) *Two phosphor bands*

819	**349**	5d multicoloured ..	10	10	☐	☐
820	**350**	9d multicoloured ..	15	15	☐	☐
821	**351**	1s multicoloured ..	25	15	☐	☐
822	**352**	1s 6d multicoloured ..	30	30	☐	☐
823	**353**	1s 9d multicoloured ..	30	30	☐	☐
		Set of 5	1·00	90	☐	☐
		First Day Cover		1·25	☐	
		Presentation Pack	3·00		☐	

354 'Mr Pickwick and Sam' (*Pickwick Papers*)

355 'Mr and Mrs Micawber' (*David Copperfield*)

356 'David Copperfield and Betsy Trotwood' (*David Copperfield*)

357 Oliver asking for more' (*Oliver Twist*)

The 5d values were issued together *se-tenant* in blocks of four within the sheet.

358 'Grasmere' (from engraving by J. Farrington, R.A.)

Literary Anniversaries. Events described on stamps

1970 (3 JUNE) *Two phosphor bands*

824	**354**	5d multicoloured ..	10	10	☐	☐
		a. Block of 4				
		Nos. 824/7 ..	90	90	☐	☐
825	**355**	5d multicoloured ..	10	10	☐	☐
826	**356**	5d multicoloured ..	10	10	☐	☐
827	**357**	5d multicoloured ..	10	10	☐	☐
828	**358**	1s 6d multicoloured ..	20	20	☐	☐
		Set of 5	1·00	55	☐	☐
		First Day Cover		2·00		☐
		Presentation Pack	3·00		☐	

359

359a (Value redrawn)

Decimal Currency

1970 (17 JUNE)–**72** 10p *and some printings of the* 50p *were issued on phosphor paper Perf* 12

829	**359**	10p cerise	1·00	75	☐	☐
830		20p olive-green ..	70	15	☐	☐
831		50p ultramarine ..	1·50	40	☐	☐
831b	**359a**	£1 black	3·50	75	☐	☐
		Set of 4	6·00	1·75	☐	☐
829/31		Presentation Pack ..	7·00		☐	
790 (or 831b), 830/1						
		Presentation Pack ..	8·00		☐	

For First Day Cover prices see page 37.

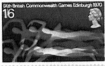

360 Runners

361 Swimmers

362 Cyclists

Ninth British Commonwealth Games

1970 (15 July) *Two phosphor bands*   Perf 13½ × 14

832	**360**	5d	pink, emerald, greenish yellow & yellow-green	10	10	□	□
833	**361**	1s 6d	greenish blue, lilac, brown and Prussian blue ..	50	50	□	.
834	**362**	1s 9d	yellow-orange, lilac, salmon and red-brown ..	50	50	□	□
	Set of 3	..	.. .. ..	1·00	1·00	□	□
	First Day Cover	..	.. ..		1·25		□
	Presentation Pack	..	..	2·50		□	

Collectors Pack 1970

1970 (14 Sept.) *Comprises Nos. 808/28 and 832/4*

	Collectors Pack	.. .. ..	24·00	□

363 1d Black (1840)

364 1s Green (1847)

365 4d Carmine (1855)

'Philympia 70' Stamp Exhibition

1970 (18 Sept.) *Two phosphor bands*   Perf 14 × 14½

835	**363**	5d	multicoloured ..	10	10	□	□
836	**364**	9d	multicoloured ..	35	35	□	□
837	**365**	1s 6d	multicoloured ..	40	40	□	□
	Set of 3	.. ..		75	75	□	□
	First Day Cover	.. .. ..			1·25		□
	Presentation Pack	.. ..		2·50		□	

366 Shepherds and Apparition of the Angel

367 Mary, Joseph, and Christ in the Manger

368 The Wise Men bearing Gifts

Christmas

1970 (25 Nov.) *Two phosphor bands (5d, 1s 6d) or one centre phosphor band (4d)*

838	**366**	4d	multicoloured ..	10	10	□	□
839	**367**	5d	multicoloured ..	10	10	□	□
840	**368**	1s 6d	multicoloured ..	35	35	□	□
	Set of 3	.. .. ..		50	50	□	□
	First Day Cover	.. ..			1·00		□
	Presentation Pack	..	2·50			□	

369

369a

Decimal Currency

1971-93. Type **369**

(a) *Printed in photogravure by Harrison & Sons (except for some ptgs of Nos, X879 and X913 which were produced by Enschedé.) with phosphor bands.* Perf 15 × 14.

X841	½p	turq-bl (2 bands) ..	10	10	□	□
X842	½p	turq-bl (1 side band) ..	60·00	25·00	□	□
X843	½p	turquoise-blue (1 centre band) ..	30	20	□	□
X844	1p	crimson (2 bands) ..	10	10	□	□
X845	1p	crim (1 centre band) ..	20	20	□	□
X846	1p	crimson ('all-over' phosphor)	20	20	□	□
X847	1p	crimson (1 side band)	1·50	1·00	□	□
X848	1½p	black (2 bands) ..	20	15	□	□
X849	2p	myr-grn (face value as in T **369**) (2 bands) ..	20	10	□	□
X850	2p	myr-grn (face value as in T **369**) 'all-over' phosphor	20	15	□	□
X851	2½p	mag (1 centre band) ..	15	10	□	□
X852	2½p	magenta (1 side band)	1·25	1·75	□	□
X853	2½p	magenta (2 bands) ..	30	75	□	□
X854	2½p	rose-red (2 bands) ..	50	60	□	□
X855	3p	ultramarine (2 bands)	20	10	□	□
X856	3p	ultram (1 centre band)	20	25	□	□
X857	3p	bright magenta (2 bands) ..	30	25	□	□
X858	3½p	olive-grey (2 bands) ..	30	30	□	□
X859	3½p	ol-grey (1 centre band)	30	15	□	□

X860	3½p purple-brown (1 centre band) ..	1·25	1·25	☐	☐
X861	4p ochre-brown (2 bands)	20	20	☐	☐
X862	4p greenish bl (2 bands)	1·50	1·50	☐	☐
X863	4p greenish blue (1 centre band) ..	1·00	1·00	☐	☐
X864	4p greenish blue (1 side band)	2·00	2·00	☐	☐
X865	4½p grey-blue (2 bands)	20	25	☐	☐
X866	5p pale violet (2 bands)	20	10	☐	☐
X867	5p claret (1 centre band)	1·50	1·50	☐	☐
X868	5½p violet (2 bands)	25	25	☐	☐
X869	5½p violet (1 centre band)	20	20	☐	☐
X870	6p light emerald (2 bands)	30	15	☐	☐
X871	6½p greenish bl (2 bands)	45	45	☐	☐
X872	6½p greenish blue (1 centre band) ..	30	15	☐	☐
X873	6½p greenish blue (1 side band) ..	60	55	☐	☐
X874	7p purple-brn (2 bands) ..	35	25	☐	☐
X875	7p purple-brown (1 centre band)	35	20	☐	☐
X876	7p purple-brown (1 side band) ..	60	75	☐	☐
X877	7½p chestnut (2 bands) ..	30	25	☐	☐
X878	8p rosine (2 bands)	25	20	☐	☐
X879	8p rosine (1 centre band)	25	15	☐	☐
X880	8p rosine (1 side band) ..	60	60	☐	☐
X881	8½p yellowish green (2 bands)	35	20	☐	☐
X882	9p yellow-orange and black (2 bands)	60	30	☐	☐
X883	9p deep violet (2 bands)	45	25	☐	☐
X884	9½p purple (2 bands)	45	30	☐	☐
X885	10p orange-brown and chestnut (2 bands) ..	40	30	☐	☐
X886	10p orange-brn (2 bands)	40	20	☐	☐
X887	10p orange-brown ('all-over' phosphor) ..	30	45	☐	☐
X888	10p orange-brown (1 centre band) ..	30	20	☐	☐
X889	10p orange-brown (1 side band) ..	60	60	☐	☐
X890	10½p yellow (2 bands) ..	40	30	☐	☐
X891	10½p blue (2 bands) ..	60	45	☐	☐
X892	11p brown-red (2 bands)	60	25	☐	☐
X893	11½p drab (1 centre band)	45	30	☐	☐
X894	11½p drab (1 side band)	60	60	☐	☐
X895	12p yellowish green (2 bands)	60	40	☐	☐
X896	12p bright emerald (1 centre band) ..	60	40	☐	☐
X897	12p bright emerald (1 side band)	75	75	☐	☐
X898	12½p light emerald (1 centre band) ..	45	25	☐	☐
X899	12½p light emerald (1 side band)	60	60	☐	☐
X900	13p pale chestnut (1 centre band) ..	45	35	☐	☐
X901	13p pale chestnut (1 side band)	60	60	☐	☐
X902	14p grey-blue (2 bands) ..	50	45	☐	☐

X903	14p dp bl (1 centre band)	60	40	☐	☐
X904	14p dp blue (1 side band)	2·50	1·75	☐	☐
X905	15p brt bl (1 centre band)	25	20	☐	☐
X906	15p brt blue (1 side band)	2·00	1·75	☐	☐
X907	15½p pale violet (2 bands) ..	45	45	☐	☐
X908	16p olive-drab (2 bands) ..	1·00	1·25	☐	☐
X909	17p grey-blue (2 bands) ..	75	75	☐	☐
X910	17p dp bl (1 centre band)	50	50	☐	☐
X911	17p dp bl (1 side band) ..	1·00	1·00	☐	☐
X912	18p dp ol-grey (2 bands)	75	75	☐	☐
X913	18p bright green (1 centre band)	30	35	☐	☐
X914	19p bright orange-red (2 bands)	1·00	1·00	☐	☐
X915	20p dull purple (2 bands)	75	40	☐	☐
X916	20p brownish black (2 bands)	1·00	1·00	☐	☐
X917	22p bright orange-red (2 bands)	1·00	1·00	☐	☐
X918	26p rosine (2 bands) ..	5·50	5·50	☐	☐
X919	31p purple (2 bands) ..	6·00	6·00	☐	☐
X920	34p ochre-brown (2 bands)	5·50	5·50	☐	☐
X921	50p ochre-brown (2 bands)	1·75	40	☐	☐
X922	50p ochre (2 bands) ..	4·50	4·50	☐	☐

(b) Printed in photogravure by Harrison and Sons on phosphorised paper. Perf 15 × 14

X924	½p turquoise-blue ..	10	10	☐	☐
X925	1p crimson	10	10	☐	☐
X926	2p myrtle-green (face value as in T **369**)	10	10	☐	☐
X927	2p deep green (smaller value as in T **369a**)	10	10	☐	☐
X928	2p myr-grn (smaller value as in T **369a**)	1·00	75	☐	☐
X929	2½p rose-red	20	20	☐	☐
X930	3p bright magenta ..	20	20	☐	☐
X931	3½p purple-brown ..	45	45	☐	☐
X932	4p greenish blue	25	20	☐	☐
X933	4p new blue	10	10	☐	☐
X934	5p pale violet	30	25	☐	☐
X935	5p dull red-brown ..	10	10	☐	☐
X936	6p olive-yellow	10	15	☐	☐
X937	7p brownish red ..	1·50	2·00	☐	☐
X938	8½p yellowish green ..	30	55	☐	☐
X939	10p orange-brown ..	30	20	☐	☐
X940	10p dull orange ..	15	15	☐	☐
X941	11p brown-red ..	75	75	☐	☐
X942	11½p ochre-brown ..	50	45	☐	☐
X943	12p yellowish green ..	45	40	☐	☐
X944	13p olive-grey	60	45	☐	☐
X945	13½p purple-brown ..	65	60	☐	☐
X946	14p grey-blue	50	40	☐	☐
X947	15p ultramarine ..	50	40	☐	☐
X948	15½p pale violet	50	40	☐	☐
X949	16p olive-drab ..	60	30	☐	☐
X950	16½p pale chestnut ..	85	75	☐	☐
X951	17p light emerald ..	70	40	☐	☐
X952	17p grey-blue	50	40	☐	☐
X953	17½p pale chestnut ..	80	80	☐	☐
X954	18p deep violet	70	75	☐	☐
X955	18p deep olive-grey ..	70	60	☐	☐
X956	19p bright orange-red	60	40	☐	☐

X957	19½p olive-grey	1·75	1·50	□ □
X958	20p dull purple	80	20	□ □
X959	20p turquoise-green ..	30	35	□ □
X960	20p brownish black	30	30	□ □
X961	20½p ultramarine	1·00	85	□ □
X962	22p blue	80	45	□ □
X963	22p yellow-green	60	55	□ □
X964	22p bright orange-red ..	60	50	□ □
X965	23p brown-red	1·10	60	□ □
X966	23p bright green	70	40	□ □
X967	24p violet	1·75	85	□ □
X968	24p Indian red	60	60	□ □
X969	24p chestnut	35	40	□ □
X970	25p purple	90	90	□ □
X971	26p rosine	90	30	□ □
X972	26p drab	70	70	□ □
X973	27p chestnut	1·00	85	□ □
X974	27p violet	75	75	□ □
X975	28p deep violet.	90	90	□ □
X976	28p ochre	75	75	□ □
X977	28p deep bluish grey ..	45	50	□ □
X978	29p ochre-brown	2·00	1·25	□ □
X979	29p deep mauve	1·00	60	□ □
X980	30p deep olive-grey ..	45	50	□ □
X981	31p purple	1·25	1·25	□ □
X982	31p ultramarine	90	90	□ □
X983	32p greenish blue	1·00	1·00	□ □
X984	33p light emerald	70	70	□ □
X985	34p ochre-brown	1·10	80	□ □
X986	34p deep bluish grey ..	1·00	80	□ □
X987	34p deep mauve	55	60	□ □
X988	35p sepia	1·25	75	□ □
X989	35p yellow	55	60	□ □
X990	37p rosine	85	85	□ □
X991	39p bright mauve	60	65	□ □

(c) Printed in photogravure by Harrison and Sons on ordinary paper. Perf 15 × 14

X992	50p ochre-brown	1·50	45	□ □
X993	75p grey-black (smaller values as T **369**a) ..	1·10	1·25	□ □

(d) Printed in photogravure by Harrison and Sons on ordinary paper or phosphorised paper. Perf 15 × 14

X994	50p ochre	75	45	□ □

(e) Printed in lithography by John Waddington. Perf 14.

X996	4p greenish blue (2 bands)	20	25	□ □
X997	4p greenish blue (phosphorised paper)	35	20	□ □
X998	20p dull purple (2 bands)	1·00	40	□ □
X999	20p dull purple (phosphorised paper)	1·25	40	□ □

(f) Printed in lithography by Questa. Perf 13½ × 14 (Nos X1000, X1003/4 and X1023) or 15 × 14 (others)

X1000	2p emerald-green (face value as in T **369**) (phosphorised paper)	20	20	□ □
	a *Perf* 15 × 14	30	20	□ □

X1001	2p bright grn and dp grn (smaller value as in T **369**a) (phosphorised paper)	35	35	□ □
X1002	4p greenish blue (phosphorised paper)	50	50	□ □
X1003	5p light violet (phosphorised paper)	40	20	□ □
X1004	5p claret (phosphorised paper)	50	20	□ □
	a *Perf* 15 × 14	50	25	□ □
X1005	13p pale chest (1 centre band)	70	70	□ □
X1006	13p pale chest (1 side band)	60	60	□ □
X1007	14p dp bl (1 centre band) ..	1·00	50	□ □
X1008	17p dp bl (1 centre band)	1·00	1·00	□ □
X1009	18p deep olive-grey (phosphorised paper)	1·00	1·00	□ □
X1010	18p dp ol-grey (2 bands)	4·00	4·00	□ □
X1011	18p bright green (1 centre band)	75	75	□ □
X1012	18p bright green (1 side band)	1·50	1·50	□ □
X1013	19p bright orange-red (phosphorised paper)	1·50	1·50	□ □
X1014	20p dull purple (phosphorised paper)	1·25	1·25	□ □
X1015	22p yell-grn (2 bands) ..	5·00	5·00	□ □
X1016	22p bright.orange-red (phosphorised paper)	1·00	1·00	□ □
X1017	24p chestnut (phosphorised paper)	60	60	□ □
X1018	24p chestnut (2 bands) ..	1·50	1·50	□ □
X1019	33p light emerald (phosphorised paper)	2·00	2·00	□ □
X1020	33p light emer (2 bands)	1·25	1·25	□ □
X1021	34p ochre-brn (2 bands)	5·00	5·00	□ □
X1022	39p brt mauve (2 bands)	2·50	2·50	□ □
X1023	75p black (face value as T **369**) (ordinary paper)	3·00	1·50	□ □
	a *Perf* 15 × 14	3·00	3·00	□ □
X1024	75p brownish grey and black (smaller value as T **369**a) (ordinary paper)	7·50	5·00	□ □

(g) Printed in lithography by Walsall. Perf 14

X1050	2p deep green (phosphorised paper)	10	10	□ □
X1051	14p deep blue (1 side band)	3·00	3·00	□ □
X1052	19p bright orange-red (2 bands)	1·00	1·00	□ □
X1053	24p chestnut (phosphorised paper)	35	40	□ □
X1054	29p deep mauve (2 bands)	3·50	3·00	□ □
X1055	29p deep mauve (phosphorised paper)	3·50	3·50	□ □
X1056	31p ultramarine (phosphorised paper)	1·25	1·25	□ □
X1057	33p light emerald (phosphorised paper)	50	55	□ □
X1058	39p bright mauve (phosphorised paper)	60	65	□ □

Presentation Pack (contains ½p (X841), 1p (X844), 1½p (X848), 2p (X849), 2½p (X851), 3p (X855), 3½p (X858), 4p (X861), 5p (X866), 6p (X870), 7½p (X877), 9p (X882))   4·00 ☐

Presentation Pack ('Scandinavia 71') (contents as above) .. .. .. 32·00 ☐

Presentation Pack (contains ½p (X841), 1p (X844), 1½p (X848), 2p (X849), 2½p (X851), 3p (X855 or X856), 3½p (X858 or X859), 4p (X861), 4½p (X865), 5p (X866), 5½p (X868 or X869), 6p (X870), 6½p (X871 or X872), 7p (X874), 7½p (X877), 8p (X878), 9p (X882), 10p (X885)) .. .. 4·00 ☐

Presentation Pack (contains ½p (X841), 1p (X844), 1½p (X848), 2p (X849), 2½p (X851), 3p (X856), 5p (X866), 6½p (X872), 7p (X874 or X875), 7½p (X877), 8p (X878), 8½p (X881), 9p (X883), 9½p (X884) 10p (X886), 10½p (X890), 11p (X892) 20p (X915), 50p (X921)) .. .. 5·00 ☐

Presentation Pack (contains 2½p (X929), 3p (X930), 4p (X996), 10½p (X891), 11½p (X893), 11½p (X942), 12p (X943), 13p (X944), 13½p (X945), 14p (X946), 15p (X947), 15½p (X948), 17p (X951), 17½p (X953), 18p (X954), 22p (X962), 25p (X970), 75p (X1023)) 16·00 ☐

Presentation Pack (Contains ½p (X924), 1p (X925), 2p (X1000), 3p (X930), 3½p (X931), 4p (X997), 5p (X1004), 10p (X888), 12½p (X898), 16p (X949), 16½p (X950), 17p (X952), 20p (X999), 20½p (X961), 23p (X965), 26p (X971), 28p (X975), 31p (X981), 50p (X992), 75p (X1023)) .. .. 22·00 ☐

Presentation Pack (contains ½p (X924), 1p (X925), 2p (X1000a), 3p (X930), 4p (X997), 5p (X1004a), 10p (X939), 13p (X900), 16p (X949), 17p (X952), 18p (X955), 20p (X999), 22p (X963), 24p (X967), 26p (X971), 28p (X975), 31p (X981), 34p (X985), 50p (X992), 75p (X1023a)) .. .. 20·00 ☐

Presentation Pack (contains 1p (X925), 2p (X1000a), 3p (X930), 4p (X997), 5p (X1004a), 7p (X937), 10p (X939), 12p (X896),

13p (X900), 17p (X952), 18p (X955), 20p (X999), 22p (X963), 24p (X967), 26p (X971), 28p (X975), 31p (X981), 34p (X985), 50p (X992), 75p (X1023a)) .. .. 16·00 ☐

Presentation Pack (contains 14p (X903), 19p (X956), 20p (X959), 23p (X966), 27p (X973), 28p (X976), 32p (X983), 35p (X988)) 9·00 ☐

Presentation Pack (contains 15p (X905), 20p (X960), 24p (X968), 29p (X979), 30p (X980), 34p (X986), 37p (X990) .. .. .. 7·00 ☐

Presentation Pack (contains 10p (X940), 17p (X910), 22p (X964), 26p (X972), 27p (X974), 31p (X982), 33p (X984) .. .. .. 6·00 ☐

Presentation Pack (contains 1p (X925), 2p (X927), 3p (X930), 4p (X933), 5p (X935), 10p (X940), 17p (X910), 20p (X959), 22p (X964), 26p (X972), 27p (X974), 30p (X980), 31p (X982), 32p (X983), 33p (X984), 37p (X990), 50p (X994), 75p (X993)) .. .. 7·00 ☐

Presentation Pack (contains 6p (X936), 18p (X913), 24p (X969), 28p (X977), 34p (X987), 35p (X989), 39p (X991)) .. .. .. 3·25 ☐

"X" NUMBERS These are provisional only and may be amended in future editions.

PHOSPHOR BANDS See notes on page 15.
Phosphor bands are applied to the stamps, after the design has been printed, by a separate cylinder. On issues with "all-over" phosphor the "band" covers the entire stamp. Parts of the stamp covered by phosphor bands, or the entire surface for "all-over" phosphor versions, appear matt.
Nos. X847, X852, X864, X873, X876, X880, X889, X894, X897, X899, X901, X906, X911, X1006 and X1012 exist with the phosphor band at the left or right of the stamp.

PHOSPHORISED PAPER. First introduced as an experiment for a limited printing of the 1s 6d value (No. 743c) in 1969 this paper has the phosphor, to activate the automatic sorting machinery, added to the paper coating before the stamps were printed. Issues on this paper have a completely shiny surface. Although not adopted after this first trial further experiments on the 8½p in 1976 led to this paper being used for new printings of current values.

For similar stamps, but with elliptical perforations see Nos. Y1667/81 in 1993.

Keep this Catalogue up to date month by month with —

The only magazine with the Stanley Gibbons Catalogue supplement – and much more besides!

Please send for a FREE COPY and subscription details to:

Hugh Jefferies
Stanley Gibbons Publications
5 Parkside, Christchurch Road,
Ringwood, Hampshire BH24 3SH
Telephone 0425 472363

QUEEN ELIZABETH II DEFINITIVE FIRST DAY COVERS

The British Post Office did not introduce special First Day of Issue postmarks for definitive issues until the first instalment of the Machin £sd series, issued 5 June 1967, although "First Day" treatment had been provided for some Regional stamps from 8 June 1964 onwards.

1952–1966

PRICES for First Day Covers listed below are for stamps, as indicated, used on illustrated envelopes and postmarked with operational cancellations.

5 Dec. 1952	1½d, 2½d (Nos. 517, 519) ..	6·00 ☐
6 July 1953	5d, 8d, 1s (Nos. 522, 525, 529)	25·00 ☐
31 Aug. 1953	½d, 1d, 2d (Nos. 515/16, 518)	20·00 ☐
2 Nov. 1953	4d, 1s 3d, 1s 6d (Nos. 521, 530/1)	50·00 ☐
18 Jan. 1954	3d, 6d, 7d (Nos. 520, 523/4)	30·00 ☐
8 Feb. 1954	9d, 10d, 11d (Nos. 526/8) ..	60·00 ☐
1 Sept. 1955	10s, £1 (Nos. 538/9)	£400 ☐
23 Sept. 1955	2s 6d, 5s (Nos. 536/7) ..	£175 ☐
19 Nov. 1957	½d, 1d, 1½d, 2d, 2½d, 3d (graphite lines) (Nos. 561/6)	60·00 ☐
9 Feb. 1959	4½d (No. 577)	45·00 ☐

1967–1989

PRICES for First Day Covers listed below are for stamps, as indicated, used on illustrated envelopes and postmarked with the special First Day of Issue handstamps. Other definitives issued during this period were not accepted for "First Day" treatment by the British Post Office.

£sd Machin Issues

5 June 1967	4d, 1s, 1s 9d (Nos.731,742, 744)	1·40 ☐
8 Aug. 1967	3d, 9d, 1s 6d (Nos.729,740, 743)	1·40 ☐
5 Feb. 1968	½d, 1d, 2d, 6d (Nos. 723/4, 726, 736)	75 ☐
1 July 1968	5d, 7d, 8d, 10d (Nos. 735, 737/8, 741)	1·10 ☐
5 March 1969	2s 6d, 5s, 10s, £1 (Nos. 787/90)	15·00 ☐

Decimal Machin Issues

17 June 1970	10p, 20p, 50p, (Nos. 829/31)	5·50 ☐
15 Feb. 1971	½p, 1p, 1½p, 2p, 2½p, 3p, 3½p, 4p, 5p, 6p, 7½p, 9p (Nos. X841, X844, X848/9, X851, X855, X858, X861, X866, X870, X877, X882) (Covers carry "POSTING DELAYED BY THE POST OFFICE STRIKE 1971" cachet) ..	2·25 ☐
11 Aug. 1971	10p (No. X885)	1·00 ☐

6 Dec. 1972	£1 (No. 831b)	7·00 ☐
24 Oct. 1973	4½p, 5½p, 8p (Nos. X865 X868, X878)	1·00 ☐
4 Sept. 1974	6½p (No. X871)	1·10 ☐
15 Jan. 1975	7p (No. X874)	75 ☐
24 Sept. 1975	8½p (No. X881)	1·25 ☐
25 Feb. 1976	9p, 9½p, 10p, 10½p, 11p, 20p (Nos. X883/4, X886, X890, X892, X915)	2·75 ☐
2 Feb. 1977	50p (No. X921)	2·25 ☐
2 Feb. 1977	£1, £2, £5 (Nos. 1026, 1027/8)	12·00 ☐
26 April. 1978	10½p (No. X891)	1·00 ☐
15 Aug. 1979	11½p, 13p, 15p (Nos. X942, X944, X947)	2·00 ☐
30 Jan. 1980	4p, 12p, 13½p, 17p, 17½p, 75p (Nos. X996, X943, X945, X951, X953, X1023)	4·50 ☐
22 Oct. 1980	3p, 22p, (Nos. X930, X962)	1·00 ☐
14 Jan. 1981	2½p, 11½p, 14p, 15½p, 18p, 25p (Nos. X929, X893, X946, X948, X954, X970)	2·25 ☐
27 Jan. 1982	5p, 12½p, 16½p, 19½p, 26p, 29p (Nos. X1004, X898, X950, X957, X971, X978) ..	3·25 ☐
30 March 1983	3½p, 16p, 17p, 20½p 23p, 28p, 31p (Nos. X931, X949, X952, X961, X965, X975, X981)	4·50 ☐
3 Aug. 1983	£1·30 (No. 1026b)	8·00 ☐
28 Aug. 1984	13p, 18p, 22p, 24p, 34p (Nos. X900, X955, X963, X967, X985)	5·00 ☐
28 Aug. 1984	£1·33 (No. 1026c)	7·50 ☐
17 Sept. 1985	£1·41 (No. 1026d)	7·00 ☐
29 Oct. 1985	7p, 12p, (Nos. X937, X896)	2·50 ☐
2 Sept. 1986	£1·50 (No. 1026e)	6·50 ☐
15 Sept. 1987	£1·60 (No. 1026f)	6·50 ☐
23 Aug. 1988	14p, 19p, 20p, 23p, 27p, 28p, 32p, 35p (Nos. X903, X956, X959, X966, X973, X976, X983, X988)	5·50 ☐
26 Sept. 1989	15p, 20p, 24p, 29p, 30p, 34p, 37p (Nos. X905, X960, X968, X979/80, X986, X990) ..	4·00 ☐
4 Sept. 1990	10p, 17p, 22p, 26p, 27p, 31p, 33p (Nos. X940, X910, X964, X972, X974, X982, X984)	3·50 ☐
10 Sept. 1991	6p, 18p, 24p, 28p, 34p, 35p, 39p (Nos. X936, X913, X969, X977, X987, X989, X991) ..	4·50 ☐

For First Day Covers of the 1989 and 1990 1st and 2nd class stamps and for the 1990 150th Anniversary of the Penny Black see pages 86, 87 and 90.

370 'A Mountain Road'
(T. P. Flanagan)

371 'Deer's Meadow'
(Tom Carr)

372 'Slieve na brock'
(Colin Middleton)

'Ulster '71' Paintings

1971 (16 JUNE) *Two phosphor bands*

881	**370**	3p multicoloured ..		10	10	☐ ☐
882	**371**	7½p multicoloured ..		50	50	☐ ☐
883	**372**	9p multicoloured ..		50	50	☐ ☐
		Set of 3		1·00	1·00	☐ ☐
		First Day Cover			1·50	☐
		Presentation Pack		5·00		☐

373 John Keats
(150th Death Anniv)

374 Thomas Gray
(Death Bicentenary)

375 Sir Walter Scott
(Birth Bicentenary)

Literary Anniversaries. Events described above

1971 (28 JULY) *Two phosphor bands*

884	**373**	3p black, gold & bl ..		10	10	☐ ☐
885	**374**	5p blk, gold & olive		50	50	☐ ☐
886	**375**	7½p black, gold & brn		50	50	☐ ☐
		Set of 3		1·00	1·00	☐ ☐
		First Day Cover			1·50	☐ ☐
		Presentation Pack		5·00		☐

376 Servicemen and Nurse
of 1921

377 Roman Centurion

378 Rugby Football, 1871

British Anniversaries. Events described on stamps

1971 (25 AUG.) *Two phosphor bands*

887	**376**	3p multicoloured ..		10	10	☐ ☐
888	**377**	7½p multicoloured ..		50	50	☐ ☐
889	**378**	9p multicoloured ..		50	50	☐ ☐
		Set of 3		1·00	1·00	☐ ☐
		First Day Cover			1·50	☐
		Presentation Pack		5·00		☐

379 Physical Sciences Building,
University College of
Wales, Aberystwyth

380 Faraday Building,
Southampton
University

381 Engineering Department,
Leicester University

382 Hexagon Restaurant,
Essex University

British Architecture (Modern University Buildings)

1971 (22 SEPT.) *Two phosphor bands*

890	**379**	3p multicoloured	10	10	□	□
891	**380**	5p multicoloured ..	20	20	□	□
892	**381**	7½p ochre, black and purple-brown..	50	50	□	□
893	**382**	9p multicoloured	90	90	□	□
		Set of 4	1·50	1·50	□	□
		First Day Cover		1·50		□
		Presentation Pack	5·00		□	

Collectors Pack 1971

1971 (29 SEPT.) *Comprises Nos. 835/40 and 881/93*

		Collectors Pack	28·00	□

383 'Dream of the Wise Men'

384 'Adoration of the Magi'

385 'Ride of the Magi'

Christmas

1971 (13 OCT.) *Two phosphor bands (3p, 7½p) or one centre phosphor band (2½p)*

894	**383**	2½p multicoloured ..	10	10	□	□
895	**384**	3p multicoloured ..	10	10	□	□
896	**385**	7½p multicoloured ..	90	90	□	□
		Set of 3	1·00	1·00	□	□
		First Day Cover		1·50		□
		Presentation Pack	4·00		□	

386 Sir James Clark Ross

387 Sir Martin Frobisher

388 Henry Hudson

389 Capt. Robert F. Scott

British Polar Explorers

1972 (16 FEB.) *Two phosphor bands*

897	**386**	3p multicoloured ..	10	10	□	□
898	**387**	5p multicoloured ..	20	20	□	□
899	**388**	7½p multicoloured ..	50	50	□	□
900	**389**	9p multicoloured ..	90	90	□	□
		Set of 4	1·50	1·50	□	□
		First Day Cover		1·50		□
		Presentation Pack	4·50		□	

390 Statuette of Tutankhamun

391 19th-century Coastguard

392 Ralph Vaughan Williams and Score

Anniversaries. Events described on stamps

1972 (26 APR.) *Two phosphor bands*

901	**390**	3p multicoloured ..	10	10	□	□
902	**391**	7½p multicoloured ..	50	50	□	□
903	**392**	9p multicoloured ..	50	50	□	□
		Set of 3	1·00	1·00	□	□
		First Day Cover		1·50		□
		Presentation Pack	4·00		□	

393 St Andrew's, Greensted-
juxta-Ongar, Essex

394 All Saints, Earls
Barton, Northants

395 St Andrew's,
Letheringsett, Norfolk

396 St Andrew's,
Helpringham, Lincs

397 St Mary the Virgin, Huish
Episcopi, Somerset

British Architecture (Village Churches)

1972 (21 JUNE) *Two phosphor bands*

904	**393**	3p multicoloured ..	10	10	☐	☐
905	**394**	4p multicoloured ..	20	20	☐	☐
906	**395**	5p multicoloured ..	20	25	☐	☐
907	**396**	7½p multicoloured ..	70	80	☐	☐
908	**397**	9p multicoloured ..	75	90	☐	☐
	Set of 5		1·75	2·00	☐	☐
	First Day Cover			3·00		☐
	Presentation Pack ..		5·00		☐	

'Belgica '72' Souvenir Pack

1972 (24 JUNE) *Comprises Nos. 894/6 and 904/8*

	Souvenir Pack	9·50		☐

398 Microphones, 1924–69

399 Horn Loudspeaker

400 TV Camera, 1972

401 Oscillator and Spark
Transmitter, 1897

Broadcasting Anniversaries. Events described on stamps

1972 (13 SEPT.) *Two phosphor bands*

909	**398**	3p multicoloured ..	10	10	☐	☐
910	**399**	5p multicoloured ..	15	20	☐	☐
911	**400**	7½p multicoloured ..	60	60	☐	☐
912	**401**	9p multicoloured ..	60	60	☐	☐
	Set of 4		1·25	1·25	☐	☐
	First Day Cover			2·00		☐
	Presentation Pack		3·50		☐	

402 Angel holding Trumpet

403 Angel playing Lute

404 Angel playing Harp

Christmas

1972 (18 Oct.) *Two phosphor bands (3p, 7½p) or one centre phosphor band (2½p)*

913	**402**	2½p multicoloured ..	10	15	☐	☐
914	**403**	3p multicoloured ..	10	15	☐	☐
915	**404**	7½p multicoloured ..	90	80	☐	☐
		Set of 3	1·00	1·00	☐	☐
		First Day Cover		1·25		☐
		Presentation Pack	2·75		☐	

407 Oak Tree

British Trees (1st issue)

1973 (28 Feb.) *Two phosphor bands*

922	**407**	9p multicoloured ..	50	50	☐	☐
		First Day Cover		1·00		☐
		Presentation Pack	2·25		☐	

See also No. 949.

405 Queen Elizabeth II and Prince Philip

406 'Europe'

Royal Silver Wedding

1972 (20 Nov.) *3p 'all-over' phosphor, 20p without phosphor*

916	**405**	3p brownish black, deep blue and silver ..	20	20	☐	☐
917		20p brownish black, reddish purple and silver ..	80	80	☐	☐
		Set of 2	1·00	1·00	☐	☐
		First Day Cover		1·25		☐
		Presentation Pack	2·25		☐	
		Presentation Pack (Japanese)	3·50		☐	
		Souvenir Book	3·00		☐	
		Gutter Pair (3p)	1·00		☐	
		Traffic Light Gutter Pair (3p)	22·00		☐	

Collectors Pack 1972

1972 (20 Nov.) *Comprises Nos. 897/917*

	Collectors Pack	28·00		☐

Nos. 920/1 were issued horizontally *se-tenant* throughout the sheet.

Britain's Entry into European Communities

1973 (3 Jan.) *Two phosphor bands*

919	**406**	3p multicoloured ..	10	10	☐	☐
920		5p multicoloured (blue jigsaw) ..	25	35	☐	☐
		a. Pair. Nos. 920/1	1·10	1·25	☐	☐
921		5p multicoloured (green jigsaw)	25	35	☐	☐
		Set of 3	1·10	70	☐	☐
		First Day Cover		1·50		☐
		Presentation Pack	2·25		☐	

408 David Livingstone

409 H. M. Stanley

The above were issued horizontally *se-tenant* throughout the sheet.

410 Sir Francis Drake

411 Sir Walter Raleigh

412 Charles Sturt

British Explorers

1973 (18 APR.) *'All-over' phosphor*

923	**408**	3p multicoloured ..	25	20	☐	☐
		a. Pair. Nos. 923/4	1·00	1·75	☐	☐
924	**409**	3p multicoloured ..	25	20	☐	☐
925	**410**	5p multicoloured ..	20	30	☐	☐
926	**411**	7½p multicoloured ..	20	30	☐	☐
927	**412**	9p multicoloured ..	25	40	☐	☐
		Set of 5	1·50	1·25	☐	☐
		First Day Cover		2·00		☐
		Presentation Pack	3·50		☐	

413   **414**

415

County Cricket 1873–1973

1973 (16 MAY) *Designs show sketches of W. G. Grace by Harry Furniss. Queen's head in gold. 'All-over' phosphor*

928	**413**	3p black and brown	10	10	☐	☐
929	**414**	7½p black and green	70	70	☐	☐
930	**415**	9p black and blue	90	90	☐	☐
		Set of 3	1·50	1·50	☐	☐
		First Day Cover		2·00		☐
		Presentation Pack	3·50		☐	
		Souvenir Book	6·25		☐	
		PHQ Card (No. 928)	50·00	£140	☐	☐

For full information on all future British issues, collectors should write to the British Post Office Philatelic Bureau, 20 Brandon Street, Edinburgh EH3 5TT

416 'Self-portrait' (Sir Joshua Reynolds)

417 'Self-portrait' (Sir Henry Raeburn)

418 'Nelly O'Brien' (Sir Joshua Reynolds)

419 'Rev R. Walker (The Skater)' (Sir Henry Raeburn)

Artistic Anniversaries. Events described on stamps

1973 (4 JULY) *'All-over' phosphor*

931	**416**	3p multicoloured ..	10	10	☐	☐
932	**417**	5p multicoloured ..	20	25	☐	☐
933	**418**	7½p multicoloured ..	45	40	☐	☐
934	**419**	9p multicoloured ..	50	50	☐	☐
		Set of 4	1·10	1·10	☐	☐
		First Day Cover		1·75		☐
		Presentation Pack	2·75		☐	

420 Court Masque Costumes

421 St Paul's Church, Covent Garden

422 Prince's Lodging, Newmarket

423 Court Masque Stage Scene

42

The 3p and 5p values were printed horizontally *se-tenant* within the sheet.

400th Anniversary of the Birth of Inigo Jones

1973 (15 AUG.) *'All-over' phosphor*

935	420	3p	deep mauve, black and gold ..	10	15	☐	☐
	a.		Pair. Nos. 935/6	35	40	☐	☐
936	421	3p	deep brown, black and gold ..	10	15	☐	☐
937	422	5p	blue, black and gold	40	45	☐	☐
	a.		Pair. Nos. 937/8	1·50	1·50	☐	☐
938	423	5p	grey-olive, black and gold	40	45	☐	☐
		Set of 4		1·60	1·10	☐	☐
		First Day Cover			2·00		☐
		Presentation Pack		3·50		☐	
		PHQ Card (No. 936)		£125	70·00	☐	☐

424 Palace of Westminster seen from Whitehall

425 Palace of Westminster seen from Millbank

19th Commonwealth Parliamentary Conference

1973 (12 SEPT.) *'All-over' phosphor*

939	424	8p	black, grey and pale buff	50	60	☐	☐
940	425	10p	gold and black	50	40	☐	☐
		Set of 2		1·00	1·00	☐	☐
		First Day Cover			1·25		☐
		Presentation Pack		2·00		☐	
		Souvenir Book		5·00		☐	
		PHQ Card (No. 939)		35·00	90·00	☐	☐

426 Princess Anne and Captain Mark Phillips

Royal Wedding

1973 (14 Nov.) *'All-over' phosphor*

941	426	3½p	violet and silver	10	10	☐	☐
942		20p	brown and silver	90	90	☐	☐
		Set of 2		1·00	1·00	☐	☐
		First Day Cover			1·25		☐
		Presentation Pack		2·00		☐	
		PHQ Card (No. 941)		8·00	22·00	☐	☐
		Set of 2 Gutter Pairs ..		6·00		☐	
		Set of 2 Traffic Light Gutter Pairs		90·00		☐	

427

428

429

430

431

432 'Good King Wenceslas, the Page and Peasant'

The 3p values depict the carol 'Good King Wenceslas' and were printed horizontally *se-tenant* within the sheet.

Christmas

1973 (28 Nov.) *One phosphor band* (3p) *or 'all-over' phosphor* (3½p)

943	427	3p	multicoloured ..	15	15	☐	☐
	a.		Strip of 5. Nos. 943/7 ..	2·75	2·50	☐	☐
944	428	3p	multicoloured ..	15	15	☐	☐
945	429	3p	multicoloured ..	15	15	☐	☐
946	430	3p	multicoloured ..	15	15	☐	☐
947	431	3p	multicoloured ..	15	15	☐	☐
948	432	3½p	multicoloured ..	15	15	☐	☐
		Set of 6	2·75	80	☐	☐
		First Day Cover		2·00		☐
		Presentation Pack ..	3·25		☐	

Collectors Pack 1973

1973 (28 Nov.) *Comprises Nos.* 919/48

	Collectors Pack	26·00		☐

433 Horse Chestnut

British Trees (2nd issue)

1974 (27 FEB.) *'All-over' phosphor*

949	**433**	10p multicoloured ..	50	50	☐	☐
		First Day Cover		1·00		☐
		Presentation Pack	2·25		☐
		PHQ Card	£100	60·00	☐	☐
		Gutter Pair	3·00		☐
		Traffic Light Gutter Pair ..	65·00		☐

434 First Motor Fire-engine, 1904

435 Prize-winning Fire-engine, 1863

436 Steam Fire-engine, 1830

437 Fire-engine, 1766

200th Anniversary of Public Fire Services

1974 (24 APR.) *'All-over' phosphor*

950	**434**	3½p multicoloured ..	10	10	☐	☐
951	**435**	5½p multicoloured ..	25	25	☐	☐
952	**436**	8p multicoloured ..	35	35	☐	☐
953	**437**	10p multicoloured ..	40	40	☐	☐
		Set of 4	1·00	1·00	☐	☐
		First Day Cover		3·00		☐
		Presentation Pack	2·50		☐
		PHQ Card (No. 950) ..	£100	50·00	☐	☐
		Set of 4 Gutter Pairs ..	4·00		☐
		Set of 4 Traffic Light Gutter Pairs	65·00		☐

438 P & O Packet Peninsular, 1888

439 Farman Biplane, 1911

440 Airmail-blue Van and Postbox, 1930

441 Imperial Airways 'C' Class Flying-boat, 1937

Centenary of Universal Postal Union

1974 (12 JUNE) *'All-over' phosphor*

954	**438**	3½p multicoloured ..	10	10	☐	☐
955	**439**	5½p multicoloured ..	20	25	☐	☐
956	**440**	8p multicoloured ..	30	35	☐	☐
957	**441**	10p multicoloured ..	50	40	☐	☐
		Set of 4	1·00	1·00	☐	☐
		First Day Cover		1·25		☐
		Presentation Pack	2·00		☐
		Set of 4 Gutter Pairs ..	4·00		☐
		Set of 4 Traffic Light Gutter Pairs	45·00		☐

442 Robert the Bruce

443 Owain Glyndŵr

444 Henry the Fifth

445 The Black Prince

Medieval Warriors

1974 (10 JULY) *'All-over' phosphor*

958	**442**	4½p multicoloured ..	10	10	☐	☐
959	**443**	5½p multicoloured ..	20	20	☐	☐
960	**444**	8p multicoloured ..	40	40	☐	☐
961	**445**	10p multicoloured ..	40	40	☐	☐
		Set of 4	1·00	1·00	☐	☐
		First Day Cover		2·50		☐
		Presentation Pack.. ..	3·50		☐
		PHQ Cards (set of 4)	30·00	24·00	☐	☐
		Set of 4 Gutter Pairs	6·00		☐
		Set of 4 Traffic Light Gutter Pairs	70·00		☐

446 Churchill in Royal Yacht Squadron Uniform

447 Prime Minister, 1940

448 Secretary for War and Air, 1919

449 War Correspondent, South Africa, 1899

Birth Centenary of Sir Winston Churchill

1974 (9 Oct.) *Queen's head and inscription in silver. 'All-over' phosphor*

962	**446**	4½p green and blue	15	15	□	□
963	**447**	5½p grey and black	20	25	□	□
964	**448**	8p rose and lake ..	50	50	□	□
965	**449**	10p stone and brown	55	50	□	□
		Set of 4	1·25	1·25	□	□
		First Day Cover		1·60		□
		Presentation Pack ..	1·75		□	
		Souvenir Book	2·50		□	
		PHQ Card (No. 963)	7·00	12·00	□	□
		Set of 4 Gutter Pairs	4·00		□	
		Set of 4 Traffic Light Gutter Pairs ..	50·00		□	

450 'Adoration of the Magi (York Minster, c. 1355)

451 'The Nativity' (St Helen's Church, Norwich, c. 1480)

452 'Virgin and Child' (Ottery St Mary Church, c. 1350)

453 'Virgin and Child' (Worcester Cathedral, c. 1224)

Christmas

1974 (27 Nov.) *Designs show church roof bosses, One phosphor band (3½p) or 'all-over' phosphor (others)*

966	**450**	3½p multicoloured ..	10	10	□	□
967	**451**	4½p multicoloured ..	10	10	□	□
968	**452**	8p multicoloured ..	45	45	□	□
969	**453**	10p multicoloured ..	50	50	□	□
		Set of 4	1·00	1·00	□	□
		First Day Cover		1·25		□
		Presentation Pack	1·75		□	
		Set of 4 Gutter Pairs	4·00		□	
		Set of 4 Traffic Light Gutter Pairs ..	50·00		□	

Collectors Pack 1974

1974 (27 Nov.) *Comprises Nos 949/69*

Collectors Pack	8·50	□

454 Invalid in Wheelchair

Health and Handicap Funds

1975 (22 Jan.) *'All-over' phosphor*

970	**454**	4½p + 1½p azure and blue ..	25	25	□	□
		First Day Cover		1·00		□
		Gutter Pair	50		□	
		Traffic Light Gutter Pair	1·00		□	

455 'Peace – Burial at Sea'

456 'Snowstorm – Steamer off a Harbour's Mouth'

457 'The Arsenal, Venice'

458 'St Laurent'

Birth Bicentenary of J. M. W. Turner

1975 (19 Feb.) *'All-over' phosphor*

971	**455**	4½p multicoloured	10	10	□	□
972	**456**	5½p multicoloured	15	15	□	□
973	**457**	8p multicoloured	40	40	□	□
974	**458**	10p multicoloured	45	45	□	□
		Set of 4	1·00	1·00	□	□
		First Day Cover		1·50		□
		Presentation Pack	2·50		□	
		PHQ Card (No. 972)	30·00	11·00	□	□
		Set of 4 Gutter Pairs	2·50		□	
		Set of 4 Traffic Light Gutter Pairs ..	7·00		□	

459 Charlotte Square, Edinburgh

460 The Rows, Chester

The above were printed horizontally *se-tenant* throughout the sheet.

461 Royal Observatory, Greenwich

462 St George's Chapel, Windsor

463 National Theatre, London

European Architectural Heritage Year

1975 (23 APR.) *'All-over' phosphor*

975	**459**	7p multicoloured ..	30	30	☐	☐
		a. Pair. Nos. 975/6	80	90	☐	☐
976	**460**	7p multicoloured ..	30	30	☐	☐
977	**461**	8p multicoloured ..	20	25	☐	☐
978	**462**	10p multicoloured ..	20	25	☐	☐
979	**463**	12p multicoloured ..	20	35	☐	☐
		Set of 5	1·25	1·25	☐	☐
		First Day Cover		2·00		☐
		Presentation Pack ..	3·00		☐	
		PHQ Cards (Nos. 975/7)	8·00	10·00	☐	☐
		Set of 5 Gutter Pairs ..	4·00		☐	
		Set of 5 Traffic Light				
		Gutter Pairs	20·00		☐	

464 Sailing Dinghies

465 Racing Keel Boats

466 Cruising Yachts

467 Multihulls

Sailing

1975 (11 JUNE) *'All-over' phosphor*

980	**464**	7p multicoloured ..	20	20	☐	☐
981	**465**	8p multicoloured ..	30	30	☐	☐
982	**466**	10p multicoloured ..	30	30	☐	☐
983	**467**	12p multicoloured ..	35	35	☐	☐
		Set of 4	1·00	1·00	☐	☐
		First Day Cover		1·50		☐
		Presentation Pack ..	1·50		☐	
		PHQ Card (No. 981)	4·50	10·00	☐	☐
		Set of 4 Gutter Pairs	2·50		☐	
		Set of 4 Traffic Light				
		Gutter Pairs	25·00		☐	

468 Stephenson's Locomotion, 1825

469 Abbotsford, 1876

470 Caerphilly Castle, 1923

471 High Speed Train, 1975

150th Anniversary of Public Railways

1975 (13 AUG.) *'All-over' phosphor*

984	**468**	7p multicoloured ..	20	20	☐	☐
985	**469**	8p multicoloured ..	25	25	☐	☐
986	**470**	10p multicoloured ..	30	30	☐	☐
987	**471**	12p multicoloured ..	35	35	☐	☐
		Set of 4	1·00	1·00	☐	☐
		First Day Cover		2·50		☐
		Presentation Pack ..	2·25		☐	
		Souvenir Book	3·00		☐	
		PHQ Cards (set of 4)	55·00	25·00	☐	☐
		Set of 4 Gutter Pairs	3·00		☐	
		Set of 4 Traffic Light				
		Gutter Pairs	12·00		☐	

472 Palace of Westminster

62nd Inter-Parliamentary Union Conference
1975 (3 SEPT.) *'All-over' phosphor*

988	**472**	12p multicoloured ..	50	50	☐	☐
		First Day Cover		1·00		☐
		Presentation Pack ..	1·25		☐	
		Gutter Pair	1·00		☐	
		Traffic Light Gutter Pair ..	3·00		☐	

473 'Emma and Mr Woodhouse' (*Emma*)

474 'Catherine Morland' (*Northanger Abbey*)

475 'Mr Darcy' (*Pride and Prejudice*)

476 'Mary and Henry Crawford' (*Mansfield Park*)

Birth Bicentenary of Jane Austen (Novelist)
1975 (22 OCT.) *'All-over' phosphor*

989	**473**	8½p multicoloured ..	20	20	☐	☐
990	**474**	10p multicoloured ..	25	25	☐	☐
991	**475**	11p multicoloured ..	30	30	☐	☐
992	**476**	13p multicoloured ..	35	35	☐	☐
		Set of 4	1·00	1·00	☐	☐
		First Day Cover		1·25		☐
		Presentation Pack ..	2·00		☐	
		PHQ Cards (set of 4) ..	16·00	15·00	☐	☐
		Set of 4 Gutter Pairs	2·50		☐	
		Set of 4 Traffic Light Gutter Pairs	8·00		☐	

477 Angels with Harp and Lute

478 Angel with Mandolin

479 Angel with Horn

480 Angel with Trumpet

Christmas
1975 (26 Nov.) *One phosphor band (6½p), phosphor-inked (8½p) (background) or 'all-over' phosphor (others)*

993	**477**	6½p multicoloured ..	20	15	☐	☐
994	**478**	8½p multicoloured ..	20	20	☐	☐
995	**479**	11p multicoloured ..	30	35	☐	☐
996	**480**	13p multicoloured ..	40	40	☐	☐
		Set of 4	1·00	1·00	☐	☐
		First Day Cover		1·25		☐
		Presentation Pack	2·00		☐	
		Set of 4 Gutter Pairs ..	2·50		☐	
		Set of 4 Traffic Light Gutter Pairs	8·00		☐	

Collectors Pack 1975
1975 (26 Nov.) *Comprises Nos.* 970/96

	Collectors Pack	7·50	☐

481 Housewife

482 Policeman

483 District Nurse

484 Industrialist

Telephone Centenary

1976 (10 MAR.) 'All-over' phosphor

997	**481**	8½p multicoloured ..	20	20	□	□
998	**482**	10p multicoloured ..	25	25	□	□
999	**483**	11p multicoloured ..	30	30	□	□
1000	**484**	13p multicoloured ..	35	35	□	□
		Set of 4	1·00	1·00	□	□
		First Day Cover		1·25		□
		Presentation Pack	2·00		□	
		Set of 4 Gutter Pairs ..	2·50		□	
		Set of 4 Traffic Light				
		Gutter Pairs	8·00		□	

485 Hewing Coal (Thomas Hepburn)

486 Machinery (Robert Owen)

487 Chimney Cleaning (Lord Shaftesbury)

488 Hands clutching Prison Bars (Elizabeth Fry)

Social Reformers

1976 (28 APR.) 'All-over phosphor

1001	**485**	8½p multicoloured ..	20	20	□	□
1002	**486**	10p multicoloured ..	25	25	□	□
1003	**487**	11p black, slate-grey and drab ..	30	30	□	□
1004	**488**	13p slate-grey, black and green	35	35	□	□
		Set of 4	1·00	1·00	□	□
		First Day Cover		1·25		□
		Presentation Pack	2·00		□	
		PHQ Card (No. 1001) ..	5·00	7·50	□	□
		Set of 4 Gutter Pairs	2·50		□	
		Set of 4 Traffic Light				
		Gutter Pairs	8·00		□	

489 Benjamin Franklin (bust by Jean-Jacques Caffieri)

Bicentenary of American Independence

1976 (2 JUNE) 'All-over' phosphor

1005	**489**	11p multicoloured ..	50	50	□	□
		First Day Cover		1·00		□
		Presentation Pack	1·25		□	
		PHQ Card	2·50	8·50	□	□
		Gutter Pair	1·00		□	
		Traffic Light Gutter Pair ..	3·00		□	

490 'Elizabeth of Glamis'

491 'Grandpa Dickson'

492 'Rosa Mundi'

493 'Sweet Briar'

Centenary of Royal National Rose Society

1976 (30 JUNE) 'All-over' phosphor

1006	**490**	8½p multicoloured ..	20	20	□	□
1007	**491**	10p multicoloured ..	30	30	□	□
1008	**492**	11p multicoloured ..	45	50	□	□
1009	**493**	13p multicoloured ..	45	40	□	□
		Set of 4	1·25	1·25	□	□
		First Day Cover		1·75		□
		Presentation Pack	2·25		□	
		PHQ Cards (set of 4) ..	30·00	14·00	□	□
		Set of 4 Gutter Pairs ..	2·50		□	
		Set of 4 Traffic Light				
		Gutter Pairs	10·00		□	

494 Archdruid

495 Morris Dancing

11P

13P

1176 1976

Highland Gathering
Na Geamannan

Eisteddfod Genedlaethol Frenhinol Cymru
Royal National Eisteddfod of Wales

496 Scots Piper   **497** Welsh Harpist

British Cultural Traditions

1976 (4 Aug.) *'All-over' phosphor*

1010	**494**	8½p multicoloured ..	20	20	☐ ☐
1011	**495**	10p multicoloured ..	25	25	☐ ☐
1012	**496**	11p multicoloured ..	30	30	☐ ☐
1013	**497**	13p multicoloured ..	35	35	☐ ☐
		Set of 4	1·00	1·00	☐ ☐
		First Day Cover		1·25	☐
		Presentation Pack ..	2·00		☐
		PHQ Cards (set of 4) ..	18·00	10·00	☐ ☐
		Set of 4 Gutter Pairs ..	2·50		☐
		Set of 4 Traffic Light Gutter Pairs	10·00		☐

William Caxton 1476   **8½P**

the foule of the fayd...

William Caxton 1476   **10P**

498 *The Canterbury Tales*   **499** *The Tretyse of Love*

William Caxton 1476   **11P**

William Caxton 1476   **13P**

500 *Game and Playe of Chesse*   **501** *Early Printing Press*

500th Anniversary of British Printing

1976 (29 Sept.) *'All-over' phosphor*

1014	**498**	8½p blk, bl & gold	20	20	☐ ☐
1015	**499**	10p blk, olive-grn & gold	25	25	☐ ☐
1016	**500**	11p blk, grey & gold ..	30	30	☐ ☐
1017	**501**	13p brn, ochre & gold	35	35	☐ ☐
		Set of 4	1·00	1·00	☐ ☐
		First Day Cover		1·25	☐
		Presentation Pack ..	2·50		☐
		PHQ Cards (set of 4)	14·00	10·00	☐ ☐
		Set of 4 Gutter Pairs	2·50		☐
		Set of 4 Traffic Light Gutter Pairs	8·00		☐

English Embroidery c.1272   **6½P**

English Embroidery c.1340   **8½P**

502 Virgin and Child   **503** Angel with Crown

English Embroidery c.1320   **11P**

English Embroidery c.1320   **13P**

504 Angel appearing to   **505** The Three Kings
Shepherds

Christmas

1976 (24 Nov.) *Designs show English mediaeval embroidery. One phosphor band (6½p) or 'all-over' phosphor (others)*

1018	**502**	6½p multicoloured ..	15	15	☐ ☐
1019	**503**	8½p multicoloured ..	20	20	☐ ☐
1020	**504**	11p multicoloured ..	35	35	☐ ☐
1021	**505**	13p multicoloured ..	40	40	☐ ☐
		Set of 4	1·00	1·00	☐ ☐
		First Day Cover		1·25	☐ ☐
		Presentation Pack ..	2·00		☐
		PHQ Cards (set of 4) ..	4·00	8·00	☐ ☐
		Set of 4 Gutter Pairs ..	2·50		☐
		Set of 4 Traffic Light Gutter Pairs ..	8·00		☐

Collectors Pack 1976

1976 (24 Nov.) *Comprises Nos. 997/1021*

Collectors Pack	10·00	☐

8½p

10p

506 Lawn Tennis   **507** Table Tennis

11p

13p

508 Squash   **509** Badminton

Racket Sports

1977 (12 Jan.) *Phosphorised paper*

1022	**506**	8½p multicoloured ..	20	20	□	□
1023	**507**	10p multicoloured ..	25	25	□	□
1024	**508**	11p multicoloured ..	30	30	□	□
1025	**509**	13p multicoloured ..	35	35	□	□
		Set of 4	1·00	1·00	□	□
		First Day Cover		1·50		□
		Presentation Pack	2·00		□	
		PHQ Cards (set of 4) ..	6·00	9·50	□	□
		Set of 4 Gutter Pairs ..	2·50		□	
		Set of 4 Traffic Light				
		Gutter Pairs	8·00		□	

510

1977 (2 Feb.)–87 *Type 510 Ordinary paper*

1026	£1 green and olive	3·00	20	□	□
1026b	£1·30 drab & dp grnish bl ..	6·50	8·00	□	·
1026c	£1·33 pale mve & grey-blk ..	6·50	8·00	□	□
1026d	£1·41 drab & dp grnish bl ..	7·00	7·50	□	□
1026e	£1·50 pale mve & grey-blk ..	6·00	4·00	□	□
1026f	£1·60 drab and dp grnish bl	6·00	6·00	□	□
1027	£2 green and brown	5·50	75	□	□
1028	£5 pink and blue	13·00	2·00	□	□
	Presentation Pack (Nos.				
	1026, 1027/8)	22·00		□	
	Presentation Pack (No.				
	1026f)	12·00		□	

For First Day Cover prices see page 37.

511 Steroids – Conform-
ational Analysis

512 Vitamin C –
Synthesis

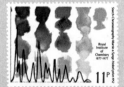

513 Starch –
Chromatography

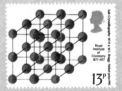

514 Salt –
Crystallography

Centenary of Royal Institute of Chemistry

1977 (2 Mar.) *'All-over' phosphor*

1029	**511**	8½p multicoloured ..	20	20	□	□
1030	**512**	10p multicoloured ..	30	30	□	□
1031	**513**	11p multicoloured ..	30	30	□	□
1032	**514**	13p multicoloured ..	30	30	□	□
		Set of 4	1·00	1·00	□	□
		First Day Cover		1·40		□
		Presentation Pack ..	2·40		□	
		PHQ Cards (set of 4) ..	7·00	10·00	□	□
		Set of 4 Gutter Pairs ..	2·50		□	
		Set of 4 Traffic Light				
		Gutter Pairs	8·00		□	

515

516

517

518

(The designs differ in the decorations of 'ER'.)

Silver Jubilee

1977 (11 May–15 June) *'All-over' phosphor.*

1033	**515**	8½p multicoloured ..	20	20	□	□
1034		9p mult (15 June) ..	25	25	□	□
1035	**516**	10p multicoloured ..	25	25	□	□
1036	**517**	11p multicoloured ..	30	30	□	□
1037	**518**	13p multicoloured ..	40	40	□	□
		Set of 5	1·25	1·25	□	□
		First Day Covers (2)		1·50		□
		Presentation Pack (ex 9p)	2·00		□	
		Souvenir Book (ex 9p) ..	4·00		□	
		PHQ Cards (set of 5) ..	12·00	8·00	□	□
		Set of 5 Gutter Pairs ..	2·75		□	
		Set of 5 Traffic Light				
		Gutter Pairs	1·25		□	

519 'Gathering of Nations'

Commonwealth Heads of Government Meeting, London

1977 (8 June) *'All-over' phosphor*

1038	**519**	13p black, deep green rose and silver ..	50	50	☐	☐
	First Day Cover			1·00		☐
	Presentation Pack		1·00		☐	
	PHQ Card		2·25	3·75	☐	☐
	Gutter Pair		1·00		☐	
	Traffic Light Gutter Pair ..		1·25		☐	

520 Hedgehog

521 Brown Hare

522 Red Squirrel

523 Otter

524 Badger

T **520/4** were printed together, *se-tenant*, throughout the sheet

British Wildlife

1977 (5 Oct.) *'All-over' phosphor*

1039	**520**	9p multicoloured ..	25	20	☐	☐
	a. Strip of 5.					
	Nos. 1039/43 ..	1·50	1·50	☐	☐
1040	**521**	9p multicoloured ..	25	20	☐	☐
1041	**522**	9p multicoloured ..	25	20	☐	☐
1042	**523**	9p multicoloured ..	25	20	☐	☐
1043	**524**	9p multicoloured ..	25	20	☐	☐
	Set of 5		1·50	90	☐	☐
	First Day Cover			2·25		☐
	Presentation Pack		2·25		☐	
	PHQ Cards (set of 5) ..		4·00	5·00	☐	☐
	Gutter Strip of 10 ..		3·75		☐	
	Traffic Light Gutter Strip of 10		4·00		☐	

525 'Three French Hens, Two Turtle Doves and a Partridge in a Pear Tree'

526 'Six Geese a-laying, Five Gold Rings, Four Colly Birds'

527 'Eight Maids a-milking, Seven Swans a-swimming'

528 'Ten Pipers piping, Nine Drummers drumming'

529 'Twelve Lords a-leaping, Eleven Ladies dancing'

530 'A Partridge in a Pear Tree'

T **525/30** depict the carol 'The Twelve Days of Christmas'. T **525/29** were printed horizontally *se-tenant* throughout the sheet.

Christmas

1977 (23 Nov.) *One centre phosphor band (7p) or 'all-over' phosphor (9p)*

1044	**525**	7p multicoloured ..	15	15	☐	☐
	a. Strip of 5					
	Nos. 1044/8 ..	90	1·00	☐	☐
1045	**526**	7p multicoloured ..	15	15	☐	☐
1046	**527**	7p multicoloured ..	15	15	☐	☐
1047	**528**	7p multicoloured ..	15	15	☐	☐
1048	**529**	7p multicoloured ..	15	15	☐	☐
1049	**530**	9p multicoloured ..	20	20	☐	☐
	Set of 6		1·00	85	☐	☐
	First Day Cover			1·40		☐
	Presentation Pack		2·00		☐	
	PHQ Cards (set of 6) ..		3·25	4·00	☐	☐
	Set of 6 Gutter Pairs ..		2·50		☐	
	Set of 6 Traffic Light Gutter Pairs		4·50		☐	

Collectors Pack 1977

1977 (23 Nov.) *Comprises Nos.* 1022/5. 1029/49

	Collectors Pack	7·00		☐

531 Oil—North Sea Production Platform

532 Coal—Modern Pithead

533 Natural Gas—Flame Rising from Sea

534 Electricity—Nuclear Power Station and Uranium Atom

Energy Resources

1978 (25 Jan.) *'All-over' phosphor*

1050	**531**	9p multicoloured	..	25	20	☐	☐
1051	**532**	10½p multicoloured	..	25	30	☐	☐
1052	**533**	11p multicoloured	..	30	30	☐	☐
1053	**534**	13p multicoloured	..	30	30	☐	☐
	Set of 4	.. ..	.. ..	1·00	1·00	☐	☐
	First Day Cover ..	.. ..			1·25		☐
	Presentation Pack	.. ..		2·00		☐	
	PHQ Cards (set of 4) ..	..	4·00	4·00	☐	☐	
	Set of 4 Gutter Pairs ..	..	2·50		☐		
	Set of 4 Traffic Light Gutter Pairs	.. ..	..	4·00		☐	

535 Tower of London

536 Holyroodhouse

537 Caernarvon Castle

538 Hampton Court Palace

British Architecture (Historic Buildings)

1978 (1 Mar.) *'All-over' phosphor*

1054	**535**	9p multicoloured	..	25	20	☐	☐
1055	**536**	10½p multicoloured	..	25	30	☐	☐
1056	**537**	11p multicoloured	..	30	30	☐	☐
1057	**538**	13p multicoloured	..	30	30	☐	☐
	Set of 4	.. ..	.. ..	1·00	1·00	☐	☐
	First Day Cover ..	.. ..			1·25		☐
	Presentation Pack	.. ..		2·00		☐	
	PHQ Cards (set of 4) ..	..	4·00	5·00	☐	☐	
	Set of 4 Gutter Pairs ..	..	2·50	-	☐		
	Set of 4 Traffic Light Gutter Pairs	.. ..		4·00		☐	
MS1058	121 × 90 mm. Nos. 1054/57			1·25	1·50	☐	☐
	First Day Cover	..			2·00		☐

No. **MS**1058 was sold at 53½p, the premium being used for the London 1980 Stamp Exhibition.

539 State Coach

540 St Edward's Crown

541 The Sovereign's Orb

542 Imperial State Crown

25th Anniversary of Coronation

1978 (31 May) *'All-over' phosphor*

1059	**539**	9p gold and blue	..	20	20	☐	☐
1060	**540**	10½p gold and red	..	25	30	☐	☐
1061	**541**	11p gold and green	..	30	30	☐	☐
1062	**542**	13p gold and violet	..	35	30	☐	☐
	Set of 4	.. ..	.. ..	1·00	1·00	☐	☐
	First Day Cover ..	.. ..			1·25		☐
	Presentation Pack	.. ..		2·00		☐	
	Souvenir Book	.. ..		4·00		☐	
	PHQ Cards (set of 4) ..	..	2·50	4·00	☐	☐	
	Set of 4 Gutter Pairs ..	..	2·50		☐		
	Set of 4 Traffic Light Gutter Pairs	.. ..	..	4·00		☐	

543 Shire Horse

544 Shetland Pony

545 Welsh Pony

546 Thoroughbred

Horses

1978 (5 JULY) *'All-over' phosphor*

1063	**543**	9p multicoloured ..	20	20	□	□
1064	**544**	10½p multicoloured ..	25	25	□	□
1065	**545**	11p multicoloured ..	30	30	□	□
1066	**546**	13p multicoloured ..	35	35	□	□
		Set of 4	1·00	1·00	□	□
		First Day Cover		1·50	□	
		Presentation Pack	2·00		□	
		PHQ Cards (set of 4)	2·50	6·00	□	□
		Set of 4 Gutter Pairs	2·50		□	
		Set of 4 Traffic Light				
		Gutter Pairs	4·00		□	

547 Penny-farthing and 1884 Safety Bicycle

548 1920 Touring Bicycles

549 Modern Small-wheel Bicycles

550 1978 Road-racers

Centenaries of Cyclists Touring Club and British Cycling Federation

1978 (2 AUG.) *'All-over' phosphor*

1067	**547**	9p multicoloured ..	20	20	□	□
1068	**548**	10½p multicoloured ..	25	25	□	□
1069	**549**	11p multicoloured ..	30	30	□	□
1070	**550**	13p multicoloured ..	35	35	□	□
		Set of 4	1·00	1·00	□	□
		First Day Cover		1·25	□	
		Presentation Pack	2·00		□	
		PHQ Cards (set of 4) ..	1·50	3·25	□	□
		Set of 4 Gutter Pairs	2·50		□	
		Set of 4 Traffic Light				
		Gutter Pairs	4·00		□	

551 Singing Carols round the Christmas Tree

552 The Waits

553 18th-Century Carol Singers

554 'The Boar's Head Carol'

Christmas

1978 (22 Nov.) *One centre phosphor band (7p) or 'all-over' phosphor (others)*

1071	**551**	7p multicoloured ..	20	20	□	□
1072	**552**	9p multicoloured ..	25	25	□	□
1073	**553**	11p multicoloured ..	30	30	□	□
1074	**554**	13p multicoloured ..	35	35	□	□
		Set of 4	1·00	1·00	□	□
		First Day Cover		1·25	□	
		Presentation Pack	1·75		□	
		PHQ Cards (set of 4) ..	1·50	4·00	□	□
		Set of 4 Gutter Pairs	2·50		□	
		Set of 4 Traffic Light				
		Gutter Pairs	3·00		□	

Collectors Pack 1978

1978 (22 Nov.) *Comprises Nos.* 1050/7. 1059/74

	Collectors Pack	7·00	□	

555 Old English Sheepdog

556 Welsh Springer Spaniel

557 West Highland Terrier   **558** Irish Setter

Dogs

1979 (7 Feb.) 'All-over' phosphor

1075	555	9p multicoloured	.	20	20	☐	☐
1076	556	10½p multicoloured	.	30	30	☐	☐
1077	557	11p multicoloured	.	30	30	☐	☐
1078	558	13p multicoloured	.	30	30	☐	☐
		Set of 4	.. ..	1·00	1·00	☐	☐
		First Day Cover			1·50		☐
		Presentation Pack		2·00		☐	
		PHQ Cards (set of 4) ..	.	3·00	5·00	☐	☐
		Set of 4 Gutter Pairs ..		2·50		☐	
		Set of 4 Traffic Light Gutter Pairs		3·75		☐	

559 Primrose

560 Daffodil

561 Bluebell

562 Snowdrop

Spring Wild Flowers

1979 (21 Mar.) 'All-over' phosphor

1079	559	9p multicoloured	..	20	20	☐	☐
1080	560	10½p multicoloured	..	30	30	☐	☐
1081	561	11p multicoloured	..	30	30	☐	☐
1082	562	13p multicoloured	..	30	30	☐	☐
		Set of 4	.. ..	1·00	1·00	☐	☐
		First Day Cover			1·50		☐
		Presentation Pack		2·00		☐	
		PHQ Cards (set of 4) ..		2·00	4·00	☐	☐
		Set of 4 Gutter Pairs ..		2·50		☐	
		Set of 4 Traffic Light Gutter Pairs		3·75		☐	

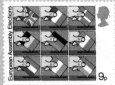

563

564

565

566

T **563/6** show hands placing the flags of the member nations into ballot boxes.

First Direct Elections to European Assembly

1979 (9 May) Phosphorised paper

1083	563	9p multicoloured	..	20	20	☐	☐
1084	564	10½p multicoloured	..	30	30	☐	☐
1085	565	11p multicoloured	..	30	30	☐	☐
1086	566	13p multicoloured	..	30	30	☐	☐
		Set of 4	.. ..	1·00	1·00	☐	☐
		First Day Cover			1·25		☐
		Presentation Pack		2·00		☐	
		PHQ Cards (set of 4) ..	..	1·50	3·50	☐	☐
		Set of 4 Gutter Pairs ..	..	2·50		☐	
		Set of 4 Traffic Light Gutter Pairs		3·75		☐	

567 'Saddling "Mahmoud" for the Derby, 1936' (Sir Alfred Munnings)

568 'The Liverpool Great National Steeple Chase, 1839' (aquatint by F. C. Turner)

569 'The First Spring Meeting, Newmarket, 1793' (J. N. Sartorius)

570 'Racing at Dorsett Ferry, Windsor, 1684' (Francis Barlow)

Horseracing Paintings and Bicentenary of The Derby (9p)

1979 (6 June) 'All-over' phosphor

1087	567	9p multicoloured	.	25	25	□	□
1088	568	10½p multicoloured	.	30	30	□	□
1089	569	11p multicoloured	.	30	30	□	□
1090	570	13p multicoloured	.	30	30	□	□
		Set of 4		1·10	1·10	□	□
		First Day Cover	..		1·50		□
		Presentation Pack		2·00		□	
		PHQ Cards (set of 4)	..	1·50	3·00	□	□
		Set of 4 Gutter Pairs	..	2·50		□	
		Set of 4 Traffic Light					
		Gutter Pairs	.. ..	3·75		□	

571 *The Tale of Peter Rabbit* (Beatrix Potter)

572 *The Wind in the Willows* (Kenneth Grahame)

573 *Winnie-the-Pooh* (A. A. Milne)

574 *Alice's Adventures in Wonderland* (Lewis Carroll)

T **571/4** depict original illustrations from the four books.

International Year of the Child

1979 (11 July) 'All-over' phosphor

1091	571	9p multicoloured	..	35	20	□	□
1092	572	10½p multicoloured	..	40	35	□	□
1093	573	11p multicoloured	..	45	40	□	□
1094	574	13p multicoloured	..	50	55	□	□
		Set of 4	.. ..	1·50	1·40	□	□
		First Day Cover	.. ..		2·00		□
		Presentation Pack	..	2·25		□	
		PHQ Cards (set of 4)	..	2·50	3·00	□	□
		Set of 4 Gutter Pairs	..	4·00		□	
		Set of 4 Traffic Light					
		Gutter Pairs	.. ..	4·75		□	

For full information on all future British issues, collectors should write to the British Post Office Philatelic Bureau, 20 Brandon Street, Edinburgh EH3 5TT

575 Sir Rowland Hill, 1795–1879

576 General Post, c. 1839

577 London Post, c. 1839

578 Uniform Postage, 1840

Death Centenary of Sir Rowland Hill (Postal Reformer)

1979 (22 Aug.–24 Oct.) 'All-over' phosphor

1095	575	10p multicoloured	..	25	25	□	□
1096	576	11½p multicoloured	..	30	35	□	□
1097	577	13p multicoloured	..	35	40	□	□
1098	578	15p multicoloured	..	50	40	□	□
		Set of 4	.. ..	1·25	1·25	□	□
		First Day Cover	.. ..		1·25		□
		Presentation Pack	..	2·00		□	
		PHQ Cards (set of 4)	..	1·50	3·00	□	□
		Set of 4 Gutter Pairs	..	2·50		□	
		Set of 4 Traffic Light					
		Gutter Pairs	.. ..	3·75		□	
MS1099		89×121 mm. Nos. 1095/8		1·25	1·25	□	□
		First Day Cover (24 Oct.)	..		1·25		□

No. **MS**1099 was sold at 59½p, the premium being used for the London 1980 Stamp Exhibition.

579 Policeman on the Beat

580 Policeman directing Traffic

13ᵖ

15ᵖ

581 Mounted Policewoman

582 River Patrol Boat

150th Anniversary of Metropolitan Police

1979 (26 SEPT.) *Phosphorised paper*

1100	**579**	10p multicoloured ..	25	25	☐	☐
1101	**580**	11½p multicoloured ..	30	35	☐	☐
1102	**581**	13p multicoloured ..	35	40	☐	☐
1103	**582**	15p multicoloured ..	50	40	☐	☐
		Set of 4	1·25	1·25	☐	☐
		First Day Cover		1·25		☐
		Presentation Pack	2·00		☐	
		PHQ Cards (set of 4)	1·50	3·00	☐	☐
		Set of 4 Gutter Pairs	2·50		☐	
		Set of 4 Traffic Light				
		Gutter Pairs	3·75		☐	

8ᵖ

10ᵖ

583 The Three Kings

584 Angel appearing to the Shepherds

11½ᵖ

13ᵖ

585 The Nativity

586 Mary and Joseph travelling to Bethlehem

15ᵖ

587 The Annunciation

Christmas

1979 (21 Nov.) *One centre phosphor band (8p) or phosphorised paper (others)*

1104	**583**	8p multicoloured ..	20	20	☐	☐
1105	**584**	10p multicoloured ..	25	25	☐	☐
1106	**585**	11½p multicoloured ..	30	35	☐	☐
1107	**586**	13p multicoloured ..	40	40	☐	☐
1108	**587**	15p multicoloured ..	50	45	☐	☐
		Set of 5	1·50	1·50	☐	☐
		First Day Cover		1·50		☐
		Presentation Pack	2·25		☐	
		PHQ Cards (set of 5)	1·50	3·50	☐	☐
		Set of 5 Gutter Pairs	3·00		☐	
		Set of 5 Traffic Light				
		Gutter Pairs	3·75		☐	

Collectors Pack 1979

1979 (21 Nov.) *Comprises Nos.* 1075/98, 1100/8

	Collectors Pack	9·00		☐

KINGFISHER 10ᵖ

DIPPER 11½ᵖ

588 Kingfisher

589 Dipper

MOORHEN 13ᵖ

YELLOW WAGTAIL 15ᵖ

590 Moorhen

591 Yellow Wagtails

Centenary of Wild Bird Protection Act

1980 (16 JAN.) *Phosphorised paper*

1109	**588**	10p multicoloured ..	25	25	☐	☐
1110	**589**	11½p multicoloured ..	30	35	☐	☐
1111	**590**	13p multicoloured ..	40	40	☐	☐
1112	**591**	15p multicoloured ..	45	45	☐	☐
		Set of 4	1·25	1·25	☐	☐
		First Day Cover		1·40		☐
		Presentation Pack	2·00		☐	
		PHQ Cards (set of 4)	1·50	3·00	☐	☐
		Set of 4 Gutter Pairs	3·00		☐	

592 *Rocket* approaching Moorish Arch, Liverpool

593 First and Second Class Carriages passing through Olive Mount Cutting

594 Third Class Carriage and Cattle Truck crossing Chat Moss

595 Horsebox and Carriage Truck near Bridgewater Canal

596 Goods Truck and Mail-coach at Manchester

T **592/6** were printed together, *se-tenant* in horizontal strips of 5 throughout the sheet.

150th Anniversary of Liverpool and Manchester Railway

1980 (12 MAR.) *Phosphorised paper*

1113	**592**	12p multicoloured	25	25	☐	☐
	a.	Strip of 5.				
		Nos. 1113/17	1·50	1·60	☐	☐
1114	**593**	12p multicoloured	25	25	☐	☐
1115	**594**	12p multicoloured	25	25	☐	☐
1116	**595**	12p multicoloured	25	25	☐	☐
1117	**596**	12p multicoloured	25	25	☐	☐
		Set of 5	1·50	1·10	☐	☐
		First Day Cover		1·60	☐	
		Presentation Pack	2·50		☐	
		PHQ Cards (set of 5)	1·50	3·75	☐	☐
		Gutter strip of 10	3·25		☐	

Minimum Price. The minimum price quoted is 10p. This represents a handling charge rather than a basis for valuing common stamps. Where the actual value of a stamp is less than 10p this may be apparent when set prices are shown, particularly for sets including a number of 10p stamps. It therefore follows that in valuing common stamps the 10p catalogue price should not be reckoned automatically since it covers a variation in real scarcity.

597 Montage of London Buildings

"London 1980" International Stamp Exhibition

1980 (9 APR–7 MAY) *Phosphorised paper. Perf* $14\frac{1}{2} \times 14$

1118	**597**	50p agate	1·50	1·50	☐	☐
		First Day Cover		1·50		☐
		Presentation Pack	2·00		☐	
		PHQ Card	50	1·50	☐	☐
		Gutter Pair	3·00		☐	
MS1119	90×123 mm. No. 1118		1·50	1·50	☐	☐
		First Day Cover (7 May)		1·50		☐

No. **MS1119** was sold at 75p, the premium being used for the exhibition.

598 Buckingham Palace

599 The Albert Memorial

600 Royal Opera House

601 Hampton Court

17½p Kensington Palace

602 Kensington Palace

607 Queen Elizabeth the Queen Mother

London Landmarks

1980 (7 MAY) *Phosphorised paper*

1120	**598**	10½p multicoloured	25	25	☐	☐
1121	**599**	12p multicoloured	30	30	☐	☐
1122	**600**	13½p multicoloured	35	35	☐	☐
1123	**601**	15p multicoloured	40	40	☐	☐
1124	**602**	17½p multicoloured	40	40	☐	☐
		Set of 5	1·50	1·50	☐	☐
		First Day Cover		1·75		☐
		Presentation Pack	2·50		☐	
		PHQ Cards (set of 5)	1·50	3·00	☐	☐
		Set of 5 Gutter Pairs	3·00		☐	

12p

603 Charlotte Brontë
(*Jane Eyre*)

13½p

604 George Eliot (*The Mill on the Floss*)

15p

605 Emily Brontë
(*Wuthering Heights*)

17½p

606 Mrs Gaskell (*North and South*)

T 603/6 show authoresses and scenes from their novels. T 603/4 also include the "Europa" C.E.P.T. emblem.

Famous Authoresses

1980 (9 JULY) *Phosphorised paper*

1125	**603**	12p multicoloured	30	30	☐	☐
1126	**604**	13½p multicoloured	35	35	☐	☐
1127	**605**	15p multicoloured	40	45	☐	☐
1128	**606**	17½p multicoloured	60	60	☐	☐
		Set of 4	1·50	1·50	☐	☐
		First Day Cover		1·50		☐
		Presentation Pack	2·50		☐	
		PHQ Cards (set of 4)	1·50	3·00	☐	☐
		Set of 4 Gutter Pairs	3·00		☐	

80th Birthday of Queen Elizabeth the Queen Mother

1980 (4 AUG.) *Phosphorised paper*

1129	**607**	12p multicoloured	50	50	☐	☐
		First Day Cover		60		☐
		PHQ Card	50	1·25	☐	☐
		Gutter Pair	1·00		☐	

12p

608 Sir Henry Wood

13½p

609 Sir Thomas Beecham

15p

610 Sir Malcolm Sargent

17½p

611 Sir John Barbirolli

British Conductors

1980 (10 SEPT.) *Phosphorised paper*

1130	**608**	12p multicoloured	30	30	☐	☐
1131	**609**	13½p multicoloured	35	40	☐	☐
1132	**610**	15p multicoloured	45	45	☐	☐
1133	**611**	17½p multicoloured	55	50	☐	☐
		Set of 4	1·50	1·50	☐	☐
		First Day Cover		1·50		☐
		Presentation Pack	2·00		☐	
		PHQ Cards (set of 4)	1·50	2·50	☐	☐
		Set of 4 Gutter Pairs	3·00		☐	

612 Running

613 Rugby

614 Boxing

615 Cricket

Sports Centenaries

1980 (10 Oct.) *Phosphorised paper. Perf* 14 × 14½

1134	**612**	12p multicoloured ..	30	30	☐	☐
1135	**613**	13½p multicoloured ..	35	40	☐	☐
1136	**614**	15p multicoloured ..	40	40	☐	☐
1137	**615**	17½p multicoloured ..	60	55	☐	☐
		Set of 4	1·50	1·50	☐	☐
		First Day Cover		1·50		☐
		Presentation Pack	2·00		☐	
		PHQ Cards (set of 4)	1·50	2·50	☐	☐
		Set of 4 Gutter Pairs	3·00		☐	

Centenaries:– 12p Amateur Athletics Association; 13½p Welsh Rugby Union; 15p Amateur Boxing Association; 17½p First England v Australia Test Match.

618 Apples and Mistletoe

619 Crown, Chains and Bell

620 Holly

Christmas

1980 (19 Nov.) *One centre phosphor band (10p) or phosphorised paper (others)*

1138	**616**	10p multicoloured ..	25	25	☐	☐
1139	**617**	12p multicoloured ..	30	35	☐	☐
1140	**618**	13½p multicoloured ..	35	40	☐	☐
1141	**619**	15p multicoloured ..	40	40	☐	☐
1142	**620**	17½p multicoloured ..	40	40	☐	☐
		Set of 5	1·50	1·60	☐	☐
		First Day Cover		1·60		☐
		Presentation Pack	2·25		☐	
		PHQ Cards (set of 5) ..	1·50	2·50	☐	☐
		Set of 5 Gutter Pairs ..	3·00		☐	

Collectors Pack 1980

1980 (19 Nov.) *Comprises Nos.* 1109/18, 1120/42

	Collectors Pack	12·00	☐

616 Christmas Tree

617 Candles

621 St. Valentine's Day

622 Morris Dancers

623 Lammastide **624** Medieval Mummers

T **621/22** also include the "Europa" C.E.P.T. emblem.

Folklore

1981 (6 Feb.) *Phosphorised paper*

1143	**621**	14p multicoloured ..	35	35	☐	☐
1144	**622**	18p multicoloured ..	45	50	☐	☐
1145	**623**	22p multicoloured ..	60	60	☐	☐
1146	**624**	25p multicoloured ..	75	70	☐	☐
		Set of 4	2·00	2·00	☐	☐
		First Day Cover		2·00		☐
		Presentation Pack ..	2·50		☐	
		PHQ Cards (set of 4) ..	1·50	2·50	☐	☐
		Set of 4 Gutter Pairs	4·00		☐	

625 Blind Man with Guide Dog **626** Hands spelling "Deaf" in Sign Language

627 Disabled Man in Wheelchair **628** Disabled Artist painting with Foot

International Year of the Disabled

1981 (25 Mar.) *Phosphorised paper*

1147	**625**	14p multicoloured ..	35	35	☐	☐
1148	**626**	18p multicoloured ..	45	50	☐	☐
1149	**627**	22p multicoloured ..	60	60	☐	☐
1150	**628**	25p multicoloured ..	75	70	☐	☐
		Set of 4	2·00	2·00	☐	☐
		First Day Cover		2·00		☐
		Presentation Pack ..	2·50		☐	
		PHQ Cards (set of 4) ..	1·50	2·75	☐	☐
		Set of 4 Gutter Pairs	4·00		☐	

629 *Aglais urticae* **630** *Maculinea arion*

631 *Inachis io*. **632** *Carterocephalus palaemon*

Butterflies

1981 (13 May) *Phosphorised paper*

1151	**629**	14p multicoloured ..	35	35	☐	☐
1152	**630**	18p multicoloured ..	50	50	☐	☐
1153	**631**	22p multicoloured ..	60	65	☐	☐
1154	**632**	25p multicoloured ..	70	75	☐	☐
		Set of 4	2·00	2·00	☐	☐
		First Day Cover		2·00		☐
		Presentation Pack ..	2·50		☐	
		PHQ Cards (set of 4) ..	2·00	3·00	☐	☐
		Set of 4 Gutter Pairs	4·00		☐	

633 Glenfinnan, Scotland **634** Derwentwater, England

635 Stackpole Head, Wales **636** Giant's Causeway, N. Ireland

637 St Kilda, Scotland

50th Anniversary of National Trust for Scotland

1981 (24 June) *Phosphorised paper*

1155	633	14p multicoloured ..	30	30	☐	☐
1156	634	18p multicoloured ..	40	40	☐	☐
1157	635	20p multicoloured ..	50	50	☐	☐
1158	636	22p multicoloured ..	60	60	☐	☐
1159	637	25p multicoloured ..	70	70	☐	☐
		Set of 5	2·25	2·25	☐	☐
		First Day Cover..		2·25		☐
		Presentation Pack	2·75		☐	
		PHQ Cards (set of 5) ..	2·00	2·75	☐	☐
		Set of 5 Gutter Pairs	4·50		☐	

638 Prince Charles and Lady Diana Spencer

Royal Wedding

1981 (22 July) *Phosphorised paper*

1160	638	14p multicoloured ..	25	25	☐	☐
1161		25p multicoloured ..	75	95	☐	☐
		Set of 2	1·00	1·00	☐	☐
		First Day Cover		2·00		☐
		Presentation Pack	2·00		☐	
		Souvenir Book	4·00		☐	
		PHQ Cards (set of 2) ..	1·00	2·75	☐	☐
		Set of 2 Gutter Pairs	2·00		☐	

639 "Expeditions"

640 "Skills"

641 "Service"   **642** "Recreation"

25th Anniversary of Duke of Edinburgh Award Scheme

1981 (12 Aug.) *Phosphorised paper. Perf* 14

1162	639	14p multicoloured ..	35	35	☐	☐
1163	640	18p multicoloured ..	50	50	☐	☐
1164	641	22p multicoloured ..	60	60	☐	☐
1165	642	25p multicoloured ..	70	70	☐	☐
		Set of 4	2·00	2·00	☐	☐
		First Day Cover..		2·00		☐
		Presentation Pack	2·50		☐	
		PHQ Cards (set of 4) ..	1·60	2·25	☐	☐
		Set of 4 Gutter Pairs	4·00		☐	

643 Cockle-Dredging   **644** Hauling Trawl Net

645 Lobster Potting   **646** Hoisting Seine Net

Fishing Industry

1981 (23 Sept.) *Phosphorised paper*

1166	643	14p multicoloured ..	35	35	☐	☐
1167	644	18p multicoloured ..	50	50	☐	☐
1168	645	22p multicoloured ..	60	60	☐	☐
1169	646	25p multicoloured ..	70	65	☐	☐
		Set of 4	2·00	2·00	☐	☐
		First Day Cover..		2·00		☐
		Presentation Pack	2·50		☐	
		PHQ Cards (set of 4) ..	2·00	2·50	☐	☐
		Set of 4 Gutter Pairs	4·00		☐	

Nos. 1166/9 were issued on the occasion of the centenary of Royal National Mission to Deep Sea Fishermen.

647 Father Christmas

648 Jesus Christ

649 Flying Angel

650 Joseph and Mary arriving at Bethlehem

651 Three Kings approaching Bethlehem

652 Charles Darwin and Giant Tortoises

653 Darwin and Marine Iguanas

654 Darwin, Cactus Ground Finch and Large Ground Finch

655 Darwin and Prehistoric Skulls

Death Centenary of Charles Darwin

1982 (10 FEB.) *Phosphorised paper*

1175	652	15½p multicoloured	..	35	35	☐	☐
1176	653	19½p multicoloured	..	60	60	☐	☐
1177	654	26p multicoloured	..	70	70	☐	☐
1178	655	29p multicoloured	..	75	75	☐	☐
		Set of 4	.. ..	2·25	2·25	☐	☐
		First Day Cover	.. ..		2·25		☐
		Presentation Pack	..	3·00		☐	
		PHQ Cards (set of 4)	..	2·50	6·50	☐	☐
		Set of 4 Gutter Pairs	..	4·50		☐	

Christmas. Children's Pictures

1981 (18 NOV.) *One phosphor band (11½p) or phosphorised paper (others)*

1170	647	11½p multicoloured	..	30	30	☐	☐
1171	648	14p multicoloured	..	40	40	☐	☐
1172	649	18p multicoloured	..	50	50	☐	☐
1173	650	22p multicoloured	..	60	60	☐	☐
1174	651	25p multicoloured	..	70	70	☐	☐
		Set of 5	.. .. ..	2·25	2·25	☐	☐
		First Day Cover	.. ..		2·25		☐
		Presentation Pack	..	2·75		☐	
		PHO Cards (set of 5)	..	2·00	3·50	☐	☐
		Set of 5 Gutter Pairs	.. ..	4·50		☐	

Collectors Pack 1981

1981 (18 NOV.) *Comprises Nos.* 1143/74

	Collectors Pack	.. .. ..	18·00	☐

656 Boys' Brigade

657 Girls' Brigade

658 Boy Scout Movement

659 Girl Guide Movement

For full information on all future British issues, collectors should write to the British Post Office Philatelic Bureau, 20 Brandon Street, Edinburgh EH3 5TT.

Youth Organizations

1982 (24 MAR.) *Phosphorised paper*

1179	**656**	15½p multicoloured	..	35	35	☐	☐
1180	**657**	19½p multicoloured		50	50	☐	☐
1181	**658**	26p multicoloured		75	75	☐	☐
1182	**659**	29p multicoloured		90	90	☐	☐
		Set of 4	.. .. ..	2·25	2·25	☐	☐
		First Day Cover	.. ..		2·25		☐
		Presentation Pack	.: ..	3·50		☐	
		PHQ Cards (set of 4)	..	2·50	6·50	☐	☐
		Set of 4 Gutter Pairs	..	4·50		☐	

Nos. 1179/82 were issued on the occasion of the 75th anniversary of the Boy Scout Movement, the 125th birth anniversary of Lord Baden-Powell and the centenary of the Boys' Brigade (1983).

660 Ballerina

661 'Harlequin'

662 'Hamlet'

663 Opera Singer

Europa. British Theatre

1982 (28 APR.) *Phosphorised paper*

1183	**660**	15½p multicoloured	..	35	35	☐	☐
1184	**661**	19½p multicoloured		50	50	☐	☐
1185	**662**	26p multicoloured		75	75	☐	☐
1186	**663**	29p multicoloured		90	90	☐	☐
		Set of 4	.. ..	2·25	2·25	☐	☐
		First Day Cover	.. ..		2·25		☐
		Presentation Pack	.. ..	3·50		☐	
		PHQ Cards (set of 4)	..	2·50	6·50	☐	☐
		Set of 4 Gutter Pairs	..	4·50		☐	

664 Henry VIII and *Mary Rose*

665 Admiral Blake and *Triumph*

666 Lord Nelson and HMS *Victory*

667 Lord Fisher and HMS *Dreadnought*

668 Viscount Cunningham and HMS *Warspite*

Maritime Heritage

1982 (16 JUNE) *Phosphorised paper*

1187	**664**	15½p multicoloured	..	35	35	☐	☐
1188	**665**	19½p multicoloured	..	60	60	☐	☐
1189	**666**	24p multicoloured	..	70	70	☐	☐
1190	**667**	26p multicoloured	..	80	80	☐	☐
1191	**668**	29p multicoloured	..	90	90	☐	☐
		Set of 5	.. .. ..	3·00	3·00	☐	☐
		First Day Cover	.. ..		3·00		☐
		Presentation Pack	..	3·50		☐	
		PHQ Cards (set of 5)	..	3·00	6·50	☐	☐
		Set of 5 Gutter Pairs	..	6·00		☐	

669 ''Strawberry Thief'' (William Morris)

670 Untitled (Steiner and Co)

671 "Cherry Orchard"
(Paul Nash)

672 "Chevron" (Andrew
Foster)

British Textiles

1982 (23 JULY) *Phosphorised paper*

1192	**669**	15½p multicoloured ..	35	35	□	□
1193	**670**	19½p multicoloured ..	55	55	□	□
1194	**671**	26p multicoloured ..	70	70	□	□
1195	**672**	29p multicoloured ..	90	90	□	□
		Set of 4	2·25	2·25	□	□
		First Day Cover		2·50	□	
		Presentation Pack	3·25		□	
		PHQ Cards (set of 4) ..	3·00	6·50	□	□
		Set of 4 Gutter Pairs ..	4·50		□	

Nos 1192/5 were issued on the occasion of the 250th birth anniversary of Sir Richard Arkwright (inventor of spinning machine).

673 Development of Communications

674 Modern Technological Aids

Information Technology

1982 (8 SEPT.) *Phosphorised paper. Perf* 14×15

1196	**673**	15½p multicoloured ..	45	50	□	□
1197	**674**	26p multicoloured ..	80	85	□	□
		Set of 2	1·25	1·25	□	□
		First Day Cover		1·50	□	
		Presentation Pack	2·00		□	
		PHQ Cards (set of 2) ..	1·50	4·50	□	□
		Set of 2 Gutter Pairs ..	2·50		□	

675 Austin "Seven" and "Metro" **676** Ford "Model T" and "Escort"

677 Jaguar "SS1" and "XJ6" **678** Rolls-Royce "Silver Ghost"
and "Silver Spirit"

British Motor Industry

1982 (13 OCT.) *Phosphorised paper. Perf* 14½×14

1198	**675**	15½p multicoloured ..	50	50	□	□
1199	**676**	19½p multicoloured ..	70	70	□	□
1200	**677**	26p multicoloured ..	85	90	□	□
1201	**678**	29p multicoloured ..	1·00	1·25	□	□
		Set of 4	2·75	3·00	□	□
		First Day Cover		3·00	□	
		Presentation Pack	3·75		□	
		PHQ Cards (set of 4)	3·00	7·00	□	□
		Set of 4 Gutter Pairs	5·50		□	

679 "While Shepherds Watched" **680** "The Holly and the Ivy"

681 "I Saw Three Ships" **682** "We Three Kings"

STANLEY GIBBONS
MAIL ORDER SERVICE

BY APPOINTMENT TO
HER MAJESTY THE QUEEN
STANLEY GIBBONS LTD.,
LONDON.
PHILATELISTS.

HOW WE CAN HELP YOU IMPROVE YOUR COLLECTION

★ SERVICE We can offer you a friendly, highly efficient service supported by 137 years of philatelic experience.

★ QUALITY The range and depth of our stock is world famous. Most items can be supplied immediately – always of the highest quality and backed by the Gibbons guarantee of authenticity

★ SAVINGS Our regular Mail Order clients have the benefit of exclusive discounts and special offers not made available elsewhere.

★ BUDGET PLANS AND INTEREST FREE payment schemes available to spread the cost

★ BACK UP STOCK of Errors, Varieties, Missing Colours, Multiples and a comprehensive stock of earlier specialist material from 1840 onwards

★ PERSONAL SERVICE from our G.B. Mail Order Specialists

> PURCHASE COMPLETE year sets and save more than 10% on unmounted mint and fine used sets, presentation packs and First Day Covers. Just tick the box in bold at the end of each year.

How to Order: If you wish to order Queen Elizabeth II commemoratives, please use the tick box system entering the total amount of your order on page IV along with your details and send to the address below. Other stamps prior to QE II can be supplied (if currently available) at the prices quoted in this catalogue, although all prices may be subject to change without notice. Please send your requirements to the same address enclosing a full description of the stamps you require and payment details.

GREAT BRITAIN MAIL ORDER SERVICE, 399 STRAND, LONDON WC2R 0LX
Tel: 071-836 8444 Fax: 071-836 7342

QUEEN ELIZABETH II — COMMEMORATIVES 1953-1968

SG NO.			Un/m	Fine Used	Pres. Pack	F.D.C.
532/35	1953	Coronation	9.00 ☐	7.00 ☐	—	40.00 ☐
557/59	1957	Scouts Jamboree	4.50 ☐	4.50 ☐	—	12.00 ☐
560		Parliament	1.00 ☐	1.00 ☐	—	90.00 ☐
567/69	1958	Commonwealth Games	2.25 ☐	2.25 ☐	—	55.00 ☐
619/20	1960	G.L.O.	3.50 ☐	3.50 ☐	—	40.00 ☐
621/22		Europa	5.00 ☐	4.50 ☐	—	28.00 ☐
623/25	1961	POSB	2.25 ☐	2.00 ☐	—	60.00 ☐
626/28		CEPT	0.60 ☐	0.50 ☐	—	2.50 ☐
629/30		Parliamentary	2.50 ☐	2.00 ☐	—	26.00 ☐
631/33	1962	NPY	2.00 ☐	1.60 ☐	—	30.00 ☐
634/35	1963	Freedom From Hunger	1.75 ☐	2.00 ☐	—	28.00 ☐
636		Paris Conference	0.50 ☐	0.40 ☐	—	12.00 ☐
637/38		Nature Week	0.60 ☐	0.60 ☐	—	14.00 ☐
639/41		Lifeboat	2.75 ☐	2.50 ☐	—	26.00 ☐
642/44		Red Cross	5.00 ☐	4.50 ☐	—	28.00 ☐
645		COMPAC	2.50 ☐	2.25 ☐	—	22.00 ☐
636/45		**Complete Commemoratives for 1963**	**11.50** ☐	**11.00** ☐	—	**110.00** ☐
646/50	1964	Shakespeare	4.00 ☐	4.00 ☐	10.00 ☐	11.00 ☐
651/54		Geographical	4.00 ☐	4.00 ☐	80.00 ☐	18.00 ☐
655/58		Botanical	4.00 ☐	4.00 ☐	80.00 ☐	18.00 ☐
659/60		Forth Road Bridge	0.60 ☐	0.50 ☐	180.00 ☐	5.00 ☐
646/60		**Complete Commemoratives for 1964**	**11.00** ☐	**11.00** ☐	**300.00** ☐	**45.00** ☐
661/62	1965	Churchill	0.60 ☐	0.40 ☐	13.00 ☐	2.00 ☐
663/64		Parliament	1.25 ☐	1.25 ☐	35.00 ☐	12.00 ☐
665/66		Salvation Army	1.10 ☐	1.10 ☐	—	20.00 ☐
667/68		Lister	1.10 ☐	1.25 ☐	—	9.50 ☐
669/70		Commonwealth Arts	1.25 ☐	1.50 ☐	—	10.00 ☐
671/76		Battle of Britain	7.00 ☐	4.25 ☐	48.00 ☐	18.00 ☐
679/80		Post Office Tower	0.75 ☐	0.85 ☐	2.50 ☐	6.00 ☐
681/82		UNO	1.25 ☐	1.10 ☐	—	11.00 ☐
683/84		ITU	1.50 ☐	1.25 ☐	—	11.00 ☐
661/84		**Complete Commemoratives for 1965**	**14.00** ☐	**11.50** ☐	**85.00** ☐	**85.00** ☐
685/86	1966	Burns	0.85 ☐	0.85 ☐	34.00 ☐	2.50 ☐
687/88		Westminster Abbey	1.00 ☐	1.00 ☐	17.00 ☐	4.50 ☐
689/92		Landscapes	1.00 ☐	1.00 ☐	—	6.00 ☐
693/95		World Cup	0.75 ☐	0.75 ☐	14.00 ☐	6.50 ☐
696/99		British Birds	1.00 ☐	0.50 ☐	7.00 ☐	6.50 ☐
700		World Cup Winners	0.20 ☐	0.20 ☐	—	2.00 ☐
701/4		Technology	1.00 ☐	1.00 ☐	7.00 ☐	3.00 ☐
705/12		Battle of Hastings	2.25 ☐	1.50 ☐	7.00 ☐	3.00 ☐
713/14		Christmas	0.45 ☐	0.45 ☐	7.00 ☐	1.50 ☐
685/714		**Complete Commemoratives for 1966**	**7.50** ☐	**6.50** ☐	**80.00** ☐	**30.00** ☐
715/16	1967	EFTA	0.40 ☐	0.40 ☐	1.50 ☐	1.50 ☐
717/22		Wild Flowers	1.40 ☐	0.65 ☐	3.00 ☐	2.50 ☐
748/50		Paintings	0.50 ☐	0.50 ☐	5.50 ☐	1.50 ☐
751		Chichester	0.25 ☐	0.25 ☐	—	1.00 ☐
752/55		Discoveries	0.60 ☐	0.50 ☐	2.00 ☐	1.00 ☐
756/58		Christmas	0.50 ☐	0.50 ☐	—	1.00 ☐
715/58		**Complete Commemoratives for 1967**	**3.00** ☐	**2.50** ☐	**10.00** ☐	**7.50** ☐
763/6	1968	Bridges	0.60 ☐	0.60 ☐	2.00 ☐	1.10 ☐
767/70		Anniversaries	0.60 ☐	0.60 ☐	3.00 ☐	3.25 ☐
771/4		Paintings	0.60 ☐	0.60 ☐	2.00 ☐	1.00 ☐
775/77		Christmas	0.50 ☐	0.50 ☐	2.00 ☐	1.00 ☐
763/77		**Complete Commemoratives for 1968**	**2.00** ☐	**2.00** ☐	**8.00** ☐	**5.60** ☐

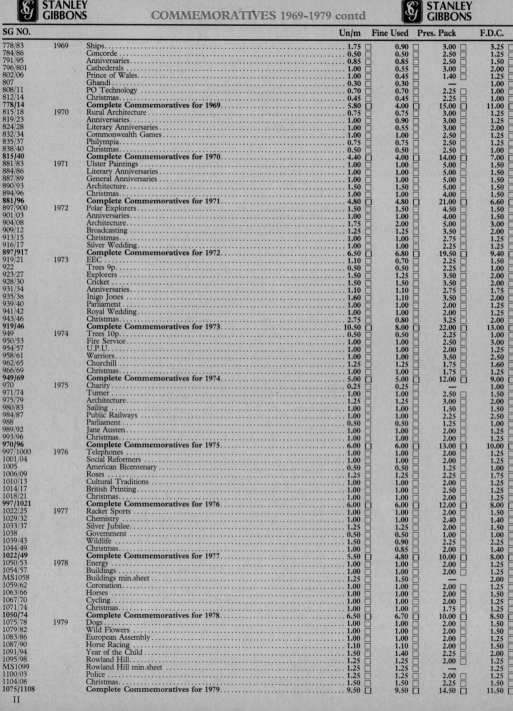

SG NO.			Un/m	Fine Used	Pres. Pack	F.D.C.
778/83	1969	Ships	1.75	0.90	3.00	3.25
784/86		Concorde	0.50	0.50	2.50	1.25
791/95		Anniversaries	0.85	0.85	2.50	1.50
796/801		Cathedrals	1.00	0.55	3.00	2.00
802/06		Prince of Wales	1.00	0.45	1.40	1.25
807		Ghandi	0.30	0.30	—	1.00
808/11		PO Technology	0.70	0.70	2.25	1.00
812/14		Christmas	0.45	0.45	2.25	1.00
778/14		**Complete Commemoratives for 1969**	**5.80**	**4.00**	**15.00**	**11.00**
815/18	1970	Rural Architecture	0.75	0.75	3.00	1.25
819/23		Anniversaries	1.00	0.90	3.00	1.25
824/28		Literary Anniversaries	1.00	0.55	3.00	2.00
832/34		Commonwealth Games	1.00	1.00	2.50	1.25
835/37		Philympia	0.75	0.75	2.50	1.25
838/40		Christmas	0.50	0.50	2.50	1.00
815/40		**Complete Commemoratives for 1970**	**4.40**	**4.00**	**14.00**	**7.00**
881/83	1971	Ulster Paintings	1.00	1.00	5.00	1.50
884/86		Literary Anniversaries	1.00	1.00	5.00	1.50
887/89		General Anniversaries	1.00	1.00	5.00	1.50
890/93		Architecture	1.50	1.50	5.00	1.50
894/96		Christmas	1.00	1.00	4.00	1.50
881/96		**Complete Commemoratives for 1971**	**4.80**	**4.80**	**21.00**	**6.60**
897/900	1972	Polar Explorers	1.50	1.50	4.50	1.50
901/03		Anniversaries	1.00	1.00	4.00	1.50
904/08		Architecture	1.75	2.00	5.00	3.00
909/12		Broadcasting	1.25	1.25	3.50	2.00
913/15		Christmas	1.00	1.00	2.75	1.25
916/17		Silver Wedding	1.00	1.00	2.25	1.25
897/917		**Complete Commemoratives for 1972**	**6.50**	**6.80**	**19.50**	**9.40**
919/21	1973	EEC	1.10	0.70	2.25	1.50
922		Trees 9p	0.50	0.50	2.25	1.00
923/27		Explorers	1.50	1.25	3.50	2.00
928/30		Cricket	1.50	1.50	3.50	2.00
931/34		Anniversaries	1.10	1.10	2.75	1.75
935/38		Inigo Jones	1.60	1.10	3.50	2.00
939/40		Parliament	1.00	1.00	2.00	1.25
941/42		Royal Wedding	1.00	1.00	2.00	1.25
943/46		Christmas	2.75	0.80	3.25	2.00
919/46		**Complete Commemoratives for 1973**	**10.50**	**8.00**	**22.00**	**13.00**
949	1974	Trees 10p	0.50	0.50	2.25	1.00
950/53		Fire Service	1.00	1.00	2.50	3.00
954/57		U.P.U.	1.00	1.00	2.00	1.25
958/61		Warriors	1.00	1.00	3.50	2.50
962/65		Churchill	1.25	1.25	1.75	1.60
966/69		Christmas	1.00	1.00	1.75	1.25
949/69		**Complete Commemoratives for 1974**	**5.00**	**5.00**	**12.00**	**9.00**
970	1975	Charity	0.25	0.25	—	1.00
971/74		Turner	1.00	1.00	2.50	1.50
975/79		Architecture	1.25	1.25	3.00	2.00
980/83		Sailing	1.00	1.00	1.50	1.50
984/87		Public Railways	1.00	1.00	2.25	2.50
988		Parliament	0.50	0.50	1.25	1.00
989/92		Jane Austen	1.00	1.00	2.00	1.25
993/96		Christmas	1.00	1.00	2.00	1.25
970/96		**Complete Commemoratives for 1975**	**6.00**	**6.00**	**13.00**	**10.00**
997/1000	1976	Telephones	1.00	1.00	2.00	1.25
1001/04		Social Reformers	1.00	1.00	2.00	1.25
1005		American Bicentenary	0.50	0.50	1.25	1.00
1006/09		Roses	1.25	1.25	2.25	1.75
1010/13		Cultural Traditions	1.00	1.00	2.00	1.25
1014/17		British Printing	1.00	1.00	2.50	1.25
1018/21		Christmas	1.00	1.00	2.00	1.25
997/1021		**Complete Commemoratives for 1976**	**6.00**	**6.00**	**12.00**	**8.00**
1022/25	1977	Racket Sports	1.00	1.00	2.00	1.50
1029/32		Chemistry	1.00	1.00	2.40	1.40
1033/37		Silver Jubilee	1.25	1.25	2.00	1.50
1038		Government	0.50	0.50	1.00	1.00
1039/43		Wildlife	1.50	0.90	2.25	2.25
1044/49		Christmas	1.00	0.85	2.00	1.40
1022/49		**Complete Commemoratives for 1977**	**5.50**	**4.80**	**10.00**	**8.00**
1050/53	1978	Energy	1.00	1.00	2.00	1.25
1054/57		Buildings	1.00	1.00	2.00	1.25
MS1058		Buildings min.sheet	1.25	1.50	—	2.00
1059/62		Coronation	1.00	1.00	2.00	1.25
1063/66		Horses	1.00	1.00	2.00	1.50
1067/70		Cycling	1.00	1.00	2.00	1.25
1071/74		Christmas	1.00	1.00	1.75	1.25
1050/74		**Complete Commemoratives for 1978**	**6.50**	**6.70**	**10.00**	**8.50**
1075/78	1979	Dogs	1.00	1.00	2.00	1.50
1079/82		Wild Flowers	1.00	1.00	2.00	1.50
1083/86		European Assembly	1.00	1.00	2.00	1.25
1087/90		Horse Racing	1.10	1.10	2.00	1.50
1091/94		Year of the Child	1.50	1.40	2.25	2.00
1095/98		Rowland Hill	1.25	1.25	2.00	1.25
MS1099		Rowland Hill min.sheet	1.25	1.25	—	1.25
1100/03		Police	1.25	1.25	2.00	1.25
1104/08		Christmas	1.50	1.50	2.25	1.50
1075/1108		**Complete Commemoratives for 1979**	**9.50**	**9.50**	**14.50**	**11.50**

SG NO.			Un/m	Fine Used	Pres. Pack	F.D.C.
1109/12	1980	Birds	1.25 □	1.25 □	2.00 □	1.40 □
1113/17		Railways	1.50 □	1.60 □	2.50 □	1.60 □
1118		London 50p	1.50 □	1.50 □	2.00 □	1.50 □
MS1119		London 1980 min.sheet	1.50 □	1.50 □	—	1.50 □
1120/24		Landmarks	1.50 □	1.50 □	2.50 □	1.75 □
1125/28		Authoresses	1.50 □	1.50 □	2.50 □	1.50 □
1129		Queen Mother's 80th	0.50 □	0.50 □	—	0.60 □
1130/33		Conductors	1.50 □	1.50 □	2.00 □	1.50 □
1134/37		Sports	1.50 □	1.50 □	2.00 □	1.50 □
1138/42		Christmas	1.50 □	1.60 □	2.25 □	1.60 □
1109/42		**Complete Commemoratives for 1980**	**12.00** □	**12.40** □	**15.50** □	**13.00** □
1143/46	1981	Folklore	2.00 □	2.00 □	2.50 □	2.00 □
1147/50		Year of the Disabled	2.00 □	2.00 □	2.50 □	2.00 □
1151/54		Butterflies	2.00 □	2.00 □	2.50 □	2.00 □
1155/59		National Trust	2.25 □	2.25 □	2.75 □	2.25 □
1160/61		Royal Wedding	1.00 □	1.00 □	2.00 □	2.00 □
1162/65		Duke of Edinburgh	2.00 □	2.00 □	2.50 □	2.00 □
1166/69		Fishing	2.00 □	2.00 □	2.50 □	2.00 □
1170/74		Christmas	2.25 □	2.25 □	2.75 □	2.25 □
1143/74		**Complete Commemoratives for 1981**	**13.50** □	**13.50** □	**18.00** □	**14.50** □
1175/78	1982	Darwin	2.25 □	2.25 □	3.00 □	2.25 □
1179/82		Youth Organisations	2.25 □	2.25 □	3.50 □	2.25 □
1183/86		Europa	2.25 □	2.25 □	3.25 □	2.25 □
1187/91		Maritime	3.00 □	3.00 □	3.50 □	3.00 □
1192/95		Textiles	2.25 □	2.25 □	3.25 □	2.50 □
1196/97		Information Technology	1.25 □	1.25 □	2.00 □	1.50 □
1198/1201		Cars	2.75 □	3.00 □	3.75 □	3.00 □
1202/06		Christmas	2.25 □	2.50 □	3.00 □	2.50 □
1175/1206		**Complete Commemoratives for 1982**	**16.00** □	**16.50** □	**22.50** □	**17.00** □
1207/10	1983	Fishes	2.25 □	2.25 □	3.00 □	2.50 □
211/14		Commonwealth Day	2.25 □	2.25 □	3.25 □	2.50 □
1215/17		Europa	2.25 □	2.50 □	3.50 □	2.75 □
1218/22		Army Uniforms	3.00 □	3.00 □	4.25 □	3.25 □
1223/26		Gardens	2.25 □	2.50 □	3.50 □	2.75 □
1227/30		Fairs	2.25 □	2.50 □	3.50 □	2.75 □
1231/35		Christmas	2.50 □	2.75 □	3.50 □	2.75 □
1207/35		**Complete Commemoratives for 1983**	**15.00** □	**15.50** □	**22.00** □	**17.00** □
1236/39	1984	Heraldic Arms	2.50 □	2.50 □	3.50 □	2.50 □
1240/44		Cattle	3.00 □	3.00 □	4.25 □	3.00 □
1245/48		Urban Renewal	2.25 □	2.50 □	3.50 □	3.00 □
1249/52		Europa	3.50 □	3.50 □	5.00 □	3.50 □
1253		Summit	1.00 □	1.00 □	—	2.00 □
1254/57		Meridian	2.50 □	2.75 □	3.75 □	2.75 □
1258/62		First Mail Coach Run	2.75 □	2.75 □	3.75 □	2.75 □
1263/66		British Council	2.75 □	2.75 □	3.50 □	2.75 □
1267/71		Christmas	3.00 □	3.00 □	3.75 □	3.00 □
1236/71		**Complete Commemoratives for 1984**	**20.50** □	**21.00** □	**27.50** □	**22.50** □
1272/76	1985	Trains	4.00 □	4.00 □	5.00 □	5.00 □
1277/81		Insects	3.25 □	3.25 □	4.00 □	3.50 □
1282/85		Europa	3.75 □	3.75 □	4.50 □	3.75 □
1286/89		Safety at Sea	3.00 □	3.00 □	4.25 □	3.75 □
1290/93		Mail Service	3.00 □	3.00 □	4.25 □	4.00 □
1294/97		Arthurian Legends	3.00 □	3.25 □	4.75 □	4.00 □
1298/1302		British Film Year	4.00 □	4.25 □	6.00 □	4.50 □
1303/07		Christmas	3.00 □	3.25 □	4.50 □	3.75 □
1272/1307		**Complete Commemoratives for 1985**	**24.00** □	**24.50** □	**33.00** □	**28.50** □
1308/11	1986	Industry Year	2.75 □	2.75 □	4.00 □	4.50 □
1312/15		Halley's Comet	3.00 □	3.00 □	4.50 □	4.50 □
1316/19		H.M. Birthday	3.50 □	3.50 □	5.00 □	4.50 □
1320/23		Europe	3.00 □	3.00 □	5.00 □	4.50 □
1324/27		Doomsday Book	3.25 □	3.25 □	5.00 □	4.25 □
1328/32		Sport	4.00 □	4.00 □	5.25 □	5.75 □
1333/34		Royal Wedding	1.25 □	1.25 □	2.00 □	2.50 □
1335		Conference	1.25 □	1.25 □	—	2.00 □
1336/40		R.A.F.	4.00 □	4.25 □	6.00 □	5.00 □
1341/46		Christmas	3.25 □	3.25 □	5.00 □	5.25 □
1308/46		**Complete Commemoratives for 1986**	**26.00** □	**26.50** □	**30.00** □	**36.00** □
1347/50	1987	Flowers	3.00 □	3.00 □	4.50 □	4.25 □
1351/54		Issac Newton	3.00 □	3.00 □	4.50 □	4.25 □
1355/58		Europa	3.00 □	3.00 □	4.50 □	4.25 □
1359/62		St.John's Ambulance	3.00 □	3.00 □	4.50 □	4.25 □
1363/66		Heraldry	3.00 □	3.00 □	4.50 □	4.25 □
1367/70		Victorian Britain	3.00 □	3.00 □	4.50 □	4.25 □
1371/74		Pottery	3.00 □	3.00 □	4.50 □	4.25 □
1375/79		Christmas	3.25 □	3.50 □	4.50 □	4.25 □
1347/79		**Complete Commemoratives for 1987**	**21.00** □	**22.00** □	**31.00** □	**30.00** □
1380/83	1988	Linnean Society	3.00 □	3.00 □	4.50 □	4.00 □
1384/87		Welsh Bible	3.00 □	3.00 □	4.50 □	4.00 □
1388/91		Sport	3.00 □	3.00 □	4.50 □	5.50 □
1392/95		Europa	3.25 □	3.25 □	4.50 □	4.25 □
1396/99		Australia	3.25 □	3.25 □	4.50 □	4.25 □
1400/04		Armada	2.75 □	2.75 □	4.00 □	3.75 □
1405/06		Edward Lear	3.00 □	3.00 □	4.50 □	4.00 □
MS1409		Edward Lear Min.Sheet	8.00 □	8.50 □	—	8.50 □
1414/18		Christmas	3.00 □	3.00 □	4.25 □	4.25 □
1380/1418		**Complete Commemoratives for 1988**	**28.50** □	**29.50** □	**31.00** □	**38.00** □

SG NO.			Un/m	Fine Used	Pres. Pack	F.D.C.
1419/22	1989	Birds	3.50 ☐	3.50 ☐	4.50 ☐	4.50 ☐
1423/27		Greetings	12.00 ☐	10.00 ☐	—	10.00 ☐
1428/31		Food and Farming	3.25 ☐	3.25 ☐	4.50 ☐	4.25 ☐
1432/35		Anniversaries	4.75 ☐	3.50 ☐	5.25 ☐	4.50 ☐
1436/39		Europa (Toys)	3.50 ☐	3.50 ☐	4.50 ☐	4.25 ☐
1440/43		Architecture	3.00 ☐	3.00 ☐	4.50 ☐	4.25 ☐
MS1444		Architecture min.sheet	6.00 ☐	6.00 ☐	—	6.00 ☐
1453/58		Microscopical Society	3.50 ☐	3.50 ☐	4.00 ☐	5.00 ☐
1457/61		Lord Mayor's Show	3.25 ☐	3.25 ☐	4.50 ☐	3.75 ☐
1462/66		Christmas	3.50 ☐	3.50 ☐	4.50 ☐	4.00 ☐
1419/66		**Complete Commemoratives for 1989**	**40.00** ☐	**38.00** ☐	**32.00** ☐	**45.00** ☐
1467/78	1990	Penny Black	4.50 ☐	4.50 ☐	5.75 ☐	6.00 ☐
1479/82		R.S.P.C.A.	3.25 ☐	3.25 ☐	5.00 ☐	5.25 ☐
1483/92		Smiles	11.00 ☐	11.00 ☐	—	12.00 ☐
1493/96		Europa	3.00 ☐	3.00 ☐	4.00 ☐	4.25 ☐
1497/1500		Queen's Award	3.00 ☐	3.00 ☐	4.00 ☐	4.50 ☐
MS1501		London 1990 min.sheet	3.50 ☐	4.00 ☐	—	5.50 ☐
1502/05		Kew Gardens	3.25 ☐	3.50 ☐	4.00 ☐	4.50 ☐
1506		Thomas Hardy	0.60 ☐	0.70 ☐	1.75 ☐	2.00 ☐
1507/10		Queen Mother's 90th	3.25 ☐	3.50 ☐	4.50 ☐	4.75 ☐
1517/21		Gallantry Awards	3.00 ☐	3.00 ☐	4.00 ☐	3.75 ☐
1522/25		Astronomy	3.00 ☐	3.00 ☐	4.00 ☐	3.75 ☐
1526/30		Christmas	3.50 ☐	3.50 ☐	4.25 ☐	4.25 ☐
1467/1530		**Complete Commemoratives for 1990**	**40.00** ☐	**40.00** ☐	**37.00** ☐	**53.00** ☐
1531/35	1991	Dogs	4.00 ☐	4.00 ☐	5.00 ☐	5.00 ☐
1536/45		Greetings	7.00 ☐	8.00 ☐	—	8.50 ☐
1546/49		Scientific Achievements	3.00 ☐	3.00 ☐	3.75 ☐	4.00 ☐
1550/59		Greetings (Type II)	3.50 ☐	4.00 ☐	—	7.50 ☐
1560/63		Europa	3.00 ☐	3.00 ☐	4.00 ☐	4.00 ☐
1564/67		Games/Rugby	3.00 ☐	3.00 ☐	4.00 ☐	4.00 ☐
1568/72		Roses	4.00 ☐	4.00 ☐	4.50 ☐	5.50 ☐
1573/77		Dinosaurs	4.50 ☐	4.50 ☐	5.00 ☐	5.50 ☐
1578/81		Ordinance Survey	3.00 ☐	3.25 ☐	4.00 ☐	4.25 ☐
1582/86		Christmas	4.00 ☐	4.00 ☐	4.25 ☐	4.50 ☐
1531/86		**Complete Commemoratives for 1991**	**35.00** ☐	**36.00** ☐	**31.00** ☐	**47.00** ☐
1587/91	1992	Wintertime	3.25 ☐	3.50 ☐	4.25 ☐	4.50 ☐
1592/1601		Greetings	3.50 ☐	4.00 ☐	4.00 ☐	7.00 ☐
1602/06		Accession	4.00 ☐	3.50 ☐	4.25 ☐	5:00 ☐
1607/10		Tennyson	3.00 ☐	3.00 ☐	3.75 ☐	4.00 ☐
1615/19		Europa	3.50 ☐	3.50 ☐	4.25 ☐	4.50 ☐
1620/23		Civil War	2.75 ☐	2.75 ☐	3.00 ☐	4.00 ☐
1624/28		Gilbert & Sullivan	3.00 ☐	3.00 ☐	3.25 ☐	4.75 ☐
1629/32		Green Issue	2.75 ☐	2.75 ☐	7.00 ☐	3.50 ☐
1633		Single European Market	0.60 ☐	0.60 ☐	1.00 ☐	1.00 ☐
1634/38		Christmas	3.00 ☐	3.00 ☐	3.00 ☐	4.00 ☐
1587/1638		**Complete Commemoratives for 1992**	**26.00** ☐	**26.00** ☐	**33.50** ☐	**38.00** ☐
1639/43	1993	Swans	2.00 ☐	2.25 ☐	2.50 ☐	3.50 ☐
1644/1653		Greetings	3.50 ☐	4.00 ☐	4.00 ☐	5.50 ☐
1654/57		Marine Time keepers	1.75 ☐	1.90 ☐	2.40 ☐	3.00 ☐
1659/63		Orchids	2.00 ☐	2.25 ☐	2.50 ☐	3.75 ☐
1767/70		Europa	1.70 ☐	2.00 ☐	2.40 ☐	3.00 ☐
1771/74		Roman Britain	1.75 ☐	2.00 ☐	2.40 ☐	3.00 ☐
1775/78		Inland Waterways	1.75 ☐	2.00 ☐	2.40 ☐	3.00 ☐
1779/83		Autumn	2.00 ☐	2.25 ☐	2.50 ☐	3.25 ☐
1784/88		Sherlock Holmes	1.75 ☐	2.00 ☐	2.25 ☐	3.00 ☐
1790/94		Christmas	2.10 ☐	2.40 ☐	2.75 ☐	3.25 ☐
1639/1794		**Complete Commemoratives for 1993**	**18.00** ☐	**20.50** ☐	**23.00** ☐	**30.50** ☐

To: Stanley Gibbons Ltd Great Britain Mail Order Service, 399 Strand, London WC2R 0LX

☐ I enclose cheque/PO made payable to Stanley Gibbons Ltd. for £ ....

☐ I have paid £ .... into Stanley Gibbons Giro Account No. 586 6006

☐ I authorise you to charge my credit card for £ ....

Total		
Postage & Handling	1	50
Total Order Value		

Type of card .... (all major cards accepted)

Expiry date

Card No.

Signature ....

Name ....   Address ....

....   Postcode ....

We will return your order form for your record together with our new price list.

Please allow 14 days for delivery (overseas customers 21 days)

3b2/gen/cbslist

IV

683 "Good King Wenceslas"

Christmas. Carols

1982 (17 Nov.) *One phosphor band (12½p) or phosphorised paper (others)*

1202	**679**	12½p multicoloured	..	30	30	☐	☐
1203	**680**	15½p multicoloured	..	40	40	☐	☐
1204	**681**	19½p multicoloured	..	50	60	☐	☐
1205	**682**	26p multicoloured	..	60	70	☐	☐
1206	**683**	29p multicoloured	..	70	80	☐	☐
		Set of 5		2·25	2·50	☐	☐
		First Day Cover			2·50	☐	
		Presentation Pack ..		3·00		☐	
		PHQ Cards (set of 5) ..		3·00	7·00	☐	☐
		Set of 5 Gutter Pairs ..		4·50		☐	

Collectors Pack 1982

1982 (17 Nov.) *Comprises Nos.* 1175/1206

	Collectors Pack ..	..	24·00	☐

684 Salmon

685 Pike

686 Trout

687 Perch

British River Fishes

1983 (26 Jan.) *Phosphorised paper*

1207	**684**	15½p multicoloured	..	35	35	☐	☐
1208	**685**	19½p multicoloured	..	55	55	☐	☐
1209	**686**	26p multicoloured	..	70	70	☐	☐
1210	**687**	29p multicoloured	..	90	90	☐	☐
		Set of 4		2·25	2·25	☐	☐
		First Day Cover			2·50	☐	
		Presentation Pack ..		3·00		☐	
		PHQ Cards (set of 4) ..		3·00	6·50	☐	☐
		Set of 4 Gutter Pairs ..		4·50		☐	

688 Tropical Island

689 Desert

690 Temperate Farmland

691 Mountain Range

Commonwealth Day. Geographical Regions

1983 (9 Mar.) *Phosphorised paper*

1211	**688**	15½p multicoloured	..	35	35	☐	☐
1212	**689**	19½p multicoloured	..	55	55	☐	☐
1213	**690**	26p multicoloured	..	70	70	☐	☐
1214	**691**	29p multicoloured	..	90	90	☐	☐
		Set of 4		2·25	2·25	☐	☐
		First Day Cover			2·50	☐	
		Presentation Pack ..		3·25		☐	
		PHQ Cards (set of 4) ..		3·00	6·50	☐	
		Set of 4 Gutter Pairs ..		4·50		☐	

692 Humber Bridge

693 Thames Flood Barrier

694 *Iolair* (oilfield emergency support vessel)

Europa. Engineering Achievements

1983 (25 MAY) *Phosphorised paper.*						
1215	**692**	16p multicoloured	..	45	45	□ □
1216	**693**	20½p multicoloured	..	95	1·10	□ □
1217	**694**	28p multicoloured	..	1·10	1·25	□ □
		Set of 3		2·25	2·50	□ □
		First Day Cover			2·75	□
		Presentation Pack		3·50		□
		PHQ Cards (set of 3)		2·50	6·00	□ □
		Set of 3 Gutter Pairs		4·50		□

695 Musketeer and Pikeman.
The Royal Scots
(1633)

696 Fusilier and Ensign. The
Royal Welch Fusiliers
(mid-18th century)

697 Riflemen. 96th Rifles
(The Royal Green
Jackets) (1805)

698 Sergeant (khaki service
uniform) and Guardsman
(full dress). The Irish
Guards (1900)

699 Paratroopers. The Parachute Regiment
(1983)

British Army Uniforms

1983 (6 JULY) *Phosphorised paper.*						
1218	**695**	16p multicoloured	..	40	40	□ □
1219	**696**	20½p multicoloured	..	60	60	□ □
1220	**697**	26p multicoloured	..	70	70	□ □
1221	**698**	28p multicoloured	..	70	70	□ □
1222	**699**	31p multicoloured	..	90	90	□ □
		Set of 5		3·00	3·00	□ □
		First Day Cover			3·25	□
		Presentation Pack		4·25		□
		PHQ Cards (set of 5) ..		3·00	6·00	□ □
		Set of 5 Gutter Pairs ..		6·00		□

Nos. 1218/22 were issued on the occasion of the 350th
anniversary of The Royal Scots, the senior line regiment of the
British Army.

700 20th-Century Garden,
Sissinghurst

701 19th-Century Garden,
Biddulph Grange

702 18th-Century Garden,
Blenheim

703 17th-Century Garden,
Pitmedden

British Gardens

1983 (24 AUG.) *Phosphorised paper. Perf* 14						
1223	**700**	16p multicoloured	..	40	40	□ □
1224	**701**	20½p multicoloured	..	50	50	□ □
1225	**702**	28p multicoloured	..	70	90	□ □
1226	**703**	31p multicoloured	..	90	1·00	□ □
		Set of 4		2·25	2·50	□ □
		First Day Cover			2·75	□
		Presentation Pack		3·50		□
		PHQ Cards (set of 4) ..		3·00	6·00	□ □
		Set of 4 Gutter Pairs		4·50		□

704 Merry-go-round

705 Big Wheel, Helter-skelter and Performing Animals

712 "Christmas Dove"
(hedge sculpture)

706 Side-shows

707 Early Produce Fair

British Fairs

1983 (5 OCT.) *Phosphorised paper.*

1227	**704**	16p multicoloured	..	40	40	☐	☐
1228	**705**	20½p multicoloured	..	50	65	☐	☐
1229	**706**	28p multicoloured	..	75	85	☐	☐
1230	**707**	31p multicoloured	..	90	90	☐	☐
		Set of 4	.. .. ..	2·25	2·50	☐	☐
		First Day Cover	.. ..		2·75		☐
		Presentation Pack	·. ..	3·50		☐	
		PHQ Cards (set of 4)	.. ..	3·00	6·00	☐	☐
		Set of 4 Gutter Pairs	..	4·50		☐	

Nos. 1227/30 were issued to mark the 850th Anniversary of St. Bartholomew's Fair, Smithfield, London.

Christmas

1983 (16 Nov.) *One phosphor band (12½p) or phosphorised paper (others)*

1231	**708**	12½p multicoloured	..	30	30	☐	☐
1232	**709**	16p multicoloured	..	35	35	☐	☐
1233	**710**	20½p multicoloured	..	60	60	☐	☐
1234	**711**	28p multicoloured	..	70	80	☐	☐
1235	**712**	31p multicoloured	..	85	1·00	☐	☐
		Set of 5	..	2·50	2·75	☐	☐
		First Day Cover	.. ..		2·75		☐
		Presentation Pack ..	.. ..	3·50		☐	
		PHQ Cards (set of 5)	..	3·00	6·00	☐	☐
		Set of 5 Gutter Pairs	..	5·00		☐	

Collectors Pack 1983

1983 (16 Nov.) *Comprises Nos. 1207/35*

	Collectors Pack	.. ..	40·00	☐

708 "Christmas Post"
(pillar-box)

709 "The Three Kings"
(chimney-pots)

713 Arms of the
College of Arms

714 Arms of King Richard III
(founder)

710 "World at Peace"
(Dove and Blackbird)

711 "Light of Christmas"
(street lamp)

715 Arms of the Earl Marshal
of England

716 Arms of the City of London

500th Anniversary of College of Arms

1984 (17 Jan) *Phosphorised paper. Perf 14½*

1236	**713**	16p multicoloured ..	40	40	☐	☐
1237	**714**	20½p multicoloured	60	60	☐	☐
1238	**715**	28p multicoloured	85	85	☐	☐
1239	**716**	31p multicoloured	95	95	☐	☐
		Set of 4	2·50	2·50	☐	☐
		First Day Cover		2·50		☐
		Presentation Pack ..	3·50		☐	
		PHQ Cards (set of 4) ..	3·00	6·00	☐	☐
		Set of 4 Gutter Pairs	5·00		☐	

717 Highland Cow

718 Chillingham Wild Bull

719 Hereford Bull

720 Welsh Black Bull

721 Irish Moiled Cow

British Cattle

1984 (6 Mar.) *Phosphorised paper.*

1240	**717**	16p multicoloured ..	40	40	☐	☐
1241	**718**	20½p multicoloured ..	65	65	☐	☐
1242	**719**	26p multicoloured ..	70	70	☐	☐
1243	**720**	28p multicoloured ..	70	70	☐	☐
1244	**721**	31p multicoloured ..	90	90	☐	☐
		Set of 5	3·00	3·00	☐	☐
		First Day Cover		3·00		☐
		Presentation Pack	4·25		☐	
		PHQ Cards (set of 5)	3·00	6·00	☐	☐
		Set of 5 Gutter Pairs	6·00		☐	

Nos. 1240/4 marked the centenary of the Highland Cattle Society and the bicentenary of the Royal Highland and Agricultural Society of Scotland.

722 Festival Hall, Liverpool

723 Milburngate Shopping Centre, Durham

724 Bush House, Bristol

725 Commercial Street Housing Scheme, Perth

Urban Renewal

1984 (10 Apr.) *Phosphorised paper.*

1245	**722**	16p multicoloured ..	40	40	☐	☐
1246	**723**	20½p multicoloured ..	60	60	☐	☐
1247	**724**	28p multicoloured ..	75	90	☐	☐
1248	**725**	31p multicoloured ..	75	90	☐	☐
		Set of 4	2·25	2·50	☐	☐
		First Day Cover		3·00		☐
		Presentation Pack	3·50		☐	
		PHQ Cards (set of 4)	3·00	6·00	☐	☐
		Set of 4 Gutter Pairs	4·50		☐	

Nos. 1245/8 mark the opening of the International Gardens Festival, Liverpool, and the 150th anniversaries of the Royal Institute of British Architects and the Chartered Institute of Building.

726 C.E.P.T. 25th Anniversary Logo

727 Abduction of Europa

Nos. 1249/50 and 1251/2 were each printed together, *se-tenant,* in horizontal pairs throughout the sheets.

Europa. 25th Anniversary of C.E.P.T. and 2nd European Parliamentary Elections

1984 (15 MAY) *Phosphorised paper.*

1249	**726**	16p greenish slate, dp blue and gold	70	70	☐	☐
		a. Horiz pair. Nos. 1249/50	1·40	1·40	☐	☐
1250	**727**	16p greenish slate, dp bl, blk and gold	70	70	☐	☐
1251	**726**	20½p Venetian red, deep magenta and gold	1·25	1·25	☐	☐
		a. Horizontal pair. Nos. 1251/2	2·50	2·50	☐	☐
1252	**727**	20½p Venetian red, deep magenta, black and gold	1·25	1·25	☐	☐
		Set of 4	3·50	3·50	☐	☐
		First Day Cover		3·50		☐
		Presentation Pack	5·00		☐	
		PHQ Cards (set of 4)	3·00	6·00	☐	☐
		Set of 4 Gutter Pairs	7·00		☐	

728 Lancaster House

London Economic Summit Conference

1984 (5 JUNE) *Phosphorised paper.*

1253	**728**	31p multicoloured	1·00	1·00	☐	☐
		First Day Cover		2·00		☐
		PHQ Card	1·00	2·75	☐	☐
		Gutter Pair	2·00		☐	

729 View of Earth from "Apollo 11"

730 Navigational Chart of English Channel

731 Greenwich Observatory

732 Sir George Airey's Transit Telescope

Centenary of Greenwich Meridian

1984 (26 JUNE) *Phosphorised paper. Perf* 14 × 14½

1254	**729**	16p multicoloured	40	40	☐	☐
1255	**730**	20½p multicoloured	65	65	☐	☐
1256	**731**	28p multicoloured	85	90	☐	☐
1257	**732**	31p multicoloured	90	1·10	☐	☐
		Set of 4	2·50	2·75	☐	☐
		First Day Cover		2·75		☐
		Presentation Pack	3·75		☐	
		PHQ Cards (set of 4)	3·00	6·00	☐	☐
		Set of 4 Gutter Pairs	5·00		☐	

733 Bath Mail Coach, 1784

734 Attack on Exeter Mail, 1816

735 Norwich Mail in Thunderstorm, 1827

736 Holyhead and Liverpool Mails leaving London, 1828

737 Edinburgh Mail Snowbound, 1831

T 733/7 were printed together, *se-tenant* in horizontal strips of 5 throughout the sheet.

Bicentenary of First Mail Coach Run, Bath and Bristol to London

1984 (31 July) *Phosphorised paper*

1258	**733**	16p multicoloured	..	60	60	☐	☐
		a. *Horiz strip of 5.*					
		Nos. 1258/62.		2·75	2·75	☐	☐
1259	**734**	16p multicoloured	..	60	60	☐	☐
1260	**735**	16p multicoloured	..	60	60	☐	☐
1261	**736**	16p multicoloured	..	60	60	☐	☐
1262	**737**	16p multicoloured	..	60	60	☐	☐
		Set of 5		2·75	2·75	☐	☐
		First Day Cover			2·75		☐
		Presentation Pack		3·75		☐	
		Souvenir Book		6·00		☐	
		PHQ Cards (set of 5)		3·00	6·50	☐	☐
		Gutter Strip of 10		5·50		☐	

738 Nigerian Clinic

739 Violinist and Acropolis, Athens

740 Building Project, Sri Lanka

741 British Council Library

50th Anniversary of The British Council

1984 (25 Sept.) *Phosphorised paper*

1263	**738**	17p multicoloured	..	50	50	☐	☐
1264	**739**	22p multicoloured	..	65	65	☐	☐
1265	**740**	31p multicoloured	..	90	90	☐	☐
1266	**741**	34p multicoloured	..	1·00	1·00	☐	☐
		Set of 4		2·75	2·75	☐	☐
		First Day Cover			2·75		☐
		Presentation Pack		3·50		☐	
		PHQ Cards (set of 4)		3·00	6·00	☐	☐
		Set of 4 Gutter Pairs		5·50		☐	

For full information on all future British issues, collectors should write to the British Post Office Philatelic Bureau, 20 Brandon Street, Edinburgh EH3 5TT.

742 The Holy Family

743 Arrival in Bethlehem

744 Shepherd and Lamb

745 Virgin and Child

746 Offering of Frankincense

Christmas

1984 (20 Nov.) *One phosphor band (13p) or phosphorised paper (others)*

1267	**742**	13p multicoloured	..	30	30	☐	☐
1268	**743**	17p multicoloured	..	50	50	☐	☐
1269	**744**	22p multicoloured	..	60	60	☐	☐
1270	**745**	31p multicoloured	..	95	95	☐	☐
1271	**746**	34p multicoloured	..	1·00	1·00	☐	☐
		Set of 5		3·00	3·00	☐	☐
		First Day Cover			3·00		☐
		Presentation Pack		3·75		☐	
		PHQ Cards (set of 5) ..		3·00	6·00	☐	☐
		Set of 5 Gutter Pairs		6·00		☐	

Collectors Pack 1984

1984 (20 Nov.) *Comprises Nos. 1236/71*

Collectors Pack	..	..	40·00	☐

Post Office Yearbook

1984 *Comprises Nos. 1236/71 in hardbound book with slip case.*

Yearbook	..	..	80·00	☐

70

747 "The Flying Scotsman"

748 "The Golden Arrow"

749 "The Cheltenham Flyer"

750 "The Royal Scot"

751 "The Cornish Riviera"

754 *Decticus verrucivorus*
(bush-cricket)

755 *Lucanus cervus* (stag beetle)

756 *Anax imperator* (dragonfly)

Famous Trains

1985 (22 JAN.) *Phosphorised paper*

1272	**747**	17p multicoloured	..	50	50	☐	☐
1273	**748**	22p multicoloured	..	70	70	☐	☐
1274	**749**	29p multicoloured	..	90	90	☐	☐
1275	**750**	31p multicoloured	..	1·00	1·00	☐	☐
1276	**751**	34p multicoloured	..	1·10	1·10	☐	☐
	Set of 5	.. ..		4·00	4·00	☐	☐
	First Day Cover	.. ..			5·00		☐
	Presentation Pack	.. ..		5·00		☐	
	PHQ Cards (set of 5)	.. ..		4·00	11·00	☐	☐
	Set of 5 *Gutter Pairs*	.. ..		8·00		☐	

Nos. 1272/6 were issued on the occasion of the 150th anniversary of the Great Western Railway Company.

Insects

1985 (12 MARCH) *Phosphorised paper*

1277	**752**	17p multicoloured	..	40	40	☐	☐
1278	**753**	22p multicoloured	..	60	60	☐	☐
1279	**754**	29p multicoloured	..	80	80	☐	☐
1280	**755**	31p multicoloured	..	90	90	☐	☐
1281	**756**	34p multicoloured	..	90	90	☐	☐
	Set of 5	.. ..		3·25	3·25	☐	☐
	First Day Cover	.. ..			3·50		☐
	Presentation Pack	.. ..		4·00		☐	
	PHQ Cards (set of 5)	.. ..		3·00	6·50	☐	☐
	Set of 5 *Gutter Pairs*	.. ..		6·50		☐	

Nos. 1277/81 were issued on the occasion of the centenaries of the Royal Entomological Society of London's Royal Charter and of the Selborne Society.

752 *Bombus terrestris* (bee)

753 *Coccinella septempunctata*
(ladybird)

757 "Water Music", by Handel

758 "The Planets", by Holst

759 "The First Cuckoo", by Delius

760 "Sea Pictures", by Elgar

Europa – European Music Year

1985 (14 MAY) *Phosphorised paper. Perf* 14½

1282	**757**	17p multicoloured	..	65	65	☐	☐
1283	**758**	22p multicoloured	..	90	90	☐	☐
1284	**759**	31p multicoloured	..	1·25	1·25	☐	☐
1285	**760**	34p multicoloured	..	1·40	1·40	☐	☐
		Set of 4	..	3·75	3·75	☐	☐
		First Day Cover	..		3·75	☐	
		Presentation Pack	..	4·50		☐	
		PHQ Cards (set of 4)	..	3·00	6·00	☐	☐
		Set of 4 Gutter Pairs	..	7·50		☐	

Nos. 1282/5 were issued on the occasion of the 300th birth anniversary of Handel.

761 R.N.L.I. Lifeboat and Signal Flags

762 Beachy Head Lighthouse and Chart

763 "Marecs A" Communications Satellite and Dish Aerials

764 Buoys

Safety at Sea

1985 (18 JUNE) *Phosphorised paper. Perf* 14

1286	**761**	17p multicoloured	..	50	50	☐	☐
1287	**762**	22p multicoloured	..	65	65	☐	☐
1288	**763**	31p multicoloured	..	1·10	1·10	☐	☐
1289	**764**	34p multicoloured	..	1·10	1·10	☐	☐
		Set of 4	..	3·00	3·00	☐	☐
		First Day Cover	..		3·75	☐	
		Presentation Pack	..	4·25		☐	
		PHQ Cards (set of 4)	..	3·00	6·00	☐	☐
		Set of 4 Gutter Pairs	..	6·00		☐	

Nos. 1286/9 were issued on the occasion of the bicentenary of the unimmersible lifeboat and the 50th anniversary of Radar.

765 Datapost Motorcyclist, City of London

766 Rural Postbus

767 Parcel Delivery in Winter

768 Town Letter Delivery

350 Years of Royal Mail Public Postal Service

1985 (30 JULY) *Phosphorised paper*

1290	**765**	17p multicoloured	..	50	50	☐	☐
1291	**766**	22p multicoloured	..	65	65	☐	☐
1292	**767**	31p multicoloured	..	1·10	1·10	☐	☐
1293	**768**	34p multicoloured	..	1·10	1·10	☐	☐
		Set of 4	..	3·00	3·00	☐	☐
		First Day Cover	..		4·00	☐	
		Presentation Pack	..	4·25		☐	
		PHQ Cards (set of 4)	..	3·00	6·00	☐	☐
		Set of 4 Gutter Pairs	..	6·00		☐	

769 King Arthur and Merlin

770 The Lady of the Lake

771 Queen Guinevere and Sir Lancelot

772 Sir Galahad

777 Alfred Hitchcock (from photo by Howard Coster)

Arthurian Legends

1985 (3 SEPT.) *Phosphorised paper*

1294	**769**	17p multicoloured	..	50	50	☐	☐
1295	**770**	22p multicoloured	..	65	75	☐	☐
1296	**771**	31p multicoloured	..	1·10	1·10	☐	☐
1297	**772**	34p multicoloured	..	1·10	1·25	☐	☐
		Set of 4		3·00	3·25	☐	☐
		First Day Cover			4·00		☐
		Presentation Pack		4·75		☐	
		PHQ Cards (set of 4)		3·00	6·00	☐	☐
		Set of 4 Gutter Pairs		6·00		☐	

Nos. 1294/7 were issued on the occasion of the 500th anniversary of the printing of Sir Thomas Malory's *Morte d'Arthur*.

British Film Year

1985 (8 OCT.) *Phosphorised paper. Perf* 14½

1298	**773**	17p multicoloured	..	50	50	☐	☐
1299	**774**	22p multicoloured	..	70	85	☐	☐
1300	**775**	29p multicoloured	..	90	1·00	☐	☐
1301	**776**	31p multicoloured	..	1·10	1·10	☐	☐
1302	**777**	34p multicoloured	..	1·25	1·25	☐	☐
		Set of 5		4·00	4·25	☐	☐
		First Day Cover			4·50		☐
		Presentation Pack		6·00		☐	
		Souvenir Book		7·00		☐	
		PHQ Cards (set of 5)		3·00	6·00	☐	☐
		Set of 5 Gutter Pairs		8·00		☐	

773 Peter Sellers (from photo by Bill Brandt)

774 David Niven (from photo by Cornell Lucas)

775 Charlie Chaplin (from photo by Lord Snowdon)

776 Vivien Leigh (from photo by Angus McBean)

778 Principal Boy

779 Genie

780 Dame

781 Good Fairy

782 Pantomime Cat

73

Christmas. Pantomime Characters

1985 (19 Nov.) *One phosphor band (12p) or phosphorised paper (others)*

1303	**778**	12p multicoloured	..	35	30	☐	☐
1304	**779**	17p multicoloured	..	45	40	☐	☐
1305	**780**	22p multicoloured	..	70	80	☐	☐
1306	**781**	31p multicoloured	..	95	1·00	☐	☐
1307	**782**	34p multicoloured	..	1·00	1·10	☐	☐
		Set of 5		3·00	3·25	☐	☐
		First Day Cover			3·75		☐
		Presentation Pack .. ..` ..		4·50		☐	
		PHQ Cards (Set of 5)		3·00	6·00	☐	☐
		Set of 5 Gutter Pairs		6·00		☐	

Collectors Pack 1985

1985 (19 Nov.) *Comprises Nos. 1272/1307*

Collectors Pack	.. .. ..	40·00	☐

Post Office Yearbook

1985 *Comprises Nos. 1272/1307 in hardbound book with slip case.*

Yearbook	.. ..	75·00	☐

783 Light Bulb and North Sea Oil Drilling Rig (Energy)

784 Thermometer and Pharmaceutical Laboratory (Health)

785 Garden Hoe and Steel Works (Steel)

786 Loaf of Bread and Cornfield (Agriculture)

Industry Year

1986 (14 Jan.) *Phosphorised paper. Perf 14½ × 14*

1308	**783**	17p multicoloured	..	45	45	☐	☐
1309	**784**	22p multicoloured	..	60	60	☐	☐
1310	**785**	31p multicoloured	..	90	90	☐	☐
1311	**786**	34p multicoloured	..	1·10	1·10	☐	☐
		Set of 4		2·75	2·75	☐	☐
		First Day Cover			4·50		☐
		Presentation Pack		4·00		☐	
		PHQ Cards (set of 4)		3·00	6·00	☐	☐
		Set of 4 Gutter Pairs		5·50		☐	

787 Dr. Edmond Halley as Comet

788 *Giotto* Spacecraft approaching Comet

789 "Twice in a Lifetime"

790 Comet orbiting Sun and Planets

Appearance of Halley's Comet

1986 (18 Feb.) *Phosphorised paper.*

1312	**787**	17p multicoloured	..	45	45	☐	☐
1313	**788**	22p multicoloured	..	70	70	☐	☐
1314	**789**	31p multicoloured	..	1·10	1·10	☐	☐
1315	**790**	34p multicoloured	..	1·10	1·10	☐	☐
		Set of 4		3·00	3·00	☐	☐
		First Day Cover			4·50		☐
		Presentation Pack ..		4·50		☐	
		PHQ Cards (set of 4)		4·00	6·00	☐	☐
		Set of 4 Gutter Pairs		6·00		☐	

791 Queen Elizabeth II in 1928, 1942 and 1952

792 Queen Elizabeth II in 1958, 1973 and 1982

Nos. 1316/17 and 1318/19 were each printed together, *se-tenant*, in horizontal pairs throughout the sheets.

60th Birthday of Queen Elizabeth II

1986 (21 Apr.) *Phosphorised paper.*

1316	**791**	17p multicoloured	..	70	70	☐	☐
		a. Horiz pair.					
		Nos.1316/17	..	1·40	1·40	☐	☐
1317	**792**	17p multicoloured	..	70	70	☐	☐
1318	**791**	34p multicoloured	..	1·25	1·25	☐	☐
		a. Horiz pair.					
		Nos.1318/19	..	2·50	2·50	☐	☐
1319	**792**	34p multicoloured	..	1·25	1·25	☐	☐
		Set of 4		3·50	3·50	☐	☐
		First Day Cover			4·50		☐
		Presentation Pack		5·00		☐	
		Souvenir Book		7·00		☐	
		PHQ Cards (set of 4)		3·00	6·00	☐	☐
		Set of 4 Gutter Pairs ..		7·00		☐	

793 Barn Owl

794 Pine Marten

795 Wild Cat

796 Natterjack Toad

Europa. Nature Conservation. Endangered Species

1986 (20 MAY) *Phosphorised paper. Perf 14½ × 14*

1320	793	17p multicoloured	..	50	50	☐	☐
1321	794	22p multicoloured	..	65	65	☐	☐
1322	795	31p multicoloured	..	1·10	1·10	☐	☐
1323	796	34p multicoloured	..	1·10	1·10	☐	☐
		Set of 4		3·00	3·00	☐	☐
		First Day Cover			4·50		☐
		Presentation Pack		5·00		☐	
		PHQ Cards (set of 4)		3·00	6·00	☐	☐
		Set of 4 Gutter Pairs		6·00		☐	

797 Peasants working in Fields

798 Freemen working at Town Trades

799 Knight and Retainers

800 Lord at Banquet

900th Anniversary of Domesday Book

1986 (17 JUNE) *Phosphorised paper*

1324	797	17p multicoloured		50	50	☐	☐
1325	798	22p multicoloured	..	75	75	☐	☐
1326	799	31p multicoloured	..	1·10	1·10	☐	☐
1327	800	34p multicoloured	..	1·25	1·25	☐	☐
		Set of 4		3·25	3·25	☐	☐
		First Day Cover			4·25		☐
		Presentation Pack		5·00		☐	
		PHQ Cards (set of 4)		3·00	6·00	☐	☐
		Set of 4 Gutter Pairs		6·50		☐	

801 Athletics

802 Rowing

803 Weightlifting

804 Rifle-Shooting

805 Hockey

Thirteenth Commonwealth Games, Edinburgh (Nos. 1328/31) and World Men's Hockey Cup, London (No. 1332)

1986 (15 JULY) *Phosphorised paper.*

1328	801	17p multicoloured	..	50	50	☐	☐
1329	802	22p multicoloured	..	70	70	☐	☐
1330	803	29p multicoloured	..	90	90	☐	☐
1331	804	31p multicoloured	..	1·10	1·10	☐	☐
1332	805	34p multicoloured	..	1·25	1·25	☐	☐
		Set of 5		4·00	4·00	☐	☐·
		First Day Cover ·..			5·75		☐
		Presentation Pack		5·25		☐	
		PHQ Cards (Set of 5)		4·00	6·00	☐	☐
		Set of 5 Gutter Pairs		8·00		☐	

No. 1332 also marked the centenary of the Hockey Association.

806 Prince Andrew and Miss Sarah Ferguson **807**

Royal Wedding

1986 (22 July) *One side band* (12p) *or phosphorised paper* (17p)

1333	**806**	12p multicoloured	..	60	60	☐	☐
1334	**807**	17p multicoloured	..	90	90	☐	☐
		Set of 2	..	1·25	1·25	☐	☐
		First Day Cover	.. .. ..		2·50		☐
		Presentation Pack	.. ..	2·00		☐	
		PHQ Cards (set of 2)	.. ..	1·50	5·00	☐	☐
		Set of 2 Gutter Pairs	.. ..	2·50		☐	

808 Stylised Cross on Ballot Paper

32nd Commonwealth Parliamentary Conference, London

1986 (19 Aug.) *Phosphorised paper. Perf* 14 × 14½

1335	**808**	34p multicoloured	..	1·25	1·25	☐	☐
		First Day Cover	.. .. ..		2·00		☐
		PHQ Card	.. ..	1·00	2·50	☐	☐
		Gutter Pair	.. .. ..	2·50		☐	

809 Lord Dowding and "Hurricane"

810 Lord Tedder and "Typhoon"

811 Lord Trenchard and "DH 9A"

812 Sir Arthur Harris and "Lancaster"

813 Lord Portal and "Mosquito"

History of the Royal Air Force

1986 (16th Sept.) *Phosphorised paper. Perf* 14½ × 14.

1336	**809**	17p multicoloured	..	50	40	☐	☐
1337	**810**	22p multicoloured	..	70	85	☐	☐
1338	**811**	29p multicoloured	..	90	1·00	☐	☐
1339	**812**	31p multicoloured	..	1·10	1·10	☐	☐
1340	**813**	34p multicoloured	..	1·25	1·25	☐	☐
		Set of 5	.. .. ..	4·00	4·25	☐	☐
		First Day Cover	.. ..		5·00		☐
		Presentation Pack	.. ..	6·00		☐	
		PHQ Cards (set of 5)	.. ..	4·00	6·50	☐	☐
		Set of 5 Gutter Pairs	.. ..	8·00		☐	

Nos. 1336/40 were issued to celebrate the 50th anniversary of the first R.A.F. Commands.

814 The Glastonbury Thorn

815 The Tanad Valley Plygain

816 The Hebrides Tribute

817 The Dewsbury Church Knell

818 The Hereford Boy Bishop

Christmas. Folk Customs

1986 One phosphor band (12p, 13p) or phosphorised paper (others)

1341	**814**	12p mult. (2 Dec.)	..	50	50	☐	☐
1342		13p mult. (18 Nov.)	..	30	30	☐	☐
1343	**815**	18p mult. (18 Nov.)	..	45	45	☐	☐
1344	**816**	22p mult. (18 Nov.)	..	65	65	☐	☐
1345	**817**	31p mult. (18 Nov.)	..	80	80	☐	☐
1346	**818**	34p mult. (18 Nov.)	..	90	90	☐	☐
	Set of 6 ..	.. ..	..	3·25	3·25	☐	☐
	First Day Covers (2)	..	..		5·25		☐
	Presentation Pack (Nos. 1342/6)		5·00			☐	
	PHQ Cards (set of 5) (Nos. 1342/6) ..	..	..	3·00	6·00	☐	☐
	Set of 6 Gutter Pairs	..	..	6·50		☐	

Collectors Pack 1986

1986 (18 Nov.) Comprises Nos. 1308/40, 1342/6
Collectors Pack .. .. .. 40·00 ☐

Post Office Yearbook

1986 Comprises Nos. 1308/40, 1342/6 in hardbound book with slip case.
Yearbook .. .. 70·00 ☐

819 North American Blanket Flower

820 Globe Thistle

821 Echeveria

822 Autumn Crocus

Flower Photographs by Alfred Lammer

1987 (20 Jan.) Phosphorised paper. Perf $14\frac{1}{2} \times 14$

1347	**819**	18p multicoloured	..	50	50	☐	☐
1348	**820**	22p multicoloured	..	65	65	☐	☐
1349	**821**	31p multicoloured	..	1·10	1·10	☐	☐
1350	**822**	34p multicoloured	..	1·10	1·10	☐	☐
	Set of 4	.. ..	..	3·00	3·00	☐	☐
	First Day Cover	..			4·25		☐
	Presentation Pack ..	..	..	4·50		☐	
	PHQ Cards (set of 4)	..	..	3·00	6·00	☐	☐
	Set of 4 Gutter Pairs	..	..	6·00		☐	

823 The Principia Mathematica

824 Motion of Bodies in Ellipses

825 Optick Treatise

826 The System of the World

300th Anniversary of The Principia Mathematica by Sir Isaac Newton

1987 (24 Mar.) Phosphorised paper.

1351	**823**	18p multicoloured	..	50	50	☐	☐
1352	**824**	22p multicoloured	..	65	65	☐	☐
1353	**825**	31p multicoloured	..	1·10	1·10	☐	☐
1354	**826**	34p multicoloured	..	1·10	1·10	☐	☐
	Set of 4	.. ..	..	3·00	3·00	☐	☐
	First Day Cover	..	..		4·25		☐
	Presentation Pack ..	..	..	4·50		☐	
	PHQ Cards (set of 4)	..	..	3·00	6·00	☐	☐
	Set of 4 Gutter Pairs	..	..	6·00		☐	

For full information on all future British issues, collectors should write to the British Post Office Philatelic Bureau, 20 Brandon Street, Edinburgh EH3 5TT

827 Willis Faber and Dumas Building, Ipswich

828 Pompidou Centre, Paris

829 Staatsgalerie, Stuttgart

830 European Investment Bank, Luxembourg

Europa. British Architects in Europe

1987 (12 MAY) *Phosphorised paper.*

1355	**827**	18p multicoloured	..	50	50	☐	☐
1356	**828**	22p multicoloured	..	65	65	☐	☐
1357	**829**	31p multicoloured	..	1·10	1·10	☐	☐
1358	**830**	34p multicoloured	..	1·10	1·10	☐	☐
		Set of 4	.. .. ..	3·00	3·00	☐	☐
		First Day Cover	.. ..		4·25	☐	
		Presentation Pack ..		4·50		☐	
		PHQ Cards (set of 4)	.. ..	3·00	6·00	☐	☐
		Set of 4 Gutter Pairs		6·00		☐	

831 Brigade Members with Ashford Litter, 1887

832 Bandaging Blitz Victim, 1940

833 Volunteer with fainting Girl, 1965

834 Transport of Transplant Organ by Air Wing, 1987

Centenary of St. John Ambulance Brigade

1987 (16 JUNE) *Phosphorised paper. Perf 14 × 14½*

1359	**831**	18p multicoloured	..	50	50	☐	☐
1360	**832**	22p multicoloured	..	65	65	☐	☐
1361	**833**	31p multicoloured	..	1·10	1·10	☐	☐
1362	**834**	34p multicoloured	..	1·10	1·10	☐	☐
		Set of 4	.. ..	3·00	3·00	☐	☐
		First Day Cover	.. ..		4·25	☐	
		Presentation Pack ..	.. ..	4·50		☐	
		PHQ Cards (set of 4)	.. ..	3·00	6·00	☐	☐
		Set of 4 Gutter Pairs	.. ..	6·00		☐	

835 Arms of the Lord Lyon King of Arms

836 Scottish Heraldic Banner of Prince Charles

837 Arms of Royal Scottish Academy of Painting, Sculpture and Architecture

838 Arms of Royal Society of Edinburgh

300th Anniversary of Revival of Order of the Thistle

1987 (21 JULY) *Phosphorised paper. Perf 14½*

1363	**835**	18p multicoloured	..	50	50	☐	☐
1364	**836**	22p multicoloured	..	65	65	☐	☐
1365	**837**	31p multicoloured	..	1·10	1·10	☐	☐
1366	**838**	34p multicoloured	..	1·10	1·10	☐	☐
		Set of 4	.. .. ..	3·00	3·00	☐	☐
		First Day Cover	.. ..		4·25	☐	
		Presentation Pack ..		4·50		☐	
		PHQ Cards (set of 4)	.. ..	3·00	6·00	☐	☐
		Set of 4 Gutter Pairs	..	6·00		☐	

839 Crystal Palace, 'Monarch of the Glen' (Landseer) and Grace Darling

840 Great Eastern, Beeton's Book of Household Management and Prince Albert

841 Albert Memorial, Ballot Box and Disraeli

842 Diamond Jubilee Emblem, Morse Key and Newspaper Placard for Relief of Mafeking

150th Anniversary of Queen Victoria's Accession

1987 (8 Sept.) *Phosphorised paper.*

1367	839	18p multicoloured	..	50	50	□	□
1368	840	22p multicoloured	..	65	65	□	□
1369	841	31p multicoloured	..	1·10	1·10	□	□
1370	842	34p multicoloured	..	1·10	1·10	□	□
		Set of 4	..	3·00	3·00	□	□
		First Day Cover ..	..		4·25	□	
		Presentation Pack ..	..	4·50		□	
		PHQ Cards (set of 4)	..	3·00	6·00	□	□
		Set of 4 Gutter Pairs ..	..	6·00		□	

843 Pot by Bernard Leach

844 Pot by Elizabeth Fritsch

845 Pot by Lucie Rie

846 Pot by Hans Coper

Studio Pottery

1987 (13 Oct.) *Phosphorised paper. Perf* $14\frac{1}{2} \times 14$

1371	843	18p multicoloured	..	50	50	□	□
1372	844	26p multicoloured	..	65	65	□	□
1373	845	31p multicoloured	..	1·10	1·10	□	□
1374	846	34p multicoloured	..	1·10	1·10	□	□
		Set of 4	..	3·00	3·00	□	□
		First Day Cover	..		4·25	□	
		Presentation Pack	..	4·50		□	
		PHQ Cards (set of 4)	..	3·00	6·00	□	□
		Set of 4 Gutter Pairs	..	6·00		□	

Nos. 1371/4 also mark the birth centenary of Bernard Leach, the potter.

847 Decorating the Christmas tree

848 Waiting for Father Christmas

849 Sleeping Child and Father Christmas in Sleigh

850 Child reading

851 Child playing Flute and Snowman

Christmas

1987 (17 Nov.) *One phosphor band* (13p) *or phosphorised paper* (*others*)

1375	847	13p multicoloured	..	30	30	□	□
1376	848	18p multicoloured	..	50	50	□	□
1377	849	26p multicoloured	..	75	75	□	□
1378	850	31p multicoloured	..	95	1·10	□	□
1379	851	34p multicoloured	..	1·10	1·25	□	□
		Set of 5	..	3·25	3·50	□	□
		First Day Cover ..	..		4·25	□	
		Presentation Pack ..	..	4·50		□	
		PHQ Cards (set of 5)	..	3·00	6·00	□	□
		Set of 5 Gutter Pairs	..	6·50		□	

Collectors Pack 1987

1987 (17 Nov.) *Comprises Nos.* 1347/79
    Collectors Pack .. .. .. 33·00 ☐

Post Office Yearbook

1987 *Comprises Nos.* 1347/79 *in hardbound book with slip case*
    Yearbook .. .. .. 45·00 ☐

852 Bull-rout (Jonathan Couch)   **853** Yellow Waterlily (Major Joshua Swatkin)

854 Whistling ("Bewick's") Swan (Edward Lear)   **855** *Morchella esculenta* (James Sowerby)

Bicentenary of Linnean Society. Archive Illustrations

1988 (19 JAN.) *Phosphorised paper*

1380	**852**	18p multicoloured	..	45	45	☐	☐
1381	**853**	26p multicoloured		70	70	☐	☐
1382	**854**	31p multicoloured	..	1·10	1·10	☐	☐
1383	**855**	34p multicoloured	..	1·10	1·10	☐	☐
		Set of 4		3·00	3·00	☐	☐
		First Day Cover			4·00		☐
		Presentation Pack		4·50		☐	
		PHQ Cards (set of 4)		3·00	6·00	☐	☐
		Set of 4 Gutter Pairs ..		6·00		☐	

856 Revd William Morgan (Bible translator, 1588)   **857** William Salesbury (New Testament translator, 1567)

858 Bishop Richard Davies (New Testament translator, 1567)   **859** Bishop Richard Parry (editor of Revised Welsh Bible, 1620)

400th Anniversary of Welsh Bible

1988 (1 MAR.) *Phosphorised paper. Perf* $14\frac{1}{2} \times 14$

1384	**856**	18p multicoloured	..	45	45	☐	☐
1385	**857**	26p multicoloured		70	70	☐	☐
1386	**858**	31p multicoloured		1·10	1·10	☐	☐
1387	**859**	34p multicoloured	..	1·10	1·10	☐	☐
		Set of 4	..	3·00	3·00	☐	☐
		First Day Cover			4·00		☐
		Presentation Pack		4·50		☐	
		PHQ Cards (set of 4)		3·00	6·00	☐	☐
		Set of 4 Gutter Pairs ..		6·00		☐	

860 Gymnastics (Centenary of British Amateur Gymnastics Association)   **861** Downhill Skiing (Ski Club of Great Britain)

862 Tennis (Centenary of Lawn Tennis Association)   **863** Football (Centenary of Football League)

Sports Organizations

1988 (22 Mar.) *Phosphorised paper. Perf* 14½

1388	860	18p multicoloured	..	45	45 □ □
1389	861	26p multicoloured		70	70 □ □
1390	862	31p multicoloured		1·10	1·10 □ □
1391	863	34p multicoloured		1·10	1·10 □ □
		Set of 4	..	3·00	3·00 □ □
		First Day Cover			5·50 □
		Presentation Pack		4·50	□
		PHQ Cards (set of 4)		2·25	5·00 □ □
		Set of 4 Gutter Pairs		6·00	□

864 *Mallard* and Mailbags on Pick-up Arms

865 Loading Transatlantic Mail on Liner *Queen Elizabeth*

866 Glasgow Tram No. 1173 and Pillar Box

867 Imperial Airways Handley Page "HP 42" and Airmail Van

Europa. Transport and Mail Services in 1930's

1988 (10 May) *Phosphorised paper*

1392	864	18p multicoloured	..	50	50 □ □
1393	865	26p multicoloured		80	80 □ □
1394	866	31p multicoloured		1·10	1·10 □ □
1395	867	34p multicoloured		1·25	1·25 □ □
		Set of 4	..	3·25	3·25 □ □
		First Day Cover			4·25 □
		Presentation Pack		4·50	□
		PHQ Cards (set of 4)		2·00	5·00 □ □
		Set of 4 Gutter Pairs		6·50	□

868 Early Settler and Sailing Clipper

869 Queen Elizabeth II with British and Australian Parliament Buildings

870 W. G. Grace (cricketer) and Tennis Racquet

871 Shakespeare, John Lennon (entertainer) and Sydney Landmarks

Nos. 1396/7 and 1398/9 were each printed together, *se-tenant*, in horizontal pairs throughout the sheets, each pair showing a background design of the Australian flag.

Bicentenary of Australian Settlement

1988 (21 June) *Phosphorised paper. Perf* 14½

1396	868	18p multicoloured	..	60	60 □ □
		a. Horiz pair.			
		Nos. 1396/7 ..	..	1·25	1·25 □ □
1397	869	18p multicoloured		60	60 □ □
1398	870	34p multicoloured		1·10	1·10 □ □
		a. Horiz pair.			
		Nos. 1398/9 ..	..	2·40	2·40 □ □
1399	871	34p multicoloured		1·10	1·10 □ □
		Set of 4		3·25	3·25 □ □
		First Day Cover			4·25 □
		Presentation Pack		4·50	□
		Souvenir Book		6·00	□
		PHQ Cards (set of 4) ..		2·00	5·00 □ □
		Set of 4 Gutter Pairs ..		6·50	□

Stamps in similar designs were also issued by Australia.

872 Spanish Galeasse off The Lizard

873 English Fleet leaving Plymouth

874 Engagement off Isle of Wight

875 Attack of English Fire-ships, Calais

876 Armada in Storm,
North Sea

Nos. 1400/4 were printed together, *se-tenant*, in horizontal strips of 5
throughout the sheet, forming a composite design.

400th Anniversary of Spanish Armada

1988 (19 JULY) *Phosphorised paper*

1400	872	18p multicoloured	..	65	65	□	□
		a. *Horiz strip of* 5.					
		Nos. 1400/4 ..		2·75	2·75	□	□
1401	873	18p multicoloured	..	65	65	□	□
1402	874	18p multicoloured	..	65	65	□	□
1403	875	18p multicoloured	..	65	65	□	□
1404	876	18p multicoloured	..	65	65	□	□
		Set of 5	..	2·75	2·75	□	□
		First Day Cover			3·75	□	
		Presentation Pack		4·00		□	
		PHQ Cards (set of 5)	..	2·50	5·50	□	□
		Gutter strip of 10		5·50		□	

877 "The Owl and the
Pussy-cat"

878 "Edward Lear as a Bird"
(self-portrait)

879 "Cat" (from alphabet
book)

880 "There was a Young Lady
whose Bonnet ..."
(limerick)

Death Centenary of Edward Lear (artist and author)

1988 (6–27 SEPT.) *Phosphorised paper*

1405	877	19p black, pale cream and carmine	50	50	□	□
1406	878	27p black, pale cream and yellow	65	80	□	□
1407	879	32p black, pale cream and emerald	1·10	1·10	□	□
1408	880	35p black, pale cream and blue	1·10	1·25	□	□
		Set of 4	3·00	3·25	□	□
		First Day Cover		4·00	□	
		Presentation Pack	4·50		□	
		PHQ Cards (set of 4)	2·00	5·00	□	□
		Set of 4 *Gutter Pairs* ..	6·00		□	
MS1409		122 × 90 mm. Nos. 1405/8	8·00	8·50	□	□
		First Day Cover (27 Sept.) ..		8·50	□	

No. **MS**1409 was sold at £1·35, the premium being used for
the "Stamp World London 90" International Stamp Exhibition.

881 Carrickfergus Castle

882 Caernarvon Castle

883 Edinburgh Castle

884 Windsor Castle

1988 (18 OCT.) *Ordinary paper*

1410	881	£1 deep green	..	..	2·25	50	□ □
1411	882	£1·50 maroon	..	..	3·25	1·00	□ □
1412	883	£2 indigo	..	..	4·50	1·50	□ □
1413	884	£5 deep brown	..	..	11·00	3·00	□ □
		Set of 4		..	19·00	5·50	□ □
		First Day Cover		..		45·00	□
		Presentation Pack			22·00		□
		Set of 4 *Gutter Pairs* ..		..	38·00		□

For similar designs, but with silhouette Queen's head see
Nos. 1611/14.

885 Journey to Bethlehem

886 Shepherds and Star

887 Three Wise Men

888 Nativity

889 The Annunciation

890 Atlantic Puffin

891 Avocet

892 Oystercatcher

893 Northern Gannet

Christmas

1988 (15 Nov.) *One phosphor band* (14p) *or phosphorised paper* (*others*)

1414	**885**	14p multicoloured	..	35	35	☐	☐
1415	**886**	19p multicoloured	..	40	45	☐	☐
1416	**887**	27p multicoloured	..	70	70	☐	☐
1417	**888**	32p multicoloured	..	90	1·00	☐	☐
1418	**889**	35p multicoloured	..	1·00	1·10	☐	☐
		Set of 5		3·00	3·25	☐	☐
		First Day Cover			4·25		☐
		Presentation Pack		4·25		☐	
		PHQ Cards (*set of 5*)		2·50	5·25	☐	☐
		Set of 5 Gutter Pairs		6·00		☐	

Collectors Pack 1988

1988 (15 Nov.) *Comprises Nos.* 1380/1408, 1414/18

Collectors Pack	..	..	30·00	☐

Post Office Yearbook

1988 *Comprises Nos.* 1380/1404. **MS**1409, 1414/18 *in hardbound book with slip case*

Yearbook	.. ..	..	40·00	☐

Centenary of Royal Society for the Protection of Birds

1989 (17 Jan.) *Phosphorised paper*

1419	**890**	19p multicoloured	..	45	45	☐	☐
1420	**891**	27p multicoloured	..	1·10	1·10	☐	☐
1421	**892**	32p multicoloured	..	1·10	1·10	☐	☐
1422	**893**	35p multicoloured	..	1·25	1·25	☐	☐
		Set of 4		3·50	3·50	☐	☐
		First Day Cover			4·50		☐
		Presentation Pack		4·50		☐	
		PHQ Cards (*set of 4*) ..		2·50	5·00	☐	☐
		Set of 4 Gutter Pairs		7·00		☐	

894 Rose

895 Cupid

896 Yachts

897 Fruit

898 Teddy Bear

Nos. 1423/7 were printed together, *se-tenant*, in horizontal strips of five, two such strips forming the booklet pane.

Greetings Booklet Stamps

1989 (31 Jan.) *Phosphorised paper*

1423	**894**	19p multicoloured	..	2·75	2·25	☐	☐
		a. *Booklet pane.*					
		Nos. 1423/7 × 2		24·00		☐	
1424	**895**	19p multicoloured	..	2·75	2·25	☐	☐
1425	**896**	19p multicoloured	..	2·75	2·25	☐	☐
1426	**897**	19p multicoloured	..	2·75	2·25	☐	☐
1427	**898**	19p multicoloured	..	2·75	2·25	☐	☐
		Set of 5	..	12·00	10·00	☐	☐
		First Day Cover			10·00		☐

899 Fruit and Vegetables

900 Meat Products

901 Dairy Produce

902 Cereal Products

Food and Farming Year

1989 (7 Mar.) *Phosphorised paper. Perf* $14 \times 14\frac{1}{2}$

1428	**899**	19p multicoloured	..	50	50	☐	☐
1429	**900**	27p multicoloured	..	80	80	☐	☐
1430	**901**	32p multicoloured	..	1·10	1·10	☐	☐
1431	**902**	35p multicoloured	..	1·25	1·25	☐	☐
		Set of 4	..	3·25	3·25	☐	☐
		First Day Cover	..		4·25		☐
		Presentation Pack		4·50		☐	
		PHQ Cards (set of 4) ..	..	2·00	5·00	☐	☐
		Set of 4 Gutter Pairs ..	..	6·50		☐	

903 Mortar Board (150th Anniv of Public Education in England)

904 Cross on Ballot Paper (3rd Direct Elections to European Parliament)

905 Posthorn (26th Postal, Telegraph and Telephone International Congress Brighton)

906 Globe (Inter-Parliamentary Union Centenary Conference, London)

Nos. 1432/3 and 1434/5 were each printed together, *se-tenant*, in horizontal pairs throughout the sheets.

Anniversaries

1989 (11 Apr.) *Phosphorised paper. Perf* $14 \times 14\frac{1}{2}$

1432	**903**	19p multicoloured	..	70	70	☐	☐
		a. *Horiz pair.*					
		Nos. 1432/3	..	2·25	2·25	☐	☐
1433	**904**	19p multicoloured	..	70	70	☐	☐
1434	**905**	35p multicoloured	..	1·25	1·25	☐	☐
		a. *Horiz pair.*					
		Nos. 1434/5	..	3·00	3·00	☐	☐
1435	**906**	35p multicoloured	..	1·25	1·25	☐	☐
		Set of 4	..	4·75	3·50	☐	☐
		First Day Cover	..		4·50		☐
		Presentation Pack	..	5·25		☐	
		PHQ Cards (set of 4) ..	..	2·00	5·00	☐	☐
		Set of 2 Gutter Pairs ..	..	5·00		. ☐	

907 Toy Train and Airplane

908 Building Bricks

909 Dice and Board Games

910 Toy Robot, Boat and Doll's House

Europa. Games and Toys

1989 (16 MAY) *Phosphorised paper*

1436	**907**	19p multicoloured	..	50	50	☐	☐
1437	**908**	27p multicoloured	..	90	90	☐	☐
1438	**909**	32p multicoloured	..	1·25	1·25	☐	☐
1439	**910**	35p multicoloured	..	1·40	1·40	☐	☐
		Set of 4		3·50	3·50	☐	☐
		First Day Cover			4·25		☐
		Presentation Pack		4·50		☐	
		PHQ Cards (set of 4)		2·00	5·00	☐	☐
		Set of 4 Gutter Pairs		7·00		☐	

911 Ironbridge, Shropshire

912 Tin Mine, St. Agnes Head, Cornwall

913 Cotton Mills, New Lanark, Strathclyde

914 Pontcysyllte Aqueduct, Clwyd

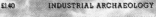

915

Industrial Archaeology

1989 (4–25 JULY) *Phosphorised paper*

1440	**911**	19p multicoloured	..	50	50	☐	☐
1441	**912**	27p multicoloured	..	80	80	☐	☐
1442	**913**	32p multicoloured	..	1·00	1·00	☐	☐
1443	**914**	35p multicoloured	..	1·10	1·10	☐	☐
		Set of 4		3·00	3·00	☐	☐
		First Day Cover			4·25		☐
		Presentation Pack		4·50		☐	
		PHQ Cards (set of 4)		2·00	5·00	☐	☐
		Set of 4 Gutter Pairs		6·50		☐	
MS1444		122 × 90 mm. **915** As Nos.					
		1440/3 but designs horizontal		6·00	6·00	☐	☐
		First Day Cover (25 July) ..			6·00		☐

No.**MS**1444 was sold at £1.40, the premium being used for the "Stamp World London 90" International Stamp Exhibition.

916

917

Booklet Stamps

1989 (22 AUG.)–**92**

(a) Printed in photogravure by Harrison and Sons. Perf 15 × 14

1445	**916**	(2nd) bright blue (1 centre band)	30	35	☐	☐
1446		(2nd) bright blue (1 side band) (20.3.90)	2·25	2·25	☐	☐
1447	**917**	(1st) black (phosphorised paper)	1·00	50	☐	☐
1448		(1st) brownish black (2 bands) (20.3.90) ..	2·25	2·25	☐	☐

(b) Printed in lithography by Walsall. Perf 14

1449	**916**	(2nd) bright blue (1 centre band)	30	35	☐	☐
1450	**917**	(1st) black (2 bands) ..	1·75	1·75	☐	☐

(c) Printed in lithography by Questa. Perf 15 × 14

1451	**916**	(2nd) bright blue (1 centre band) (19.9.89)	30	35	☐	☐
1451*a*		(2nd) bright blue (1 side band) (25.2.92) ..	1·00	1·00	☐	☐
1452	**917**	(1st) black (phosphorised paper) (19.9.89)	1·10	1·10	☐	☐
		First Day Cover (Nos. 1445, 1447)		3·50		☐

For similar stamps showing changed colours see Nos. 1511/16 and for those with elliptical perforations Nos. 1664/6.

No. 1451*a* exists with the phosphor band at the left or right of the stamp.

918 Snowflake (× 10)

919 *Calliphora erythrocephala* (fly) (× 5)

920 Blood Cells (× 500)

921 Microchip (× 600)

150th Anniversary of Royal Microscopical Society

1989 (5 Sept.) *Phosphorised paper. Perf* 14½ × 14

1453	**918**	19p multicoloured	..	50	50	☐ ☐
1454	**919**	27p multicoloured	..	85	85	☐ ☐
1455	**920**	32p multicoloured	..	1·25	1·25	☐ ☐
1456	**921**	35p multicoloured	..	1·40	1·40	☐ ☐
		Set of 4	..	3·50	3·50	☐ ☐
		First Day Cover			5·00	☐
		Presentation Pack ..	..	4·00		☐
		PHQ Cards (set of 4) ..	..	2·00	5·00	☐ ☐
		Set of 4 Gutter Pairs ..	..	7·00		☐

922 Royal Mail Coach

923 Escort of Blues and Royals

924 Lord Mayor's Coach

925 Coach Team passing St Paul's

926 Blues and Royals Drum Horse

Nos. 1457/61 were printed together, *se-tenant*, in horizontal strips of 5 throughout the sheet, forming a composite design.

Lord Mayor's Show, London

1989 (17 Oct.) *Phosphorised paper*

1457	**922**	20p multicoloured	..	60	60	☐ ☐
		a. Horiz strip of 5. Nos. 1457/61	..	3·25	3·25	☐ ☐
1458	**923**	20p multicoloured		60	60	☐ ☐
1459	**924**	20p multicoloured		60	60	☐ ☐
1460	**925**	20p multicoloured		60	60	☐ ☐
1461	**926**	20p multicoloured		60	60	☐ ☐
		Set of 5		3·25	2·75	☐ ☐
		First Day Cover			3·75	☐
		Presentation Pack ..	..	4·50		☐
		PHQ Cards (set of 5) ..	..	2·50	5·00	☐ ☐
		Gutter Strip of 10 ..	..	6·50		☐

Nos. 1457/61 commemorate the 800th anniversary of the installation of the first Lord Mayor of London.

927 14th-century Peasants from Stained-glass Window

928 Arches and Roundels, West Front

929 Octagon Tower

930 Arcade from West Transept

931 Triple Arch from West Front

Christmas. 800th Anniversary of Ely Cathedral

1989 (14 Nov.) *One phosphor band (Nos. 1462/3) or phosphorised paper (others)*

1462	**927**	15p gold, silver and blue	35	35	□	□
1463	**928**	15p + 1p gold, silver and blue	50	40	□	□
1464	**929**	20p + 1p gold, silver and rosine	60	50	□	□
1465	**930**	34p + 1p gold, silver and emerald	1·25	1·40	□	□
1466	**931**	37p + 1p gold, silver and yellow-olive	1·25	1·40	□	□
		Set of 5	3·50	3·50	□	□
		First Day Cover		4·00	□	
		Presentation Pack	4·50		□	
		PHQ Cards (set of 5)	2·50	5·00	□	□
		Set of 5 Gutter Pairs	7·00		□	

Collectors Pack 1989

1989 (14 Nov.) *Comprises Nos. 1419/22, 1428/43 and 1453/66*

Collectors Pack	28·00	□

Post Office Yearbook

1989 (14 Nov) *Comprises Nos. 1419/22, 1428/44 and 1453/66 in hardback book with slip case.*

Yearbook	45·00	□

932 Queen Victoria and Queen Elizabeth II

150th Anniversary of the Penny Black

1990 (10 Jan.–12 June)

(a) Printed in photogravure by Harrison and Sons. Perf 15 × 14

1467	**932**	15p bright blue (1 centre band)	50	50	□	□
1468		15p bright blue (1 side band) (30 Jan) ..	1·50	1·50	□	□
1469		20p brownish black and cream (phosphorised paper) ..	75	75	□	□
1470		20p brnish blk & cream (2 bands) (30 Jan) ..	1·50	1·50	□	□
1471		29p deep mauve (phosphorised paper) ..	1·00	1·00	□	□
1472		29p deep mauve (2 bands) (20 Mar) ..	4·50	4·50	□	□
1473		34p deep bluish grey (phosphorised paper)	1·25	1·25	□	□
1474		37p rosine (phosphorised paper)	1·40	1·40	□	□
		Set of 5 (Nos. 1467, 1469, 1471, 1473/4)	4·50	4·50	□	□
		First Day Cover (Nos. 1467, 1469, 1471, 1473/4) ..		6·00	□	
		Presentation Pack (Nos. 1467, 1469, 1471, 1473/4) ..	5·75		□	

(b) Litho Walsall. Perf 14 (30 Jan)

1475	**932**	15p bright blue (1 centre band)	60	60	□	□
1476		20p brnish blk & cream (phosphorised paper)	80	80	□	□

(c) Litho Questa. Perf 15 × 14 (17 Apr)

1477	**932**	15p bright blue (1 centre band)	1·00	1·00	□	□
1478		20p brnish black (phosphorised paper) ..	1·25	1·25	□	□

No. 1468 exists with the phosphor band at the left or right of the stamp.

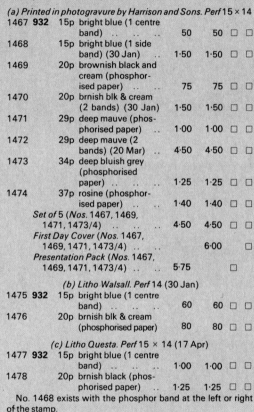

933 Kitten

934 Rabbit

935 Duckling

936 Puppy

150th Anniversary of Royal Society for Prevention of Cruelty to Animals

1990 (23 Jan.) *Phosphorised paper. Perf* 14 × 14½.

1479	**933**	20p multicoloured	..	50	50	☐	☐
1480	**934**	29p multicoloured	..	80	80	☐	☐
1481	**935**	34p multicoloured	..	1·10	1·10	☐	☐
1482	**936**	37p multicoloured	..	1·10	1·10	☐	☐
		Set of 4		3·25	3·25	☐	☐
		First Day Cover			5·25		☐
		Presentation Pack		5·00		☐	
		PHQ Cards (set of 4) ..		2·50	5·50	☐	☐
		Set of 4 Gutter Pairs		6·50		☐	

937 Teddy Bear

938 Dennis the Menace

939 Punch

940 Cheshire Cat

941 The Man in the Moon

942 The Laughing Policeman

943 Clown

944 Mona Lisa

945 Queen of Hearts

946 Stan Laurel (comedian)

T **937/46** were printed together, *se-tenant*, in booklet panes of 10.

Greetings Booklet Stamps. "Smiles"

1990 (6 Feb.) *Two phosphor bands*

1483	**937**	20p multicoloured	..	1·25	1·25	☐	☐
		a. Booklet pane.					
		Nos. 1483/92	..	11·00		☐	
1484	**938**	20p multicoloured	..	1·25	1·25	☐	☐
1485	**939**	20p multicoloured	..	1·25	1·25	☐	☐
1486	**940**	20p multicoloured	..	1·25	1·25	☐	☐
1487	**941**	20p multicoloured	..	1·25	1·25	☐	☐
1488	**942**	20p multicoloured	..	1·25	1·25	☐	☐
1489	**943**	20p multicoloured	..	1·25	1·25	☐	☐
1490	**944**	20p multicoloured	..	1·25	1·25	☐	☐
1491	**945**	20p multicoloured	..	1·25	1·25	☐	☐
1492	**946**	20p gold and grey-black		1·25	1·25	☐	☐
		Set of 10		11·00	11·00	☐	☐
		First Day Cover			12·00		☐

For those designs with the face value expressed as "1st" see Nos. 1550/9.

947 Alexandra Palace ("Stamp World London 90" Exhibition)

948 Glasgow School of Art

949 British Philatelic Bureau, Edinburgh

950 Templeton Carpet Factory, Glasgow

Europa (Nos. 1493 and 1495) and "Glasgow 1990 European City of Culture" (Nos. 1494 and 1496)

1990 (6 MAR.) *Phosphorised paper*

1493	**947**	20p multicoloured	..	50	50	☐	☐
1494	**948**	20p multicoloured	..	50	50	☐	☐
1495	**949**	29p multicoloured	..	1·10	1·10	☐	☐
1496	**950**	37p multicoloured	..	1·25	1·25	☐	☐
		Set of 4	..	3·00	3·00	☐	☐
		First Day Cover	..		4·25	☐	
		Presentation Pack	..	4·00		☐	
		PHQ Cards (set of 4)	..	2·50	5·25	☐	☐
		Set of 4 Gutter Pairs	..	6·00		☐	

951 Export Achievement Award

952 Technological Achievement Award

Nos. 1497/8 and 1499/500 were each printed together, *se-tenant*, in horizontal pairs throughout the sheets.

25th Anniversary of Queen's Awards for Export and Technology

1990 (10 APR.) *Phosphorised paper. Perf* 14 × 14½.

1497	**951**	20p multicoloured	..	55	55	☐	☐
		a. Horiz pair.					
		Nos. 1497/8 ..	..	1·10	1·10	☐	☐
1498	**952**	20p multicoloured	..	55	55	☐	☐
1499	**951**	37p multicoloured	..	1·10	1·10	☐	☐
		a. Horiz pair.					
		Nos. 1499/500 ..	..	2·25	2·25	☐	☐
1500	**952**	37p multicoloured	..	1·10	1·10	☐	☐
		Set of 4 ..	..	3·00	3·00	☐	☐
		First Day Cover	..		4·50	☐	
		Presentation Pack	..	4·00		☐	
		PHQ Cards (set of 4)	..	2·50	5·25	☐	☐
		Set of 2 Gutter Pairs	..	6·00		☐	

953

"Stamp World 90" International Stamp Exhibition, London

1990 (3 MAY.) *Sheet* 122 × 90 *mm. Phosphorised paper*

MS1501	**953**	20p. brownish black						
		and cream	..	..	..	3·50	4·00	☐ ☐
		First Day Cover	..	..			5·50	☐
		Souvenir Book (Nos. 1467,						
		1469, 1471, 1473/4 *and*						
		MS1501)	..	..	..	12·00		☐

No. **MS**1501 was sold at £1, the premium being used for the exhibition.

954 Cycad and Sir Joseph Banks Building

955 Stone Pine and Princess of Wales Conservatory

956 Willow Tree and Palm House

957 Cedar Tree and Pagoda

150th Anniversary of Kew Gardens

1990 (5 JUNE) *Phosphorised paper*

1502	**954**	20p multicoloured	..	50	50	☐	☐
1503	**955**	29p multicoloured	..	80	80	☐	☐

1504	**956**	34p multicoloured	..	1·10	1·25	☐	☐
1505	**957**	37p multicoloured	..	1·25	1·40	☐	☐
		Set of 4	.. .. ..	3·25	3·50	☐	☐
		First Day Cover			4·50		☐
		Presentation Pack	.. ..	4·00		☐	
		PHQ Cards (set of 4)	..	2·50	5·00	☐	☐
		Set of 4 Gutter Pairs		6·50		☐	

958 Thomas Hardy and Clyffe Clump, Dorset

150th Birth Anniversary of Thomas Hardy (author)

1990 (10 JULY) *Phosphorised paper*

1506	**958**	20p multicoloured	..	60	70	☐	☐
		First Day Cover			2·00		☐
		Presentation Pack	.. ..	1·75		☐	
		PHQ Card	.. ..	75	2·00	☐	
		Gutter Pair	.. .. ..	1·25		☐	

959 Queen Elizabeth the Queen Mother

960 Queen Elizabeth

961 Elizabeth, Duchess of York

962 Lady Elizabeth Bowes-Lyon

90th Birthday of Queen Elizabeth the Queen Mother

1990 (2 AUG.) *Phosphorised paper*

1507	**959**	20p multicoloured	50	50	☐	☐
1508	**960**	29p silver, indigo and grey-blue	80	80	☐	☐

1509	**961**	34p multicoloured	..	1·10	1·25	☐	☐
1510	**962**	37p silver, sepia and stone	..	1·25	1·40	☐	☐
		Set of 4	.. ..	3·25	3·50	☐	☐
		First Day Cover			4·75		☐
		Presentation Pack	..	4·50		☐	
		PHQ Cards (set of 4)		2·50	5·50	☐	☐
		Set of 4 Gutter Pairs ..	..	6·50		☐	

Booklet Stamps

1990 (7 AUG.)-**92** *As Types* **916/17**, *but colours changed*

(a) Photo Harrison, Perf 15 × 14

1511	**916**	(2nd) dp blue (1 centre band)	.. ..	50	50	☐	☐
1512	**917**	(1st) brt orge-red (phosphorised paper)	..	40	40	☐	☐

(a) Litho Questa. Perf 15 × 14

1513	**916**	(2nd) dp blue (1 centre band)	.. ..	60	60	☐	☐
1514	**917**	(1st) brt orge-red (phosphorised paper)	..	40	40	☐	☐
1514*a*		(1st) brt orange-red (2 bands) (25.2.92)	..	1·25	1·25	☐	☐

(c) Litho Walsall. Perf 14

1515	**916**	(2nd) dp blue (1 centre band)	.. ..	50	50	☐	☐
1516	**917**	(1st) brt orge-red (phosphorised paper)	..	40	40	☐	☐
		c. Perf 13	.. ..	1·50	1·50		☐
		First Day Cover (Nos. 1515/16)		3·00		☐

For similar stamps with elliptical perforations see Nos. 1664/6.

963 Victoria Cross

964 George Cross

965 Distinguished Service Cross and Distinguished Service Medal

966 Military Cross and Military Medal

967 Distinguished Flying Cross and Distinguished Flying Medal

Gallantry Awards

1990 (11 Sept.) *Phosphorised paper*

1517	**963**	20p multicoloured	..	65	65	☐	☐
1518	**964**	20p multicoloured	..	65	65	☐	☐
1519	**965**	20p multicoloured	..	65	65	☐	☐
1520	**966**	20p multicoloured	..	65	65	☐	☐
1521	**967**	20p multicoloured	..	65	65	☐	☐
		Set of 5	..	3·00	3·00	☐	☐
		First Day Cover	..		3·75	☐	
		Presentation Pack ..	..	4·00		☐	
		PHQ Cards (set of 5)	..	3·00	5·50	☐	☐
		Set of 5 Gutter Pairs	..	6·00		☐	

968 Armagh Observatory, Jodrell Bank Radio Telescope and La Palma Telescope

969 Newton's Moon and Tides Diagram with Early Telescopes

970 Greenwich Old Observatory and Early Astronomical Equipment

971 Stonehenge, Gyroscope and Navigating by Stars

Astronomy

1990 (16 Oct.) *Phosphorised paper. Perf* $14 \times 14\frac{1}{2}$

1522	**968**	22p multicoloured	..	50	40	☐	☐
1523	**969**	26p multicoloured	..	80	90	☐	☐
1524	**970**	31p multicoloured	..	1·00	1·00	☐	☐
1525	**971**	37p multicoloured	..	1·10	1·10	☐	☐
		Set of 4	..	3·00	3·00	☐	☐
		First Day Cover	..		3·75	☐	
		Presentation Pack ..	..	4·00		☐	
		PHQ Cards (set of 4)	..	2·50	5·50	☐	☐
		Set of 4 Gutter Pairs	..	6·00		☐	

Nos. 1522/5 commemorate the centenary of the British Astronomical Association and the bicentenary of the Armagh Observatory.

972 Building a Snowman

973 Fetching the Christmas Tree

974 Carol Singing

975 Tobogganing

976 Ice-skating

Christmas

1990 (13 Nov.) *One phosphor band* (17p) *or phosphorised paper (others)*

1526	**972**	17p multicoloured	..	45	35	☐	☐
1527	**973**	22p multicoloured	..	55	65	☐	☐
1528	**974**	26p multicoloured	..	80	80	☐	☐
1529	**975**	31p multicoloured	..	1·00	1·00	☐	☐
1530	**976**	37p multicoloured	..	1·10	1·10	☐	☐
		Set of 5	..	3·50	3·50	☐	☐
		First Day Cover	..		4·25	☐	
		Presentation Pack ..	..	4·25		☐	
		PHQ Cards (set of 5)	..	3·25	6·00	☐	☐
		Set of 5 Gutter Pairs	..	7·00		☐	

Collectors Pack 1990

1990 (13 Nov.) *Comprises Nos.* 1479/82, 1493/1510 *and* 1517/30

	Collectors Pack	..	..	28·00	☐

Post Office Yearbook

1990 *Comprises Nos.* 1479/82, 1493/500, 1502/10 *and* 1517/30 *in hardback book with slip case.*

	Yearbook	..	..	..	40·00	☐

KING CHARLES SPANIEL
GEORGE STUBBS

977 "King Charles Spaniel"

A POINTER
GEORGE STUBBS

978 "A Pointer"

TWO HOUNDS IN A LANDSCAPE
GEORGE STUBBS

979 "Two Hounds in a Landscape"

A ROUGH DOG
GEORGE STUBBS

980 "A Rough Dog"

FINO AND TINY
GEORGE STUBBS

981 "Fino and Tiny"

Dogs. Paintings by George Stubbs

1991 (8 JAN.) *Phosphorised paper. Perf* 14 × 14½

1531	**977**	22p multicoloured	..	75	75	☐	☐
1532	**978**	26p multicoloured	..	80	80	☐	☐
1533	**979**	31p multicoloured	..	85	85	☐	☐
1534	**980**	33p multicoloured	..	95	95	☐	☐
1535	**981**	37p multicoloured	..	1·10	1·10	☐	☐
	Set of 5	.. .. ..	..	4·00	4·00	☐	☐
	First Day Cover	.. ..	..		5·00		☐
	Presentation Pack	.. ..	..	5·00		☐	
	PHQ Cards (set of 5)	.. ..	..	3·25	6·00	☐	☐
	Set of 5 *Gutter Pairs*	.. ..		8·00		☐	

983 Shooting Star and Rainbow

982 Thrush's Nest

984 Magpies and Charm Bracelet

985 Black Cat

986 Common Kingfisher with Key

987 Mallard and Frog

988 Four-leaf Clover in Boot and Match Box

989 Pot of Gold at End of Rainbow

990 Heart-shaped Butterflies

991 Wishing Well and Sixpence

T **982/91** were printed together, *se-tenant*, in booklet panes of 10, the backgrounds of the stamps forming a composite design.

Greetings Booklet Stamps. "Good Luck"

1991 (5 FEB.) *Two phosphor bands.*

1536	**982**	(1st) multicoloured	..	75	90	☐	☐
		a. Booklet pane. Nos.					
		1536/45 *plus* 12 *half*					
		stamp-size labels	..	7·00		☐	
1537	**983**	(1st) multicoloured	..	75	90	☐	☐
1538	**984**	(1st) multicoloured	..	75	90	☐	☐
1539	**985**	(1st) multicoloured	..	75	90	☐	☐
1540	**986**	(1st) multicoloured	..	75	90	☐	☐
1541	**987**	(1st) multicoloured	..	75	90	☐	☐
1542	**988**	(1st) multicoloured	..	75	90	☐	☐
1543	**989**	(1st) multicoloured	..	75	90	☐	☐
1544	**990**	(1st) multicoloured	..	75	90	☐	☐
1545	**991**	(1st) multicoloured	..	75	90	☐	☐
		Set of 10	.. .. ..	7·00	8·00	☐	
		First Day Cover	.. ..		8·50		☐

992 Michael Faraday (inventor of electric motor) (Birth Bicentenary)

993 Charles Babbage (computer science pioneer) (Birth Bicentenary)

994 Radar Sweep of East Anglia (50th Anniv of Discovery by Sir Robert Watson-Watt)

995 Gloster E28/39 Aircraft over East Anglia (50th Anniv of First Flight of Sir Frank Whittle's Jet Engine)

Scientific Achievements

1991 (5 MAR.) *Phosphorised paper*

1546	**992**	22p multicoloured	..	65	65	☐	☐
1547	**993**	22p multicoloured	..	65	65	☐	☐
1548	**994**	31p multicoloured	..	95	95	☐	☐
1549	**995**	37p multicoloured	..	1·10	1·10	☐	☐
		Set of 4	.. ..	3·00	3·00	☐	☐
		First Day Cover	.. .. ..		4·00	☐	
		Presentation Pack	.. ..	3·75		☐	
		PHQ Cards (*set of* 4)	.. ..	3·00	5·50	☐	☐
		Set of 4 *Gutter Pairs*	.. ..	6·00		☐	

996 Teddy Bear

Nos. 1550/9 were printed together, *se-tenant*, in booklet panes of 10.

1991 (26 MAR.) *As Nos.* 1483/92, *but inscribed* "1st" *as* T **996**. *Two phosphor bands.*

1550	**996**	(1st) multicoloured	..	40	45	☐	☐
		a. *Booklet pane. Nos.* 1550/9 *plus* 12 *half stamp-size labels*	..	3·50		☐	
1551	**938**	(1st) multicoloured	..	40	45	☐	☐
1552	**939**	(1st) multicoloured	..	40	45	☐	☐
1553	**940**	(1st) multicoloured	· ..	40	45	☐	☐
1554	**941**	(1st) multicoloured	..	40	45	☐	☐
1555	**942**	(1st) multicoloured	..	40	45	☐	☐
1556	**943**	(1st) multicoloured	..	40	45	☐	☐
1557	**944**	(1st) multicoloured	· ..	40	45	☐	☐
1558	**945**	(1st) multicoloured	..	40	45	☐	☐
1559	**946**	(1st) multicoloured	..	40	45	☐	☐
		Set of 10	.. .. ..	3·50	4·00	☐	☐
		First Day Cover	.. .. ..		7·50	☐	

997 Man looking at Space

998

999 Space looking at Man

1000

Nos. 1560/1 and 1562/3 were each printed together, *se-tenant*, in horizontal pairs throughout the sheets, each pair forming a composite design.

Europa. Europe in Space

1991 (23 APR.) *Phosphorised paper.*

1560	**997**	22p multicoloured	..	55	55	☐	☐
		a. *Horiz pair. Nos.* 1560/1		1·10	1·10	☐	☐
1561	**998**	22p multicoloured	..	55	55	☐	☐
1562	**999**	37p multicoloured	..	1·10	1·10	☐	☐
		a. *Horiz pair. Nos.* 1562/3		2·25	2·25	☐	☐
1563	**1000**	37p multicoloured	..	1·10	1·10	☐	☐
		Set of 4	.. ..	3·00	3·00	☐	☐
		First Day Cover	.. ..		4·00	☐	
		Presentation Pack	.. ..	4·00		☐	
		PHQ Cards (*set of* 4)	.. ..	3·00	5·50	☐	☐
		Set of 2 *Gutter Pairs*	.. ..	6·00		☐	

1001 Fencing

1002 Hurdling

1003 Diving

1004 Rugby

World Student Games, Sheffield (Nos. 1564/6) and World Cup Rugby Championship, London (No. 1567)

1991 (11 JUNE) *Phosphorised paper. Perf* $14\frac{1}{2} \times 14$

1564	**1001**	22p multicoloured	..	50	50	☐	☐
1565	**1002**	26p multicoloured	..	80	80	☐	☐
1566	**1003**	31p multicoloured	..	95	95	☐	☐
1567	**1004**	37p multicoloured	..	1·10	1·10	☐	☐
	Set of 4		.. .. ..	3·00	3·00	☐	☐
	First Day Cover	.. .. ..		4·00		☐	
	Presentation Pack	.. ..		4·00		☐	
	PHQ Cards (set of 4)	.. .._		3·00	5·50	☐	☐
	Set of 4 Gutter Pairs	.. ..		6·00		☐	

1005 "Silver Jubilee"

1006 "Mme Alfred Carrière"

1007 *Rosa moyesii*

1008 "Harvest Fayre"

1009 "Mutabilis"

9th World Congress of Roses, Belfast

1991 (16 JULY) *Phosphorised paper. Perf* $14\frac{1}{2} \times 14$

1568	**1005**	22p multicoloured	..	75	50	☐	☐
1569	**1006**	26p multicoloured	..	80	80	☐	☐
1570	**1007**	31p multicoloured	..	85	85	☐	☐
1571	**1008**	33p multicoloured	..	95	95	☐	☐
1572	**1009**	37p multicoloured	..	1·10	1·25	☐	☐
	Set of 5	.. .. ..		4·00	4·00	☐	☐
	First Day Cover	.. ..			5·50		☐
	Presentation Pack	.. ..		4·50		☐	
	PHQ Cards (set of 5)	.. ..		3·25	6·50	☐	☐
	Set of 5 Gutter Pairs	.. ..		8·00		☐	

1010 Iguanodon

1011 Stegosaurus

1012 Tyrannosaurus

1013 Protoceratops

1014 Triceratops

150th Anniversary of Dinosaurs' Identification by Owen

1991 (20 Aug.) *Phosphorised paper. Perf* $14\frac{1}{2} \times 14$

1573	**1010**	22p multicoloured	..	75	50	☐	☐
1574	**1011**	26p multicoloured	..	90	1·00	☐	☐
1575	**1012**	31p multicoloured	..	1·00	1·10	☐	☐
1576	**1013**	33p multicoloured	..	1·10	1·10	☐	☐
1577	**1014**	37p multicoloured	..	1·25	1·25	☐	☐
		Set of 5	.. .. ..	4·50	4·50	☐	☐
		First Day Cover			5·50		☐
		Presentation Pack	.. ..	5·00		☐	
		PHQ Cards (set of 5)	.. ..	3·25	6·00	☐	☐
		Set of 5 Gutter Pairs	.. ..	9·00		☐	

1015 Map of 1816

1016 Map of 1906

1017 Map of 1959

1018 Map of 1991

Bicentenary of Ordnance Survey. Maps of Hamstreet, Kent

1991 (17 Sept.) *Phosphorised paper. Perf* $14\frac{1}{2} \times 14$

1578	**1015**	24p multicoloured	..	50	50	☐	☐
1579	**1016**	28p multicoloured	..	80	85	☐	☐
1580	**1017**	33p multicoloured	..	95	1·00	☐	☐
1581	**1018**	39p multicoloured	..	1·10	1·25	☐	☐
		Set of 4	.. .. ..	3·00	3·25	☐	☐
		First Day Cover	.. ..		4·25		☐
		Presentation Pack	..	4·00		☐	
		PHQ Cards (set of 4)	..	3·00	6·00	☐	☐
		Set of 4 Gutter Pairs	.. ..	6·00		☐	

1019 Adoration of the Magi

1020 Mary and Baby Jesus in the Stable

1021 The Holy Family and Angel

1022 The Annunciation

1023 The Flight into Egypt

Christmas. Illuminated Manuscripts from the Bodleian Library, Oxford

1991 (12 Nov.) *One phosphor band* (18p) *or phosphorised paper* (*others*)

1582	**1019**	18p multicoloured	..	70	40	☐	☐
1583	**1020**	24p multicoloured	..	80	50	☐	☐
1584	**1021**	28p multicoloured	..	85	1·00	☐	☐
1585	**1022**	33p multicoloured	..	95	1·10	☐	☐
1586	**1023**	39p multicoloured	..	1·10	1·40	☐	☐
		Set of 5	.. .. ..	4·00	4·00	☐	☐
		First Day Cover	.. .. ..		4·50		☐
		Presentation Pack	.. ..	4·25		☐	
		PHQ Cards (set of 5)	.. ..	3·00	6·00	☐	☐
		Set of 5 Gutter Pairs	.. ..	8·00		☐	

Collectors Pack 1991

1991 (12 Nov.) *Comprises Nos.* 1531/5, 1546/9 *and* 1560/86.
Collectors Pack   25·00   ☐

Post Office Yearbook

1991 *Comprises Nos.* 1531/5, 1546/9 *and* 1560/86. *in hardback book with slip case.*
Yearbook   50·00   ☐

1024 Fallow Deer in Scottish Forest

1025 Hare on North Yorkshire Moors

1031 Key

1032 Model Car and Cigarette Cards

1026 Fox in the Fens

1027 Redwing and Home Counties Village

1033 Compass and Map

1034 Pocket Watch

1035 1854 1d. Red Stamp and Pen

1036 Pearl Necklace

1028 Welsh Mountain Sheep in Snowdonia

1037 Marbles

1038 Bucket, Spade and Starfish

T **1029/38** were printed together, *se-tenant*, in booklet panes of 10, the backgrounds of the stamps forming a composite design.

The Four Seasons. Wintertime

1992 (14 JAN.) *One phosphor band* (18p) *or phosphorised paper* (*others*)

1587	**1024**	18p multicoloured	..	45	50	☐ ☐
1588	**1025**	24p multicoloured	..	60	65	☐ ☐
1589	**1026**	28p multicoloured	..	70	75	☐ ☐
1590	**1027**	33p multicoloured	..	85	90	☐ ☐
1591	**1028**	39p multicoloured	..	1·00	1·10	☐ ☐
		Set of 5	.. .. ..	3·25	3·50	☐ ☐
		First Day Cover ..	..		4·50	☐
		Presentation Pack	..	4·25		☐
		PHQ Cards (set of 5) ..	..	3·00	6·50	☐ ☐
		Set of 5 Gutter Pairs ..	..	6·50		☐

Greetings Stamps. "Memories".

1992 (28 JAN.) *Two phosphor bands*

1592	**1029**	(1st) multicoloured	..	40	45	☐ ☐
		a. Booklet pane. Nos.				
		1592/1601 *plus*				
		12 *half stamp-size*				
		labels	.. .. ..	3·50		☐
1593	**1030**	(1st) multicoloured	..	40	45	☐ ☐
1594	**1031**	(1st) multicoloured	..	40	45	☐ ☐
1595	**1032**	(1st) multicoloured	..	40	45	☐ ☐
1596	**1033**	(1st) multicoloured	..	40	45	☐ ☐
1597	**1034**	(1st) multicoloured	..	40	45	☐ ☐
1598	**1035**	(1st) multicoloured	..	40	45	☐ ☐
1599	**1036**	(1st) multicoloured	..	40	45	☐ ☐
1600	**1037**	(1st) multicoloured	..	40	45	☐ ☐
1601	**1038**	(1st) multicoloured	..	40	45	☐ ☐
		Set of 10	..	3·50	4·00	☐ ☐
		Presentation Pack	.. ..	4·00		☐
		First Day Cover ..	.. ..		7·00	☐

1029 Flower Spray

1030 Double Locket

1039 Queen Elizabeth in Coronation Robes and Parliamentary Emblem

1040 Queen Elizabeth in Garter Robes and Archiepiscopal Arms

1041 Queen Elizabeth with Baby Prince Andrew and Royal Arms

1042 Queen Elizabeth at Trooping the Colour and Service Emblems

1046 Tennyson in 1856 and "April Love" (Arthur Hughes)

1047 Tennyson as a Young Man and "Mariana" (Dante Gabriel Rossetti)

Death Centenary of Alfred, Lord Tennyson (poet)

1992 (10 MAR.) *Phosphorised paper. Perf* $14\frac{1}{2} \times 14$

1607	**1044**	24p multicoloured	..	50	50	☐	☐
1608	**1045**	28p multicoloured	..	65	65	☐	☐
1609	**1046**	33p multicoloured	..	1·10	1·10	☐	☐
1610	**1047**	39p multicoloured	..	1·10	1·10	☐	☐
		Set of 4	.. .. ..	3·00	3·00	☐	☐
		First Day Cover			4·00		☐
		Presentation Pack		3·75		☐	
		PHQ Cards (set of 4)		2·50	5·00	☐	☐
		Set of 4 Gutter Pairs		6·00		☐	

CARRICKFERGUS CASTLE   **1048** Carrickfergus Castle

Queen Elizabeth and Commonwealth Emblem

1044 Tennyson in 1888 and "The Beguiling of Merlin" (Sir Edward Burne-Jones)

1045 Tennyson in 1864 and "I am Sick of the Shadows" (John Waterhouse)

1043 Queen Elizabeth and Commonwealth Emblem

Nos. 1602/6 were printed together, *se-tenant*, in horizontal strips of 5 throughout the sheet, forming a composite design.

40th Anniversary of Accession

1992 (6 FEB.) *Two phosphor bands. Perf* $14\frac{1}{2} \times 14$.

1602	**1039**	24p multicoloured	..	60	65	☐	☐
		a. Horiz strip of 5.					
		Nos. 1602/6	..	4·00	3·50	☐	☐
1603	**1040**	24p multicoloured	..	60	65	☐	☐
1604	**1041**	24p multicoloured	..	60	65	☐	☐
1605	**1042**	24p multicoloured	..	60	65	☐	☐
1606	**1043**	24p multicoloured	..	60	65	☐	☐
		Set of 5		4·00	3·00	☐	☐
		First Day Cover			5·00		☐
		Presentation Pack		4·25		☐	
		PHQ Cards (set of 5)		3·00	5·00	☐	☐
		Gutter strip of 10		8·00		☐	

1992 (24 MAR) *Designs as Nos.* 1410/13, *but showing Queen's head in silhouette as T* **1048**. *Perf* 15 x 14 (*with one elliptical hole on each vertical side*)

1611	**1048**	£1 bottle green and					
		gold†		1·50	1·50	☐	☐
1612	**882**	£1·50 maroon and					
		gold†		2·25	2·25	☐	☐
1613	**883**	£2 indigo and gold† ..		3·00	3·00	☐	☐
1614	**884**	£5 deep brown and					
		gold†		7·50	7·50	☐	☐
		Set of 4		13·00	13·00	☐	☐
		First Day Cover			4·75		☐
		Presentation Pack		14·50		☐	
		PHQ Cards (set of 4)		1·40		☐	
		Set of 4 Gutter Pairs		27·00		☐	

†The Queen's head on these stamps is printed in optically variable ink which changes colour from gold to green when viewed from different angles.

PHQ cards for Nos. 1611/14 were not issued until 2 March 1993.

1049 British Olympic Association Logo (Olympic Games, Barcelona)

1050 British Paralympic Association Symbol (Paralympics '92, Barcelona)

1051 *Santa Maria* (500th Anniv of Discovery of America by Columbus)

1052 *Kaisei* (cadet sailing ship) (Grand Regatta Columbus, 1992)

1053 British Pavilion, "EXPO '92", Seville

Nos. 1615/16 were printed together, *se-tenant*, in horizontal pairs throughout the sheet.

Europa. International Events

1992 (7 APR.) *Phosphorised paper. Perf* $14 \times 14\frac{1}{2}$

1615	**1049**	24p multicoloured	..	65	65	☐ ☐
		a. Horiz pair.				
		Nos. 1615/16		1·25	1·25	☐ ☐
1616	**1050**	24p multicoloured	..	65	65	☐ ☐
1617	**1051**	24p multicoloured	..	65	65	☐ ☐
1618	**1052**	39p multicoloured	..	1·00	1·10	☐ ☐
1619	**1053**	39p multicoloured	..	1·00	1·10	☐ ☐
		Set of 5		3·50	3·50	☐ ☐
		First Day Cover			4·50	☐
		Presentation Pack ..		4·25		☐
		PHQ Cards (*set of 5*) ..		3·00	6·00	☐ ☐
		Set of 4 Gutter Pairs ..		6·50		☐

1054 Pikeman

1055 Drummer

1056 Musketeer

1057 Standard Bearer

350th Anniversary of the Civil War

1992 (16 JUNE) *Phosphorised paper. Perf* $14\frac{1}{2} \times 14$

1620	**1054**	24p multicoloured	..	55	55	☐ ☐
1621	**1055**	28p multicoloured	..	70	70	☐ ☐
1622	**1056**	33p multicoloured	..	85	85	☐ ☐
1623	**1057**	39p multicoloured	..	95	95	☐ ☐
		Set of 4		2·75	2·75	☐
		First Day Cover ..			4·00	☐
		Presentation Pack		3·00		☐
		PHQ Cards (*set of 4*) ..		1·40	5·00	☐ ☐
		Set of 4 Gutter Pairs		5·50		☐

1058 *The Yeomen of the Guard*

1059 *The Gondoliers*

1060 *The Mikado*

1061 *The Pirates of Penzance*

1062 *Iolanthe*

1067 European Star

150th Birth Anniversary of Sir Arthur Sullivan (composer). Gilbert and Sullivan Operas

1992 (21 JULY) *One phosphor band (18p) or phosphorised paper (others). Perf 14½ × 14*

1624	**1058**	18p multicoloured	..	40	45	☐	☐
1625	**1059**	24p multicoloured		55	55	☐	☐
1626	**1060**	28p multicoloured		65	65	☐	☐
1627	**1061**	33p multicoloured		80	80	☐	☐
1628	**1062**	39p multicoloured		95	95	☐	☐
		Set of 5	.. ..	3·00	3·00	☐	☐
		First Day Cover ..	..		4·75		☐
		Presentation Pack	..	3·25		☐	
		PHQ Cards (set of 5) ..		1·50	6·00	☐	☐
		Set of 5 Gutter Pairs ..		6·00		☐	

Single European Market

1992 (13 OCT.) *Phosphorised paper*

1633	**1067**	24p multicoloured	..	60	60	☐	☐
		First Day Cover ..	.. ..		1·00		☐
		Presentation Pack	..	1·00		☐	
		PHQ Card ..	.. ..	50	1·50	☐	☐
		Gutter Pair ..	.. ..	1·25		☐	

1063 "Acid Rain Kills"

1064 "Ozone Layer"

1068 "Angel Gabriel", St. James's, Pangbourne

1069 "Madonna and Child", St. Mary's, Bilbury

1065 "Greenhouse Effect"

1066 "Bird of Hope"

1070 "King with Gold", Our Lady and St. Peter, Leatherhead

1071 "Shepherds", All Saints, Porthcawl

Protection of the Environment. Children's Paintings

1992 (15 SEPT.) *Phosphorised paper. Perf 14 × 14½*

1629	**1063**	24p multicoloured	..	60	45	☐	☐
1630	**1064**	28p multicoloured		75	80	☐	☐
1631	**1065**	33p multicoloured		80	90	☐	☐
1632	**1066**	39p multicoloured		90	90	☐	☐
		Set of 4	.. ..	2·75	2·75	☐	☐
		First Day Cover ..	..		3·50		☐
		Presentation Pack	..	3·00		☐	
		PHQ Cards (set of 4) ..		1·40	5·50	☐	☐
		Set of 4 Gutter Pairs ..		5·50		☐	

1072 "Kings with Frankincense and Myrrh", Our Lady and St. Peter, Leatherhead

Christmas. Stained Glass Windows

1992 (10 Nov.) *One phosphor band (18p) or phosphorised paper (others).*

1634	**1068**	18p multicoloured	..	40	35	☐	☐
1635	**1069**	24p multicoloured		55	60	☐	☐
1636	**1070**	28p multicoloured		65	65	☐	☐
1637	**1071**	33p multicoloured		80	85	☐	☐
1638	**1072**	39p multicoloured	..	95	95	☐	☐
		Set of 5		3·00	3·00	☐	☐
		First Day Cover			4·00		☐
		Presentation Pack		3·50		☐	
		PHQ Cards (set of 5)		1·50	5·50	☐	☐
		Set of 5 Gutter Pairs		6·00		☐	

Collectors Pack 1992

1992 (10 Nov.) *Comprises Nos. 1587/91, 1602/10 and 1615/38*

	Collectors Pack	24·00		☐

Post Office Yearbook

1992 (11 Nov.) *Comprises Nos. 1587/91, 1602/10 and 1615/38 in hardback book with slip case.*

	Yearbook	29·00		☐

1077 Young Swan and the Fleet

600th Anniversary of Abbotsbury Swannery

1993 (19 JAN.) *One phosphor band (18p) or phosphorised paper (others)*

1639	**1073**	18p multicoloured	..	30	35	☐	☐
1640	**1074**	24p multicoloured	..	40	45	☐	☐
1641	**1075**	28p multicoloured	..	45	50	☐	☐
1642	**1076**	33p multicoloured	..	50	55	☐	☐
1643	**1077**	39p multicoloured	..	60	65	☐	☐
		Set of 5		2·00	2·25	☐	☐
		First Day Cover			3·50		☐
		Presentation Pack		2·50		☐	
		PHQ Cards (set of 5)		1·50	4·50	☐	☐
		Set of 5 Gutter Pairs		4·25		☐	

1073 Mute Swan Cob and St. Catherine's, Abbotsbury

1074 Cygnet and Decoy

1078 Long John Silver and Parrot (*Treasure Island*)

1079 Tweedledum and Tweedledee (*Alice Through the Looking-Glass*)

1075 Swans and Cygnet

1076 Eggs in Nest and Tithe Barn, Abbotsbury

1080 William (*William* books)

1081 Mole and Toad (*The Wind in the Willows*)

1082 Teacher and Wilfred ("The Bash Street Kids")

1083 Peter Rabbit and Mrs. Rabbit (*The Tale of Peter Rabbit*)

1084 Snowman and Father Christmas (*The Snowman*)

1085 The Big Friendly Giant and Sophie (*The BFG*)

1086 Bill Badger and Rupert Bear

1087 Aladdin and the Genie

T **1078/87** were printed together, *se-tenant*, in booklet panes of 10.

Greetings Stamps. "Gift Giving"

1993 (29 FEB.) *Two phosphor bands. Perf* 15 x 14 (*with one elliptical hole on each vertical side*)

1644	**1078**	(1st) multicoloured	..	40	45	☐	☐
		a. Booklet pane. Nos. 1644/53 plus 20 half stamp-size labels	.. .. ..	3·50		☐	
1645	**1079**	(1st) gold, cream and black	..	40	45	☐	☐
1646	**1080**	(1st) multicoloured	..	40	45	☐	☐
1647	**1081**	(1st) multicoloured	..	40	45	☐	☐
1648	**1082**	(1st) multicoloured	..	40	45	☐	☐
1649	**1083**	(1st) multicoloured	..	40	45	☐	☐
1650	**1084**	(1st) multicoloured	..	40	45	☐	☐
1651	**1085**	(1st) multicoloured	..	40	45	☐	☐
1652	**1086**	(1st) multicoloured	..	40	45	☐	☐
1653	**1087**	(1st) multicoloured	..	40	45	☐	☐
		Set of 10	..	3·50	4·00	☐	☐
		First Day Cover ..	..		5·50		☐
		Presentation Pack	..	4·00		☐	
		PHQ Cards (set of 10) ..	..	3·00	7·75	☐	☐

1088 Decorated Enamel Dial

1089 Escapement, Remontoire and Fusee

1090 Balance, Spring and Temperature Compensator

1091 Back of Movement

300th Birth Anniversary of John Harrison (inventor of the marine chronometer). Details of "H4" Clock

1993 (16 FEB.) *Phosphorised paper. Perf* 14½ x 14

1654	**1088**	24p multicoloured	..	40	45	☐	☐
1655	**1089**	28p multicoloured	..	45	50	☐	☐
1656	**1090**	33p multicoloured	..	50	55	☐	☐
1657	**1091**	39p multicoloured	..	60	65	☐	☐
		Set of 4	..	1·75	1·90	☐	☐
		First Day Cover ..	..		3·00		☐
		Presentation Pack	..	2·40		☐	
		PHQ Cards (set of 4) ..	..	1·40	4·00	☐	☐
		Set of 4 Gutter Pairs	..	3·75		☐	

1092 Britannia

1993 (2 MAR.) *Granite paper. Perf* 14 x 14½ (*with two elliptical holes on each horizontal side*)

1658	**1092**	£10 multicoloured	..	15·00	16·00	☐	☐
		First Day Cover ..	..		22·00		☐
		Presentation Pack	..	16·00		☐	
		PHQ Card ..	..	35	22·00	☐	☐

1093 *Dendrobium hellwigianum*

1094 *Paphiopedilum Maudiae "Magnificum"*

1095 *Cymbidium lowianum*

1096 *Vanda Rothschildiana*

1097 *Dendrobium vexillarius var albiviride*

14th World Orchid Conference, Glasgow

1993 (16 MAR.) *One phosphor band* (18p.) *or phosphorised paper* (others).

1659	**1093**	18p multicoloured	..	30	35	☐ ☐
1660	**1094**	24p multicoloured	..	40	45	☐ ☐
1661	**1095**	28p multicoloured	..	45	50	☐ ☐
1662	**1096**	33p multicoloured	..	50	55	☐ ☐
1663	**1097**	39p multicoloured	..	60	65	☐ ☐
		Set of 5	.. ..	2·00	2·25	☐ ☐
		First Day Cover			3·75	☐
		Presentation Pack	.. ..	2·50		☐
		PHQ Cards (*set of 5*)	.. ..	1·50	4·50	☐ ☐
		Set of 5 Gutter Pairs	.. ..	4·25		☐

Booklet Stamps

1993 (6 APR.–7 SEPT.) *As T* **916/17**, *but perf* 15 × 14 (*with one elliptical hole on each vertical side*)

(*a*) *Photo Harrison*

1663a	**916**	(2nd) bright blue (centre band)	30	35	☐ ☐
1664	**917**	(1st) bright orange-red (phosphorised paper)	30	35	☐ ☐

(*b*) *Litho Questa or Walsall*

1665	**916**	(2nd) bright blue (1 centre band)	30	35	☐ ☐
1666	**917**	(1st) bright orange-red (2 phosphor bands)	40	45	☐ ☐

1993. *As Nos.* X841, *etc, but perf* 15 × 14 (*with one elliptical hole on each vertical side*)

(*a*) *Photo Enschede. Two phosphor bands*

Y1667	**369**	1p crimson	..	10	10	☐ ☐
Y1670		5p dull red-brown	..	10	10	☐ ☐
Y1671		6p yellow-olive	..	10	15	☐ ☐
Y1672		10p dull orange..	..	15	20	☐ ☐
Y1674		29p grey ..	..	45	50	☐ ☐
Y1675		30p deep olive-grey	..	55	60	☐ ☐
Y1676		35p yellow..	..	55	60	☐ ☐
Y1677		36p ultramarine	..	55	60	☐ ☐
Y1678		38p rosine ..	..	60	65	☐ ☐
Y1679		41p drab	..	65	70	☐ ☐

(*b*) *Photo Harrison*

Y1700	**369**	19p sage-green (1 centre band) ..	30	35	☐ ☐
Y1701		25p rose (phosphorised paper)	40	45	☐ ☐
Y1702		35p yellow (phosphorised paper)	55	60	☐ ☐
Y1703		41p drab (phosphorised paper).. ..	65	70	☐ ☐

(*c*) *Litho Walsall. Two phosphor bands*

Y1750	**369**	25p rose ..	40	45	☐ ☐
Y1751		35p yellow	55	60	☐ ☐
Y1752		41p drab	65	70	☐ ☐
		First Day Cover (*Nos.* Y1674, Y1677/9, Y1700/1) (26.10.93)		3·75	☐
		Presentation Pack (*Nos.* ¥1674, Y1677/9, Y1700/1*)*..	3·25		☐

Nos. Y1702/3 were only issued in coils and Nos. Y1750/2 only in booklets.

1098 "Family Group"
(bronze sculpture)
(Henry Moore)

1099 "Kew Gardens"
(lithograph) (Edward
Bawden)

1100 "St. Francis and the
Birds" (Stanley
Spencer)

1101 "Still Life: Odyssey
I" (Ben Nicholson)

Europa. Contemporary Art

1993 (11 MAY) *Phosphorised paper. Perf* 14 x 14½

1767	**1098**	24p multicoloured	..	40	45	☐	☐
1768	**1099**	28p multicoloured		45	50	☐	☐
1769	**1100**	33p multicoloured		50	55	☐	☐
1770	**1101**	39p multicoloured		60	65	☐	☐
	Set of 4	.. .. ..		1·75	2·00	☐	☐
	First Day Cover	..			3·00		☐
	Presentation Pack	..		2·40		☐	
	PHQ Cards (set of 4)	..		1·40	4·00	☐	☐
	Set of 4 Gutter Pairs	..		3·75			☐

1102 Emperor Claudius
(from gold coin)

1103 Emperor Hadrian
(bronze head)

1104 Goddess Roma
(from gemstone)

1105 Christ (Hinton St.
Mary mosaic)

Roman Britain

1993 (15 JUNE) *Phosphorised paper with two phosphor
bands. Perf* 14 x 14½

1771	**1102**	24p multicoloured	..	40	45	☐	☐
1772	**1103**	28p multicoloured		45	50	☐	☐
1773	**1104**	33p multicoloured		50	55	☐	☐
1774	**1105**	39p multicoloured		60	65	☐	☐
	Set of 4	.. ..		1·75	2·00	☐	☐
	First Day Cover	..			3·00		☐
	Presentation Pack	..		2·40		☐	
	PHQ Cards (set of 4)	..		1·40	4·00	☐	☐

1106 *Midland Maid* and
other Narrow Boats,
Grand Junction Canal

1107 *Yorkshire Maid* and
other Humber Keels,
Stainforth and Keadby
Canal

1108 *Valley Princess* and
other Horse-drawn
Barges, Brecknock and
Abergavenny Canal

1109 Steam Barges,
including *Pride of
Scotland*, and Fishing
Boats, Crinan Canal

Inland Waterways

1993 (20 JULY) *Two phosphor bands. Perf* 14 x 14½

1775	**1106**	24p multicoloured	..	40	45	☐	☐
1776	**1107**	28p multicoloured		45	50	☐	☐
1777	**1108**	33p multicoloured		50	55	☐	☐
1778	**1109**	39p multicoloured		60	65	☐	☐
	Set of 4	.. ..		1·75	2·00	☐	☐
	First Day Cover	.. ..			3·00		☐
	Presentation Pack	..		2·40		☐	
	PHQ Cards (set of 4)	..		1·40	4·00	☐	☐
	Set of 4 Gutter Pairs	..		3·75			☐

Nos. 1775/8 commemorate the bicentenaries of the Acts
of Parliament authorising the canals depicted.

1110 Horse Chestnut

1111 Blackberry

1112 Hazel

1113 Rowan

1114 Pear

1119 The Final Problem

The Four Seasons. Autumn. Fruits and Leaves

1993 (11 SEPT.) *One phosphor band* (18p) *or phosphorised paper* (*others*)

1779	1110	18p multicoloured	..	30	35	☐ ☐
1780	1111	24p multicoloured	..	40	45	☐ ☐
1781	1112	28p multicoloured	..	45	50	☐ ☐
1782	1113	33p multicoloured	..	50	55	☐ ☐
1783	1114	39p multicoloured	..	60	65	☐ ☐
		Set of 5		2·00	2·25	☐ ☐
		First Day Cover			3·25	☐
		Presentation Pack		2·50		☐
		PHQ Cards (*set of 5*) ..		1·50	4·50	☐ ☐
		Set of 5 Gutter Pairs ..		4·25		☐

T**1115/19** were printed together, *se-tenant*, in horizontal strips of 5 throughout the sheet.

Sherlock Holmes. Centenary of the Publication of The Final Problem

1993 (11 OCT.) *Phosphorised paper. Perf* 14 x 14½

1784	1115	24p multicoloured	..	40	45	☐ ☐
		a. *Horiz strip. Nos.*				
		1784/8..		1·75	2·00	☐ ☐
1785	1116	24p multicoloured	..	40	45	☐ ☐
1786	1117	24p multicoloured	..	40	45	☐ ☐
1787	1118	24p multicoloured	..	40	45	☐ ☐
1788	1119	24p multicoloured	..	40	45	☐ ☐
		Set of 5		1·75	2·00	☐ ☐
		First Day Cover			3·00	☐
		Presentation Pack ..		2·25		☐
		PHQ Cards (*set of 5*) ..		1·50	4·00	☐ ☐
		Gutter strip of 10		3·75		☐

1115 The Reigate Squire

1116 The Hound of the Baskervilles

1120

Self-adhesive Booklet Stamp

1993 (19 OCT.) *Two phosphor bands. Perf* 14 x 15 (*with one elliptical hole on each vertical side*)

1789	1120	(1st) orange-red.. ..		40	45	☐ ☐
		First Day Cover			1·25	☐
		Presentation Pack (*booklet*				
		pane of 20)		7·50		☐
		PHQ Card		30	60	☐ ☐

1117 The Six Napoleons

1118 The Greek Interpreter

Minimum Price. The minimum price quoted is 10p. This represents a handling charge rather than a basis for valuing common stamps. Where the actual value of a stamp is less than 10p this may be apparent when set prices are shown, particularly for sets including a number of 10p stamps. It therefore follows that in valuing common stamps the 10p catalogue price should not be reckoned automatically since it covers a variation in real scarcity.

1121 Bob Cratchit and Tiny Tim

1122 Mr. and Mrs. Fezziwig

1123 Scrooge

1124 The Prize Turkey

1125 Mr. Scrooge's Nephew

Christmas. 150th Anniversary of Publication of A Christmas Carol

1993 (9 Nov.) *One phosphor band.* (19p) *or phosphorised paper* (others)

1790	**1121**	19p multicoloured	..	30	35	□	□
1791	**1122**	25p multicoloured	..	40	45	□	□
1792	**1123**	30p multicoloured	..	45	50	□	□
1793	**1124**	35p multicoloured	..	55	60	□	□
1794	**1125**	41p multicoloured	..	65	70	□	□
		Set of 5		2·10	2·25	□	□
		First Day Cover			3·25		□
		Presentation Pack		2·75		□	
		PHQ Cards (*set of* 5)		1·90	5·25	□	□
		Set of 5 *Gutter Pairs*		4·50			□

Collectors Pack 1993

1993 (9 Nov.) *Comprises Nos.* 1639/43, 1654/7, 1659/63, 1767/88 *and* 1790/4

	Collectors Pack	19·00		□	

Post Office Yearbook

1993 (9 Nov.) *Comprises Nos.* 1639/43, 1654/7, 1659/63, 1767/88 *and* 1790/4 *in hardback book with slip case*

	Yearbook	32·00		□	

REGIONAL ISSUES

PERFORATION AND WATERMARK. All the following Regional stamps are perforated 15×14 and are watermarked Type **179**, unless otherwise stated.

For listing of First Day Covers see pages 110/11.

1 Northern Ireland

N 1   N 2   N 3   N 4

1958–67

NI1	N 1	3d lilac	20	10 □ □
		p. One centre phosphor band	20	15 □ □
NI2		4d blue	20	15 □ □
		p. Two phosphor bands	20	15 □ □
NI3	N 2	6d purple	20	20 □ □
NI4		9d bronze-green (2 phosphor bands)	30	50 □ □
NI5	N 3	1s 3d green	30	50 □ □
NI6		1s 6d blue (2 phosphor bands)	30	50 □ □

1968–69 *One centre phosphor band (Nos. NI8/9) or two phosphor bands (others). No wmk*

NI7	N 1	4d blue	20	15 □ □
NI8		4d sepia	20	15 □ □
NI9		4d vermilion	20	20 □ □
NI10		5d blue	20	20 □ □
NI11	N 3	1s 6d blue	2·00	3·00 □ □
		Presentation Pack (comprises Nos. NI1p, NI4/6, NI8/10)	3·00	□

Decimal Currency
1971–91 *Type N 4. No wmk*
(a) Printed in photogravure with phosphor bands

NI12	2½p magenta (1 centre band)	75	25 □ □
NI13	3p ultramarine (2 bands)	40	15 □ □
NI14	3p ultramarine (1 centre band)	20	15 □ □
NI15	3½p olive-grey (2 bands)	20	20 □ □
NI16	3½p olive-grey (1 centre band)	20	25 □ □
NI17	4½p grey-blue (2 bands)	25	25 □ □
NI18	5p violet (2 bands)	1·50	1·50 □ □
NI19	5½p violet (2 bands)	20	20 □ □
NI20	5½p violet (1 centre band)	20	20 □ □
NI21	6½p blue (1 centre band)	20	20 □ □
NI22	7p brown (1 centre band)	35	25 □ □
NI23	7½p chestnut (2 bands)	2·25	2·25 □ □
NI24	8p rosine (2 bands)	30	30 □ □
NI25	8½p yellow-green (2 bands)	30	30 □ □
NI26	9p violet (2 bands)	30	30 □ □
NI27	10p orange-brown (2 bands)	35	35 □ □
NI28	10p orange-brown (1 centre band)	35	35 □ □
NI29	10½p blue (2 bands)	40	40 □ □
NI30	11p scarlet (2 bands)	40	40 □ □

(b) Printed in photogravure on phosphorised paper

NI31	12p yellowish green	50	45 □ □
NI32	13½p purple-brown	60	70 □ □
NI33	15p ultramarine	60	50 □ □

(c) Printed in lithography. Perf 14 (11½p, 12½p, 14p, (No. NI38), 15½p, 16p, 18p, (No. NI45), 19½p, 20½p, 22p, (No. NI52), 26p, (No. NI58) 28p (No. NI60), or 15×14 (others).

NI34	11½p drab (1 side band)	80	60 □ □
NI35	12p brt emer (1 side band)	50	50 □ □
NI36	12½p light emer (1 side band)	50	40 □ □
	a. Perf 15 × 14	4·50	4·50 □ □
NI37	13p pale chest (1 side band)	70	35 □ □
NI38	14p grey-blue (phosphorised paper)	70	50 □ □
NI39	14p dp blue (1 centre band)	55	35 □ □
NI40	15p brt blue (1 centre band)	60	30 □ □
NI41	15½p pale violet (phosphorised paper)	80	65 □ □
NI42	16p drab (phosphorised paper)	90	1·00 □ □
	a. Perf 15 × 14	7·00	5·00 □ □
NI43	17p grey-blue (phosphorised paper)	80	40 □ □
NI44	17p deep blue (1 centre band)	50	40 □ □
NI45	18p dp violet (phosphorised paper)	80	80 □ □
NI46	18p olive-grey (phosphorised paper)	80	70 □ □
NI47	18p brt grn (1 centre band)	30	35 □ □
	a. Perf 14	75	75 □ □
NI47b	18p brt grn (1 side band)	2·00	2·00 □ □
NI48	19p bright orange-red (phosphorised paper)	60	60 □ □
NI49	19½p olive-grey (phosphorised paper)	1·75	1·75 □ □
NI50	20p brownish black (phosphorised paper)	30	30 □ □
NI51	20½p ultramarine (phosphorised paper)	4·00	4·00 □ □
NI52	22p blue (phosphorised paper)	90	1·10 □ □
NI53	22p yellow-green (phosphorised paper)	85	1·10 □ □
NI54	22p bright orange-red (phosphorised paper)	85	40 □ □
NI55	23p bright green (phosphorised paper)	80	1·10 □ □
NI56	24p Indian red (phosphorised paper)	70	1·10 □ □
NI57	24p chestnut (phosphorised paper)	40	45 □ □
NI57a	24p chestnut (2 bands)	2·00	2·00 □ □

NI58	26p rosine (phosphorised paper)	90	1·25	☐	☐
	a. Perf 15 × 14	2·00	2·00	☐	☐
NI59	26p drab (phosphorised paper)	40	45	☐	☐
NI60	28p deep violet-blue (phosphorised paper)	1·00	1·00	☐	☐
	a. Perf 15 × 14	80	80	☐	☐
NI61	28p deep bluish grey (phosphorised paper)	45	50	☐	☐
NI62	31p bright purple (phosphorised paper)	1·10	1·10	☐	☐
NI63	32p greenish blue (phosphorised paper)	1·10	1·10	☐	☐
NI64	34p deep bluish grey (phosphorised paper)	1·00	1·00	☐	☐
NI65	37p rosine (phosphorised paper)	1·00	1·00	☐	☐
NI66	39p bright mauve (phosphorised paper)	60	65	☐	☐

Presentation Pack (contains 2½p (NI12), 3p (NI13), 5p (NI18), 7½p (NI23)) .. ..   4·00   ☐

Presentation Pack (contains 3p (NI14), 3½p (NI15), 5½p (NI19), 8p (NI24) later with 4½p (NI17) added) .. ..   2·25   ☐

Presentation Pack (contains 6½p (NI21), 8½p (NI25), 10p (NI27), 11p (NI30)) .. ..   1·75   ☐

Presentation Pack (contains 7p (NI22), 9p (NI26), 10½p (NI29), 11½p (NI34), 12p (NI31), 13½p (NI32), 14p (NI38), 15p (NI33), 18p (NI45), 22p (NI52)) ..   7·00   ☐

Presentation Pack (contains 10p (NI28), 12½p (NI36), 16p (NI42), 20½p (NI51), 26p (NI58), 28p (NI60)) ..   7·00   ☐

Presentation Pack (contains 10p (NI28), 13p (NI37), 16p (NI42a), 17p (NI43), 22p (NI53), 26p (NI58), 28p (NI60), 31p (NI62)) ..   10·00   ☐

Presentation Pack (contains 12p (NI35), 13p (NI37), 17p (NI43), 18p (NI46), 22p (NI53), 26p (NI58a), 28p (NI60a), 31p (NI62)) ..   9·00   ☐

Presentation Pack (contains 14p, 19p, 23p, 32p from Northern Ireland, Scotland and Wales (Nos. NI39, NI48, NI55, NI63, S54, S61, S66, S75, W40, W50, W57, W66))   8·00   ☐

Presentation Pack (contains 15p, 20p, 24p, 34p from Northern Ireland, Scotland and Wales (Nos. NI40, NI50, NI56, NI64, S56, S63, S68, S76, W41, W52, W58, W67))   7·50   ☐

Presentation Pack (contains 17p, 22p, 26p, 37p, from Northern Ireland, Scotland and Wales (Nos. NI44, NI54, NI59, NI65, S58, S65, S71, S77, W45, W56, W62, W68))   8·50   ☐

Presentation Pack (contains 18p, 24p, 28p, 39p from Northern Ireland, Scotland and Wales (Nos. NI47, NI57, NI61, NI66, S60, S69, S73, S78, W48, W59, W64, W69))   5·50   ☐

2 Scotland

S 1   S 2   S 3   S 4

1958–67

S1	S 1	3d	lilac	20	15	☐ ☐
		p.	Two phosphor bands	12·00	1·00	☐ ☐
		pa.	One side band	20	25	☐ ☐
		pb.	One centre band	20	15	☐ ☐
S2		4d	blue	20	10	☐ ☐
		p.	Two phosphor bands	20	20	☐ ☐
S3	S 2	6d	purple	20	15	☐ ☐
		p.	Two phosphor bands	20	25	☐ ☐
S4		9d	bronze-green (2 phosphor bands)	30	30	☐ ☐
S5	S 3	1s 3d	green	30	30	☐ ☐
		p.	Two phosphor bands	30	30	☐ ☐
S6		1s 6d	blue (2 phosphor bands)	35	30	☐ ☐

No. S1*pa* exists with the phosphor band at the left or right of the stamp.

1967–70 One centre phosphor band (Nos. S7, S9/10) or two phosphor bands (others). No wmk

S7	S 1	3d	lilac	10	15	☐ ☐
S8		4d	blue	10	15	☐ ☐
S9		4d	sepia	10	10	☐ ☐
S10		4d	vermilion	10	10	☐ ☐
S11		5d	blue	20	10	☐ ☐
S12	S 2	9d	bronze-green	5·00	5·50	☐ ☐
S13	S 3	1s 6d	blue	1·40	1·00	☐ ☐
			Presentation Pack (containing Nos. S3, S5p, S7, S9/13)	13·00		☐

Decimal Currency

1971–93 Type S 4. No wmk

(a) Printed in photogravure by Harrison and Sons with phosphor bands. Perf 15 × 14.

S14	2½p	magenta (1 centre band)	25	15	☐ ☐
S15	3p	ultramarine (2 bands)	30	15	☐ ☐
S16	3p	ultramarine (1 centre band)	15	15	☐ ☐
S17	3½p	olive-grey (2 bands)	20	20	☐ ☐
S18	3½p	ol-grey (1 centre band)	20	20	☐ ☐
S19	4½p	grey-blue (2 bands)	25	20	☐ ☐
S20	5p	violet (2 bands)	1·50	1·50	☐ ☐
S21	5½p	violet (2 bands)	20	20	☐ ☐
S22	5½p	violet (1 centre band)	20	20	☐ ☐
S23	6½p	blue (1 centre band)	20	20	☐ ☐
S24	7p	brown (1 centre band)	25	25	☐ ☐
S25	7½p	chestnut (2 bands)	1·75	1·75	☐ ☐
S26	8p	rosine (2 bands)	30	40	☐ ☐
S27	8½p	yellow-green (2 bands)	30	30	☐ ☐
S28	9p	violet (2 bands)	30	30	☐ ☐
S29	10p	orange-brown (2 bands)	35	30	☐ ☐
S30	10p	orange-brown (1 centre band)	35	35	☐ ☐
S31	10½p	blue (2 bands)	45	35	☐ ☐
S32	11p	scarlet (2 bands)	45	35	☐ ☐

(b) Printed in photogravure by Harrison and Sons on phosphorised paper. Perf 15 × 14.

S33	12p	yellowish green	50	30	☐ ☐
S34	13½p	purple-brown	60	65	☐ ☐
S35	15p	ultramarine	60	45	☐ ☐

(c) Printed in lithography by John Waddington. One side phosphor band (11½p, 12p, 12½p, 13p) or phosphorised paper (others). Perf 13½ × 14

S36	11½p	drab	85	60	☐ ☐
S37	12p	bright emerald	90	70	☐ ☐
S38	12½p	light emerald	50	40	☐ ☐
S39	13p	pale chestnut	60	30	☐ ☐
S40	14p	grey-blue	60	50	☐ ☐
S41	15½p	pale violet	70	65	☐ ☐
S42	16p	drab	70	45	☐ ☐
S43	17p	grey-blue	3·25	2·00	☐ ☐
S44	18p	deep violet	80	80	☐ ☐
S45	19½p	olive-grey	1·75	1·75	☐ ☐
S46	20½p	ultramarine	4·00	4·00	☐ ☐
S47	22p	blue	80	1·10	☐ ☐
S48	22p	yellow-green	1·00	1·10	☐ ☐
S49	26p	rosine	1·00	1·10	☐ ☐
S50	28p	deep violet-blue	1·00	1·10	☐ ☐
S51	31p	bright purple	1·40	1·10	☐ ☐

(d) Printed in lithography by Questa. Perf 15 × 14

S52	12p	brt emer (1 side band)	1·50	1·00	☐ ☐
S53	13p	pale chest (1 side band)	60	30	☐ ☐
S54	14p	dp blue (1 centre band)	40	30	☐ ☐
S55	14p	deep blue (1 side band)	60	1·00	☐ ☐
S56	15p	bright blue (1 centre band)	50	30	☐ ☐
S57	17p	grey-blue (phosphorised paper)	3·50	2·00	☐ ☐
S58	17p	dp blue (1 centre band)	50	35	☐ ☐
S59	18p	olive-grey (phosphorised paper)	80	1·50	☐ ☐
S60	18p	brt green (1 centre band)	30	35	☐ ☐
		a. Perf 14	30	35	☐ ☐
S60b	18p	brt grn (1 side band)	2·00	2·00	☐ ☐
S61	19p	bright orange-red (phosphorised paper)	60	45	☐ ☐
S62	19p	brt orange-red (2 bands)	1·40	1·40	☐ ☐
S63	20p	brownish black (phosphorised paper)	60	30	☐ ☐
S64	22p	yell-grn (phosphorised paper)	80	1·10	☐ ☐
S65	22p	bright orange-red (phosphorised paper)	90	40	☐ ☐
S66	23p	brt green (phosphorised paper)	90	1·10	☐ ☐
S67	23p	bright green (2 bands)	5·50	5·50	☐ ☐

S68	24p	Indian red (phosphorised paper)	.. .. ..	70	70	□ □
S69	24p	chestnut (phosphorised paper)	.. .. ..	40	45	□ □
		a. Perf 14	.. .. ..	75	75	□ □
S69*b*	24p	chestnut (2 bands)	..	2·00	2·00	□ □
S70	26p	rosine (phosphorised paper)	.. .. ..	70	70	□ □
S71	26p	drab (phosphorised paper)	.. .. ..	40	45	□ □
S72	28p	deep violet-blue (phosphorised paper)	..	85	75	□ □
S73	28p	deep bluish grey (phosphorised paper)	..	45	50	□ □
		a. Perf 14	.. .. ..	1·00	1·00	□ □
S74	31p	bright purple (phosphorised paper)	..	1·50	1·50	□ □
S75	32p	greenish blue (phosphorised paper)	..	1·10	1·00	□ □
S76	34p	deep bluish grey (phosphorised paper)	..	1·00	1·00	□ □
S77	37p	rosine (phosphorised paper)	.. .. ..	1·00	1·00	□ □
S78	39p	bright mauve (phosphorised paper)	..	60	65	□ □
		a. Perf 14	.. .. ..	1·60	1·25	□ □

Presentation Pack (*contains* 2½p (S14), 3p (S15), 5p (S20), 7½p (S25))	4·00	□
Presentation Pack (*contains* 3p (S16), 3½p (S17), 5½p (S21), 8p (S26) *later with* 4½p (S19) *added*)	2·25	□
Presentation Pack (*contains* 6½p (S23), 8½p (S27), 10p (S29), 11p (S32))	1·75	□
Presentation Pack (*contains* 7p (S24), 9p (S28), 10½p (S31), 11½p (S36), 12p (S33), 13½p (S34), 14p (S40), 15p (S35), 18p (S44), 22p (S47)) ..	7·00	□
Presentation Pack (*contains* 10p (S30), 12½p (S38), 16p (S42), 20½p (S46), 26p (S49), 28p (S50))	7·00	□
Presentation Pack (*contains* 10p (S30), 13p (S39), 16p (S42), 17p (S43), 22p (S48), 26p (S49), 28p (S50), 31p (S51))	9·50	□
Presentation Pack (*contains* 12p, (S52), 13p (S53), 17p (S57), 18p (S59), 22p (S64), 26p (S70), 28p (S72), 31p (S74))	9·00	□

For combined packs containing values from all three Regions see under Northern Ireland.

3 Wales and Monmouthshire

W 1   W 2   W 3   W 4

1958–67

W1	W 1	3d lilac	20	10 ☐ ☐
		p. One centre phosphor band ..	20	15 ☐ ☐
W2		4d blue	20	15 ☐ ☐
		p. Two phosphor bands	20	15 ☐ ☐
W3	W 2	6d purple	40	20 ☐ ☐
W4		9d bronze-green (2 phosphor bands)	30	35 ☐ ☐
W5	W 3	1s 3d green	30	30 ☐ ☐
W6		1s 6d blue (2 phosphor bands)	35	30 ☐ ☐

1967–69 *One centre phosphor band* (Nos. W7, W9/10) *or two phosphor bands* (others). *No wmk*

W7	W 1	3d lilac	20	10 ☐ ☐
W8		4d blue	20	10 ☐ ☐
W9		4d sepia	20	10 ☐ ☐
W10		4d vermilion	20	20 ☐ ☐
W11		5d blue	20	10 ☐ ☐
W12	W 3	1s 6d blue	3·00	3·00 ☐ ☐
		Presentation Pack (comprises Nos. W4, W6/7, W9/11) ..	2·50	☐

Decimal Currency

1971–92 *Type* W 4. *No wmk*

(a) Printed in photogravure with phosphor bands

W13	2½p magenta (1 centre band)	20	15 ☐ ☐
W14	3p ultramarine (2 bands)	25	15 ☐ ☐
W15	3p ultramarine (1 centre band)	20	20 ☐ ☐
W16	3½p olive-grey (2 bands) ..	20	25 ☐ ☐
W17	3½p olive-grey (1 centre band)	20	25 ☐ ☐
W18	4½p grey-blue (2 bands) ..	25	20 ☐ ☐
W19	5p violet (2 bands)	1·50	1·50 ☐ ☐
W20	5½p violet (2 bands)	20	25 ☐ ☐
W21	5½p violet (1 centre band) ..	20	25 ☐ ☐
W22	6½p blue (1 centre band) ..	20	20 ☐ ☐
W23	7p brown (1 centre band) ..	25	25 ☐ ☐
W24	7½p chestnut (2 bands) ..	2·00	2·25 ☐ ☐
W25	8p rosine (2 bands)	30	30 ☐ ☐
W26	8½p yellow-green (2 bands) ..	30	30 ☐ ☐
W27	9p violet (2 bands)	30	30 ☐ ☐
W28	10p orange-brown (2 bands)	35	30 ☐ ☐
W29	10p orange-brown (1 centre band)	35	30 ☐ ☐
W30	10½p blue (2 bands)	40	35 ☐ ☐
W31	11p scarlet (2 bands) ..	40	45 ☐ ☐

(b) Printed in photogravure on phosphorised paper

W32	12p yellowish green	50	45 ☐ ☐
W33	13½p purple-brown	60	70 ☐ ☐
W34	15p ultramarine	60	50 ☐ ☐

(c) *Printed in lithography. Perf* 14 (11½p, 12½p, 14p (No. W39), 15½p, 16p, 18p, (No. W42), 19½p, 20½p, 22p, (No. W58), 26p, (No. W61), 28p) *or* 15 × 14 (others).

W35	11½p drab (1 side band) ..	85	60 ☐ ☐
W36	12p brt emer (1 side band)	2·00	1·10 ☐ ☐
W37	12½p light emer (1 side band)..	60	60 ☐ ☐
	a. Perf 15 × 14 ..	7·00	6·00 ☐ ☐
W38	13p pale chest (1 side band)..	50	35 ☐ ☐
W39	14p grey-blue (phosphorised paper)	65	50 ☐ ☐
W40	14p dp blue (1 centre band) ..	55	30 ☐ ☐
W41	15p brt blue (1 centre band)..	40	30 ☐ ☐
W42	15½p pale violet (phosphorised paper)	80	65 ☐ ☐
W43	16p drab (phosphorised paper)	1·50	1·25 ☐ ☐
	a. Perf 15 × 14 ..	1·50	1·25 ☐ ☐
W44	17p grey-blue (phosphorised paper)	70	55 ☐ ☐
W45	17p deep blue (1 centre band)	50	35 ☐ ☐
W46	18p deep violet (phosphorised paper)	80	75 ☐ ☐
W47	18p olive-grey (phosphorised paper)	1·00	45 ☐ ☐
W48	18p brt grn (1 centre band)	30	35 ☐ ☐
	a. Perf 14	1·00	1·00 ☐ ☐
W49	18p brt green (1 side band)	75	75 ☐ ☐
W50	19p bright orange-red (phosphorised paper)	60	45 ☐ ☐
W51	19½p olive-grey (phosphorised paper)	1·75	1·75 ☐ ☐
W52	20p brownish black (phosphorised paper) ..	30	30 ☐ ☐
W53	20½p ultramarine (phosphorised paper)	5·00	4·00 ☐ ☐
W54	22p blue (phosphorised paper)	1·00	1·00 ☐ ☐
W55	22p yell-green (phosphorised paper)	80	1·10 ☐ ☐
W56	22p bright orange-red (phosphorised paper) ..	60	50 ☐ ☐
W57	23p brt green (phosphorised paper)	80	1·10 ☐ ☐
W58	24p Indian red (phosphorised paper)	70	1·10 ☐ ☐
W59	24p chestnut (phosphorised paper)	40	45 ☐ ☐
	a. Perf 14	1·00	1·00 ☐ ☐
W60	24p chestnut (2 bands) ..	85	85 ☐ ☐

W61	26p	rosine (phosphorised paper)	90	1·10	☐ ☐
	a.	*Perf* 15 × 14	4·00	4·00	☐ ☐
W62	26p	drab (phosphorised paper)	70	70	☐ ☐
W63	28p	dp viol-blue (phosphorised paper)	1·00	1·10	☐ ☐
	a.	*Perf* 15 × 14	70	65	☐ ☐
W64	28p	deep bluish grey (phosphorised paper)	45	50	☐ ☐
W65	31p	brt purple (phosphorised paper)	1·00	1·10	☐ ☐
W66	32p	greenish blue (phosphorised paper)	1·10	1·10	☐ ☐
W67	34p	deep bluish grey (phosphorised paper) ..	1·00	1·00	☐ ☐
W68	37p	rosine (phosphorised paper)	1·00	1·00	☐ ☐
W69	39p	bright mauve (phosphorised paper)	60	65	☐ ☐

Presentation Pack (*contains* 2½p (W13), 3p (W14), 5p (W19), 7½p (W24))	4·00	☐
Presentation Pack (*contains* 3p (W15), 3½p (W16), 5½p (W20), 8p (W25), *later with* 4½p (W18) *added*)	2·25	☐
Presentation Pack (*contains* 6½p (W22), 8½p (W26), 10p (W28), 11p (W31))	1·75	☐
Presentation Pack (*contains* 7p (W23), 9p (W27), 10½p (W30), 11½p (W35), 12p (W32), 13½p (W33), 14p (W39), 15p (W34), 18p (W46), 22p (W53))	7·00	☐
Presentation Pack (*contains* 10p (W29), 12½p (W37), 16p (W43), 20½p (W53), 26p (W61), 28p (W63)) ..	7·00	☐
Presentation Pack (*contains* 10p (W29), 13p (W38), 16p (W43a), 17p (W44), 22p (W55), 26p (W61), 28p (W63), 31p (W65)) ..	9·50	☐
Presentation Pack (*contains* 12p (W36), 13p (W38), 17p (W44), 18p (W47), 22p (W55), 26p (W61a), 28p (W63a), 31p (W65)) ..	9·50	☐

No. W49 exists with the phosphor band at the left or the right of the stamp.

For combined packs containing values from all three Regions see under Northern Ireland.

ISLE OF MAN

Regional Issues

1   2   3

1958–67 *Wmk* **179**   *Perf* 15×14

1	**1**	2½d red	45	80	☐ ☐
2	**2**	3d lilac	20	10	☐ ☐
		p. One centre phosphor band	20	30	☐ ☐
3		4d blue	1·50	1·10	☐ ☐
		p. Two phosphor bands ..	20	15	☐ ☐

1968–69 *One centre phosphor band* (*Nos.* 5/6) *or two phosphor bands* (*others*). *No wmk*

4	**2**	4d blue	20	25	☐ ☐
5		4d sepia	20	30	☐ ☐
6		4d vermilion ..	45	60	☐ ☐
7		5d blue	45	60	☐ ☐

Decimal Currency

1971 (7 JULY) *One centre phosphor band* (2½p) *or two phosphor bands* (*others*). *No wmk*

8	**3**	2½p magenta	20	15	☐ ☐
9		3p ultramarine ..	20	15	☐ ☐
10		5p violet	70	75	☐ ☐
11		7½p chestnut	70	90	☐ ☐
		Presentation Pack	2·00		☐

For comprehensive listings of the Independent Administration issues of the Isle of Man, see Stanley Gibbons *Collect Channel Islands and Isle of Man Stamps*.

CHANNEL ISLANDS
1 General Issue

C 1 Gathering Vraic   C 2 Islanders gathering Vraic

Third Anniversary of Liberation

1948 (10 MAY) *Wmk Type* **127**   *Perf* 15×14

C1	**C 1**	1d red	20	20	☐ ☐
C2	**C 2**	2½d blue	30	30	☐ ☐
		First Day Cover	18·00		☐

2 Guernsey

(a) War Occupation Issues

Stamps issued under British authority during the German Occupation.

1   2   3

1941–44 *Rouletted.* (a) *White paper. No wmk*

1*f*	1	½d green	..	..	2·50	2·75	□ □
2		1d red ..	..	..	2·50	1·25	□ □
3*a*		2½d blue	..	..	5·50	4·50	□ □

(b) *Bluish French bank-note paper. Wmk loops*

4	1	½d green	..	..	18·00	20·00	□ □
5		1d red ..	..	..	8·00	25·00	□ □

(b) Regional Issues

1958–67 *Wmk 179*   *Perf 15 × 14*

6	2	2½d red ..	..	..	35	40	□ □
7	3	3d lilac	..	..	35	30	□ □
		p. One centre phosphor band			20	20	□ □
8		4d blue	..	..	25	30	□ □
		p. Two phosphor bands	..		20	20	□ □

1968–69 *One centre phosphor band (Nos. 10/11) or two phosphor bands (others). No wmk*

9	3	4d blue	..	..	10	25	□ □
10		4d sepia	..	..	15	20	□ □
11		4d vermilion	..	..	15	30	□ □
12		5d blue	..	..	15	30	□ □

For comprehensive listings of the Independent Postal Administration issues of Guernsey, see Stanley Gibbons *Collect Channel Islands and Isle of Man Stamps.*

3 Jersey

(a) War Occupation Issues

Stamps issued under British authority during the German Occupation.

1   2 Old Jersey Farm   3 Portelet Bay

4 Corbière Lighthouse   5 Elizabeth Castle

6 Mont Orgueil Castle   7 Gathering Vraic (seaweed)

1941–42 *White paper. No wmk*   *Perf 11*

1	1	½d green	..	..	3·75	2·50	□ □
2		1d red ..	..	..	4·00	2·75	□ □

1943 *No wmk*   *Perf 13½*

3	2	½d green	..	..	7·00	5·50	□ □
4	3	1d red ..	..	..	1·50	50	□ □
5	4	1½d brown	..	..	2·50	3·00	□ □
6	5	2d orange	..	..	4·00	2·25	□ □
7*a*	6	2½d blue	..	..	75	1·50	□ □
8	7	3d violet	..	..	1·00	2·75	□ □
		Set of 6	..	..	15·00	12·50	□ □

(b) Regional Issues

8   9

1958–67 *Wmk 179*   *Perf 15 × 14*

9	8	2½d red	..	..	35	50	□ □
10	9	3d lilac	..	..	35	30	□ □
		p. One centre phospnor band			20	20	□ □
11		4d blue	..	..	25	30	□ □
		p. Two phosphor bands	..		20	25	□ □

1968–69 *One centre phosphor band (4d values) or two phosphor bands (5d). No wmk*

12	9	4d sepia	..	..	20	25	□ □
13		4d vermilion	..	..	20	30	□ □
14		5d blue	..	..	20	40	□ □

For comprehensive listings of the Independent Postal Administration issues of Jersey, see Stanley Gibbons *Collect Channel Islands and Isle of Man Stamps.*

REGIONAL FIRST DAY COVERS

PRICES for First Day Covers listed below are for stamps, as indicated, used on illustrated envelopes and postmarked with operational cancellations (before 1964) or with special First Day of Issue cancellations (1964 onwards). First Day postmarks of 8 June 1964 and 7 February 1966 were of the machine cancellation "envelope" type.

£sd Issues

18 Aug. 1958	Guernsey 3d (No. 7)	8·00	☐
	Isle of Man 3d (No. 2)	20·00	☐
	Jersey 3d (No. 10)	8·00	☐
	Northern Ireland 3d (No. NI1)	20·00	☐
	Scotland 3d (No. S1)	6·00	☐
	Wales 3d (No. W1)	6·00	☐
29 Sept. 1958	Northern Ireland 6d, 1s 3d (Nos. NI3, NI5)	25·00	☐
	Scotland 6d, 1s 3d (Nos S3, S5)	12·00	☐
	Wales 6d, 1s 3d (Nos. W3, W5)	12·00	☐
8 June 1964	Guernsey 2½d (No. 6)	15·00	☐
	Isle of Man 2½d (No. 1)	20·00	☐
	Jersey 2½d (No. 9)	15·00	☐
7 Feb. 1966	Guernsey 4d (No. 8)	7·00	☐
	Isle of Man 4d (No. 3)	7·00	☐
	Jersey 4d (No. 11)	7·00	☐
	Northern Ireland 4d (No. NI2)	4·00	☐
	Scotland 4d (No. S2)	4·00	☐
	Wales 4d (No. W2)	4·00	☐
1 March 1967	Northern Ireland 9d, 1s 6d (Nos. NI4, NI6)	1·50	☐
	Scotland 9d, 1s 6d (Nos. S4, S6)	1·50	☐
	Wales 9d, 1s 6d (Nos. W4, W6)	1·50	☐
4 Sept. 1968	Guernsey 4d, 5d (Nos. 10, 12)	1·00	☐
	Isle of Man 4d, 5d (Nos. 5, 7)	1·75	☐
	Jersey 4d, 5d (Nos. 12, 14) ..	1·25	☐
	Northern Ireland 4d, 5d (Nos. NI8, NI10)	50	☐
	Scotland 4d, 5d (Nos. S9, S11)	50	☐
	Wales 4d, 5d (Nos. W9, W11)	50	☐

Decimal Issues

7 July 1971	Isle of Man 2½p, 3p, 5p, 7½p (Nos. 8/11)	3·50	☐
	Northern Ireland 2½p, 3p, 5p, 7½p (Nos. NI12/13, NI18, NI23)	4·50	☐
	Scotland 2½p, 3p, 5p, 7½p (Nos. S14/15, S20, S25)	2·50	☐
	Wales 2½p, 3p, 5p, 7½p (Nos. W13/14, W19, W24)	2·50	☐
23 Jan. 1974	Northern Ireland 3p, 3½p, 5½p, 8p (Nos. NI14/15, NI19, NI24)	1·50	☐
	Scotland 3p, 3½p, 5½p, 8p (Nos. S16/17, S21, S26)	1·50	☐
	Wales 3p, 3½p, 5½p, 8p (Nos. W15/16, W20, W25)	1·50	☐

6 Nov. 1974	Northern Ireland 4½p, (No. NI17)	1·00	☐
	Scotland 4½p (No. S19)	1·00	☐
	Wales 4½p (No. W18)	1·00	☐
14 Jan. 1976	Northern Ireland 6½p, 8½p (Nos. NI21, NI25)	60	☐
	Scotland 6½p, 8½p (Nos. S23, S27)	60	☐
	Wales 6½p, 8½p (Nos. W22, W26)	60	☐
20 Oct. 1976	Northern Ireland 10p, 11p (Nos. NI27, NI30)	1·00	☐
	Scotland 10p, 11p (Nos. S29, S32)	75	☐
	Wales 10p, 11p (Nos. W28, W31)	75	☐
18 Jan. 1978	Northern Ireland 7p, 9p, 10½p (Nos. NI22, NI26, NI29) ..	1·00	☐
	Scotland 7p, 9p, 10½p (Nos. S24, S28, S31)	75	☐
	Wales 7p, 9p, 10½p (Nos. W23, W27, W30)	75	☐
23 July 1980	Northern Ireland 12p, 13½p, 15p (Nos. NI31/3)	2·00	☐
	Scotland 12p, 13½p, 15p (Nos. S33/5)	1·75	☐
	Wales 12p, 13½p, 15p (Nos. W32/4)	1·75	☐
8 April 1981	Northern Ireland 11½p, 14p, 18p, 22p (Nos. NI34, NI38, NI45, NI52)	2·00	☐
	Scotland 11½p, 14p, 18p, 22p (Nos. S36, S40, S44, S47)	1·75	☐
	Wales 11½p, 14p, 18p, 22p (Nos. W35, W39, W46, W54)	1·75	☐
24 Feb. 1982	Northern Ireland 12½p, 15½p, 19½p, 26p (Nos. NI36, NI41, NI49, NI58)	4·25	☐
	Scotland 12½p, 15½p, 19½p, 26p (Nos. S38, S41, S45, S49)	3·75	☐
	Wales 12½p, 15½p, 19½p, 26p (Nos. W37, W42, W51, W61)	4·25	☐
27 April 1983	Northern Ireland 16p, 20½p, 28p (Nos. NI42, NI51, NI60)	6·50	☐
	Scotland 16p, 20½p, 28p (Nos. S42, S46, S50)	6·00	☐
	Wales 16p, 20½p, 28p (Nos. W43, W53, W63)	6·50	☐
23 Oct. 1984	Northern Ireland 13p, 17p, 22p, 31p (Nos. NI37, NI43, NI53, NI62)	4·50	☐
	Scotland 13p, 17p, 22p, 31p (Nos. S39, S43, S48, S51)	4·50	☐
	Wales 13p, 17p, 22p, 31p (Nos. W38, W44, W55, W65)	4·50	☐

Date	Description	Price	
7 Jan. 1986	*Northern Ireland* 12*p* (*No.* NI35)	1·25	☐
	Scotland 12*p* (*No.* S37) ..	1·25	☐
	Wales 12*p* (*No.* W36)	1·25	☐
6 Jan. 1987	*Northern Ireland* 18*p* (*No.* NI46)	2·00	☐
	Scotland 18*p* (*No.* S59)	2·00	☐
	Wales 18*p* (*No.* W47)	2·00	☐
8 Nov. 1988	*Northern Ireland* 14*p*, 19*p*, 23*p*, 32*p* (*Nos.* NI39, NI48, NI55, NI63)	4·50	☐
	Scotland 14*p*, 19*p*, 23*p*, 32*p* (*Nos.* S54, S61, S66, S75)	4·50	☐
	Wales 14*p*, 19*p*, 23*p*, 32*p* (*Nos.* W40, W50, W57, W66)	4·50	☐
28 Nov. 1989	*Northern Ireland* 15*p*, 20*p*, 24*p*, 34*p* (*Nos.* NI40, NI50, NI56, NI64)	4·00	☐
	Scotland 15*p*, 20*p*, 24*p*, 34*p* (*Nos.* S56, S63, S68, S76)	4·00	☐
	Wales 15*p*, 20*p*, 24*p*, 34*p* (*Nos.* W41, W52, W58, W67)	4·00	☐
4 Dec. 1990	*Northern Ireland* 17*p*, 22*p*, 26*p*, 37*p*, (*Nos.* NI44, NI54, NI59, NI65)	4·50	☐
	Scotland 17*p*, 22*p*, 26*p*, 37*p*, (*Nos.* S58, S65, S71, S77)	4·50	☐
	Wales 17*p*, 22*p*, 26*p*, 37*p* (*Nos.* W45, W56, W62, W68)	4·50	☐
3 Dec. 1991	*Northern Ireland* 18*p*, 24*p*, 28*p*, 39*p*, (*Nos.* NI47, NI57, NI61, NI66)	4·00	☐
	Scotland 18*p*, 24*p*, 28*p*, 39*p*, (*Nos.* S60, S69, S73, S78)	4·00	☐
	Wales 18*p*, 24*p*, 28*p*, 39*p*, (*Nos.* W48, W59, W64, W69)	4·00	☐

POSTAGE DUE STAMPS

PERFORATION. All postage due stamps are perf 14 × 15.

D 1   D 2

1914–23 Wmk Type **96** (*Royal Cypher* ('*Simple*')) *sideways*

D1	D 1	½d green	50	50	☐	☐
D2		1d red	50	50	☐	☐
D3		1½d brown	40·00	15·00	☐	☐
D4		2d black	50	40	☐	☐
D5		3d violet	2·00	1·00	☐	☐
D6		4d green	25·00	3·00	☐	☐
D7		5d brown	5·00	2·00	☐	☐
D8		1s blue	25·00	2·50	☐	☐
	Set of 8		90·00	22·00	☐	☐

1924–31 Wmk Type **107** (*Block* G v R) *sideways*

D10	D 1	½d green	50	30	☐	☐
D11		1d red	50	30	☐	☐
D12		1½d brown	35·00	15·00	☐	☐
D13		2d black	1·00	40	☐	☐
D14		3d violet	1·50	40	☐	☐
D15		4d green	10·00	2·00	☐	☐
D16		5d brown	24·00	20·00	☐	☐
D17		1s blue	6·00	75	☐	☐
D18	D 2	2s 6d purple/*yellow* ..	30·00	1·75	☐	☐
	Set of 9		95·00	40·00	☐	☐

1936–37 Wmk Type **125** (E 8 R) *sideways*

D19	D 1	½d green	7·50	6·00	☐	☐
D20		1d red	1·50	1·60	☐	☐
D21		2d black	7·00	6·00	☐	☐
D22		3d violet	1·50	1·60	☐	☐
D23		4d green	23·00	17·00	☐	☐
D24a		5d brown	15·00	17·00	☐	☐
D25		1s blue	11·00	4·75	☐	☐
D26	D 2	2s 6d purple/*yellow*	£250	8·50	☐	☐
	Set of 8		£300	60·00	☐	☐

1937–38 Wmk Type **127** (G vi R) *sideways*

D27	D 1	½d green	8·00	3·25	☐	☐
D28		1d red	2·50	40	☐	☐
D29		2d black	2·50	40	☐	☐
D30		3d violet	10·00	40	☐	☐
D31		4d green	60·00	7·50	☐	☐
D32		5d brown	10·00	1·00	☐	☐
D33		1s blue	55·00	1·00	☐	☐
D34	D 2	2s 6d purple/*yellow* ..	55·00	3·00	☐	☐
	Set of 8		£180	15·00	☐	☐

1951–52 *Colours changed and new value* (1½d). *Wmk Type* **127** (G vi R) *sideways*

D35	D 1	½d orange	1·50	2·00	☐	☐
D36		1d blue	1·00	75	☐	☐
D37		1½d green	1·50	1·75	☐	☐
D38		4d blue	26·00	9·00	☐	☐
D39		1s brown	23·00	4·00	☐	☐
	Set of 5		48·00	16·00	☐	☐

1954–55 Wmk Type **153** (*Mult. Tudor Crown and* E 2 R) *sideways*

D40	D 1	½d orange	.. ..	4·00	2·50	□	□
D41		2d black	.. ..	2·00	2·00	□	□
D42		3d violet	.. ..	42·00	25·00	□	□
D43		4d blue	.. ..	15·00	16·00	□	□
D44		5d brown	.. ..	20·00	6·50	□	□
D45	D 2	2s 6d purple/*yellow*	..	£120	3·00	□	□
		Set of 6		£180	50·00	□	□

1955–57 Wmk Type **165** (*Mult. St Edward's Crown and* E 2 R) *sideways*

D46	D 1	½d orange	.. ..	1·50	2·25	□	□
D47		1d blue	.. ..	4·00	1·25	□	□
D48		1½d green	.. ..	3·75	3·75	□	□
D49		2d black	.. ..	35·00	3·00	□	□
D50		3d violet	.. ..	4·50	1·25	□	□
D51		4d blue	.. ..	18·00	3·00	□	□
D52		5d brown	.. ..	27·00	2·00	□	□
D53		1s brown	.. ..	65·00	1·25	□	□
D54	D 2	2s 6d purple/*yellow*	..	£160	7·50	□	□
D55		5s red/*yellow*	..	90·00	19·00	□	□
		Set of 10	.. .. ..	£375	40·00	□	□

1959–63 Wmk Type **179** (*Mult. St Edward's Crown*) *sideways*

D56	D 1	½d orange	.. ..	10	45	□	□
D57		1d blue	.. ..	10	15	□	□
D58		1½d green	.. ..	90	2·00	□	□
D59		2d black	.. ..	1·25	30	□	□
D60		3d violet	.. ..	40	15	□	□
D61		4d blue	.. ..	40	20	□	□
D62		5d brown	.. ..	45	45	□	□
D63		6d purple	.. ..	60	30	□	□
D64		1s brown	.. ..	1·40	25	□	□
D65	D 2	2s 6d purple/*yellow*	..	4·00	45	□	□
D66		5s red/*yellow*	..	7·50	80	□	□
D67		10s blue/*yellow*	..	9·00	4·00	□	□
D68		£1 black/*yellow*	..	45·00	7·00	□	□
		Set of 13	.. ..	60·00	15·00	□	□

1968–69 *Design size* 22½ × 19 *mm No wmk*

D69	D 1	2d black	.. ..	40	40	□	□
D70		3d violet	.. ..	25	40	□	□
D71		4d blue	.. ..	25	40	□	□
D72		5d orange-brown	..	4·50	5·25	□	□
D73		6d purple	.. ..	80	60	□	□
D74		1s brown	.. ..	80	1·00	□	□
		Set of 6	.. .. ..	6·50	7·00	□	□

1968–69 *Design size* 21½ × 17½ *mm No wmk*

D75	D 1	4d blue	.. ..	5·00		□	□
D76		8d red	.. ..	1·25		□	□

D 3

D 4

Decimal Currency

1970–77 *No wmk*

D77	D 3	½p turquoise-blue		10	20	□	□
D78		1p reddish purple		10	15	□	□
D79		2p myrtle-green	..	10	15	□	□
D80		3p ultramarine		15	15	□	□
D81		4p yellow-brown	..	15	15	□	□
D82		5p violet	.. ..	20	20	□	□
D83		7p red-brown	..	35	45	□	□
D84	D 4	10p red	.. ..	30	20	□	□
D85		11p green	..	50	60	□	□
D86		20p brown	..	60	50	□	□
D87		50p ultramarine	..	1·50	40	□	□
D88		£1 black	..	2·75	60	□	□
D89		£5 orange-yellow and black		25·00	2·00	□	□
		Set of 13	..	30·00	5·00	□	□

D77/82, D84, D86/8 *Presentation Pack* .. 10·00 □

D77/88 *Presentation Pack* .. 6·00 □

D 5

D 6

1982 *No wmk*

D 90	D 5	1p lake	.. ..	10	10	□	□
D 91		2p bright blue	..	10	10	□	□
D 92		3p deep mauve	..	10	15	□	□
D 93		4p deep blue	..	10	20	□	□
D 94		5p sepia	.. ..	10	20	□	□
D 95	D 6	10p light brown	..	15	25	□	□
D 96		20p olive-green	..	30	30	□	□
D 97		25p deep greenish blue		40	70	□	□
D 98		50p grey-black	..	75	50	□	□
D 99		£1 red	.. ..	1·50	50	□	□
D100		£2 turquoise-blue	..	3·00	50	□	□
D101		£5 dull orange	..	7·50	50	□	□
		Set of 12	..	12·50	3·75	□	□
		Set of 12 *Gutter Pairs*	..	30·00		□	
		Presentation Pack	..	14·00		□	

ROYAL MAIL POSTAGE LABELS

These imperforate labels were issued as an experiment by the Post Office. Special microprocessor controlled machines were installed at post offices in Cambridge, London, Shirley (Southampton) and Windsor to provide an after-hours sales service to the public. The machines printed and dispensed the labels according to the coins inserted and the buttons operated by the customer. Values were initially available in $\frac{1}{2}$p steps to 16p and in addition, the labels were sold at philatelic counters in two packs containing either 3 values ($3\frac{1}{2}$, $12\frac{1}{2}$, 16p) or 32 values ($\frac{1}{2}$p to 16p).

From 28 August 1984 the machines were adjusted to provide values up to 17p. After 31 December 1984 labels including $\frac{1}{2}$p values were withdrawn. The machines were taken out of service on 30 April 1985.

Machine postage-paid impression in red on phosphorised paper with grey-green background design. No watermark. Imperforate.

1984 (1 May–28 Aug)				
Set of 32 ($\frac{1}{2}$p to 16p)	..	20·00	30·00	☐ ☐
Set of 3 ($3\frac{1}{2}$p, $12\frac{1}{2}$p, 16p)		4·00	4·50	☐ ☐
Set of 3 on First Day Cover				
(1 May)			6·50	☐
Set of 2 ($16\frac{1}{2}$p, 17p)				
(28 August)		6·00	6·00	☐ ☐

OFFICIAL STAMPS

Various Stamps of Queen Victoria and King Edward VII Overprinted in Black.

I.R.	**I. R.**	**O. W.**
OFFICIAL	**OFFICIAL**	**OFFICIAL**
(O 1)	(O 2)	(O 3)
ARMY	**ARMY**	
OFFICIAL	**OFFICIAL**	**GOVᵀ PARCELS**
(O 4)	(O 5)	(O 7)
BOARD OF EDUCATION	**R.H. OFFICIAL**	**ADMIRALTY OFFICIAL**
(O 8)	(O 9)	(O 10)

1 Inland Revenue

Overprinted with Types O 1 or O 2 (5s, 10s, £1)

1882–1901 *Queen Victoria*

O 1	52	$\frac{1}{2}$d green	..	..	12·00	3·00	☐ ☐
O 5		$\frac{1}{2}$d blue	..	..	25·00	15·00	☐ ☐
O13	67	$\frac{1}{2}$d vermilion		..	1·50	50	☐ ☐
O17		$\frac{1}{2}$d green	..		4·00	3·00	☐ ☐
O 3	57	1d lilac (Die II)	..		1·50	65	☐ ☐
O 6	64	$2\frac{1}{2}$d lilac	..	..	£110	35·00	☐ ☐
O14	70	$2\frac{1}{2}$d purple on blue			50·00	4·00	☐ ☐
O 4	43	6d grey (Plate 18)	..		75·00	20·00	☐ ☐
O18	75	6d purple on red	..		£100	22·00	☐ ☐
O 7	65	1s green	..	..	£2500	£450	☐ ☐
O15	78	1s green	..	..	£200	20·00	☐ ☐
O19		1s green and red	.		£600	£100	☐ ☐
O 9	59	5s red	..	..	£1300	£400	☐ ☐
O10	60	10s blue	..	..	£2250	£475	☐ ☐
O11	61	£1 brown (Wmk Crowns)	..	..	£18000		☐ ☐
O12		£1 brown (Wmk Orbs)	..	..	£25000		☐ ☐
O16		£1 green	..	..	£3750	£450	☐ ☐

1902–04 *King Edward VII*

O20	79	½d blue-green	17·00	1·50 ☐ ☐
O21		1d red	10·00	70 ☐ ☐
O22	82	2½d blue	£400	60·00 ☐ ☐
O23	79	6d purple	£85000	£65000 ☐ ☐
O24	89	1s green and red	£500	65·00 ☐ ☐
O25	91	5s red	£4000	£1300 ☐ ☐
O26	92	10s blue	£15000	£9500 ☐ ☐
O27	93	£1 green	£12000	£6000 ☐ ☐

2 Office of Works

Overprinted with Type O 3

1896–1902 *Queen Victoria*

O31	67	½d vermilion	90·00	40·00 ☐ ☐
O32		½d green	£150	75·00 ☐ ☐
O33	57	1d lilac (Die II)	£150	40·00 ☐ ☐
O34	74	5d dull pur & bl	£750	£150 ☐ ☐
O35	77	10d dull pur & red	£1300	£225 ☐ ☐

1902–03 *King Edward VII*

O36	79	½d blue-green	£350	80·00 ☐ ☐
O37		1d red	£350	80·00 ☐ ☐
O38	81	2d green and red	£600	75·00 ☐ ☐
O39	82	2½d blue	£700	£200 ☐ ☐
O40	88	10d purple and red	£5000	£1500 ☐ ☐

3 Army

Overprinted with Types O 4 (½d, 1d) or O 5 (2½d, 6d)

1896–1901 *Queen Victoria*

O41	67	½d vermilion	1·50	75 ☐ ☐
O42		½d green	1·75	4·00 ☐ ☐
O43	57	1d lilac (Die II)	1·50	75 ☐ ☐
O44	70	2½d purple on blue	4·00	3·00 ☐ ☐
O45	75	6d purple on red	16·00	10·00 ☐ ☐

Overprinted with Type O 4

1902 *King Edward VII*

O48	79	½d blue-green	2·00	65 ☐ ☐
O49		1d red	1·50	55 ☐ ☐
O50		6d purple	60·00	32·00 ☐ ☐

4 Government Parcels

Overprinted with Type O 7

1883–1900 *Queen Victoria*

O69	57	1d lilac (Die II)	28·00	8·00 ☐ ☐
O61	62	1½d lilac	£100	25·00 ☐ ☐
O65	68	1½d purple and green	14·00	2·00 ☐ ☐
O70	69	2d green and red	45·00	7·00 ☐ ☐
O71	73	4½d green and red	£100	75·00 ☐ ☐
O62	63	6d green	£800	£275 ☐ ☐
O66	75	6d purple on red	28·00	10·00 ☐ ☐
O63	64	9d green	£650	£180 ☐ ☐
O67	76	9d purple and blue	55·00	15·00 ☐ ☐
O64	44	1s brown (Plate 13)	£425	70·00 ☐ ☐
O64c		1s brown (Plate 14)	£750	£110 ☐ ☐
O68	78	1s green	£120	70·00 ☐ ☐
O72		1s green and red	£160	50·00 ☐ ☐

1902 *King Edward VII*

O74	79	1d red	17·00	6·00 ☐ ☐
O75	81	2d green and red	65·00	18·00 ☐ ☐
O76	79	6d purple	£100	18·00 ☐ ☐
O77	87	9d purple and blue	£225	50·00 ☐ ☐
O78	89	1s green and red	£350	85·00 ☐ ☐

5 Board of Education

Overprinted with Type O 8

1902 *Queen Victoria*

O81	74	5d dull pur & bl	£525	£100 ☐ ☐
O82	78	1s green and red	£950	£375 ☐ ☐

1902–04 *King Edward VII*

O83	79	½d blue-green	18·00	6·00 ☐ ☐
O84		1d red	18·00	5·00 ☐ ☐
O85	82	2½d blue	£500	50·00 ☐ ☐
O86	85	5d purple and blue	£2000	£950 ☐ ☐
O87	89	1s green and red	£35000	£25000 ☐ ☐

6 Royal Household

Overprinted with Type O 9

1902 *King Edward VII*

O91	79	½d blue-green	£150	95·00 ☐ ☐
O92		1d red	£130	85·00 ☐ ☐

7 Admiralty

Overprinted with Type O 10

1903 *King Edward VII*

O107	79	½d blue-green	7·00	4·00 ☐ ☐
O102		1d red	5·00	2·50 ☐ ☐
O103	80	1½d purple and green	60·00	45·00 ☐ ☐
O104	81	2d green and red	£100	50·00 ☐ ☐
O105	82	2½d blue	£120	40·00 ☐ ☐
O106	83	3d purple on yellow	£100	38·00 ☐ ☐

Minimum Price. The minimum price quoted is 10p. This represents a handling charge rather than a basis for valuing common stamps. Where the actual value of a stamp is less than 10p this may be apparent when set prices are shown, particularly for sets including a number of 10p stamps. It therefore follows that in valuing common stamps the 10p catalogue price should not be reckoned automatically since it covers a variation in real scarcity.

Stanley Gibbons STANDARD Great Britain Album

Based on the popular DAVO Great Britain standard album and therefore including all the following special features.

- ★ High Capacity
- ★ Superb Quality Materials
- ★ Handmade to the Highest Specifications
- ★ Attractive Cover Design
- ★ Selected Stamp Illustrations
- ★ Professional Layout
- ★ Luxury Slip Case
- ★ Exceptional Value for Money

PLUS – we have added extra pages for the Machin definitives providing spaces for the popular phosphor band variations.

Because of its large size and high capacity, it is able to house an entire Great Britain collection from 1840 to 1992 in a single volume and it therefore represents fantastic value for money when compared with other albums, some of which are already in three separate volumes.

POSITIVELY THE BEST VALUE
GREAT BRITAIN ALBUM ON THE MARKET

Item 5284STSG **Stanley Gibbons Standard Great Britain Album 1840–1992** £39.95

FREE 1993 supplement with every album ordered before 28th January 1994.

Note: The 1993 supplement for the Stanley Gibbons Great Britain Standard Album (Item 5284ST93) will be published in January, price to be announced.

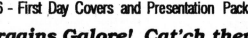

A GUIDE TO THE DECIMAL DEFINITIVES
Some hints on how to sort and collect them

The small-size decimal 'Machin' definitives have been around for over twenty years now and during that time have been subject to numerous experiments and changes in their method of production; not to mention the host of variants available from coils and booklet panes and a good number of unintentional errors and varieties thrown in for good measure.

This has resulted in one of the most interesting stamp issues ever with a great many collectors studying it in tremendous detail. It does not have to be complicated however and each collector can make his own decision as to the depth into which he wishes to go into it.

Taking just one stamp of each value and colour there are at present nearly 100 items to collect, while *Collect British Stamps*, which differentiates between the photogravure and lithographic printings and the phosphorised paper and phosphor banded issues, now lists over 200 different stamps and if you add the various non-value indicator (NVI) stamps (SG 1445-52, 1511-16 and 1664-66) this takes the total even higher. Beyond this there are all sorts of possibilities — gum differences, varying phosphor band widths and lengths, value positions, paper types and head sizes to mention only a few —

It is my intention in this article to take a few of these factors and describe briefly how one can differentiate between them.

Sorting Litho and Photogravure Printings

Let us take first the method of printing. This catalogue currently divides the main decimal Machins listing (X841-X1058) into six different sections;

(a) Photogravure printed by Harrison and Sons with phosphor bands.

(b) Photogravure printed by Harrisons on phosphorised paper.

(c) Photogravure printed by Harrisons on ordinary paper.

(d) Lithographically (Litho) printed by John Waddington.

(e) Litho printed by Questa

(f) Litho printed by Walsall

NVI stamps and the stamps with large oval (elliptical) perforation holes are listed separately, the latter in a new section beginning at Y1667.

There is therefore a basic distinction between stamps printed by photogravure and those printed by lithography. Sorting the two is not as difficult as it sounds and with a little experience it should become easy to tell which method of production was employed for a particular stamp. All you need is a reasonably good glass giving a magnification of ×4 or more (×10 is even better!).

The image on a photogravure stamp is created from a pattern or 'screen', of minute dots which are not evident when looking at the stamp without a glass but show up quite clearly under magnification, especially in the Queen's face and around the margin of the stamp design where it meets the white background of the paper. Now look at the value; here also, what looks to the naked eye like a straight line is in fact made up of rows of tiny little dots.

'Screens' of dots are also used in the production of litho printed stamps but they are only required where the printer is attempting to produce shades and tints as is necessary in the Queen's head portion of the stamp. Where solid colour is used, as in the background of the majority of values, there is no need to resort to a

The tiny dots of the printing screen give uneven edges to the values on photogravure stamps (left). Litho values have clean, clear outlines (right).

screen of dots and the background is printed as a solid mass of colour. If you look at the margins or the values of stamps produced in this way you will not see any evidence of dots — just a clear clean break between the inked portion of the stamp and the uninked white of the paper.

Unfortunately this simple test is rather complicated by the fact that on some of the first litho printed Machins, notably the early 5p values in light violet and claret printed by Questa, the background of the stamp was produced, not by printing in solid colour but with a screen of dots. Magnification of these stamps however shows the screened background of the Litho stamps to be much coarser than the photogravure versions. Strangely enough the early 2p and 75p values of Questa and the 4p of John Waddington, although having dark, solid backgrounds all showed evidence of screening dots around the stamp margins but none in the values so the 'dot' test remains valid.

As an aside it is worth mentioning that the regionals are a lot more complex in this regard but since there is no regional value which has been printed by both photogravure and litho, this fortunately does not present too much of a problem.

In this article in last year's edition of *Collect British Stamps* I remarked that it was fortunate that, among the Litho printed Machins, there were only three values which had been produced by more than one printer (plus the 1st and 2nd class NVIs and the 15p and 20p Penny Black Anniversary stamps of 1990) and that all of these could be differentiated by measuring the perforations. At that time all the Questa stamps were perf 15×14 while those of Waddington (in the case of the 4p) and Walsall (all the others) were perf 14.

This has now been complicated by the fact that the booklets containing 2nd class NVI stamps issued in April 1993 are all perf 15×14 (with an extra large oval, or elliptical perforation hole between each stamp in the pane) — whether they come from Questa or Walsall printings. The work of the two printers is not differentiated in this catalogue as they do not, individually, conform to the criteria for separate listing but with a little experience and a magnifying glass it should not be too difficult to identify them.

The main areas of difference are in the crown and hair and in the folds of Her Majesty's dress. As can be seen in the illustrations on page 132, individual folds in the dress, lines of shading in the hair and jewels in the crown are much more clearly defined on the Walsall printing than they are on the Questa version. This is especially noticeable in the central diadem in the crown where the jewels stand out on the Walsall stamp but are almost 'lost' in the Questa one.

There are other differences, particularly in the phosphor bands which run across the perforations on Walsall stamps, while the Questa types have 'bars of phosphor' which stop just short of the tops and bottom edges, these are most clearly seen using an ultraviolet lamp but they can also be seen with a reasonably powerful magnifying glass.

After a while it should become a fairly simple job to sort litho and photogravure printings 'at a glance', the generally softer more subtle tonal quality of the latter being superior to the flatter, harsher image which even the best litho printing can achieve.

Similarly the work of the two litho printers should become more or less immediately identifiable with a little experience.

Much of the interest surrounding the decimal Machins stems from the depth to which they can be studied and the vast number of collectable varieties which have been issued. The existence of many of these stamps can be attributed to nothing more than the need to provide values to cover new postage rates (i.e. inflation), however it is also true that, just as technology has resulted in huge advances in almost every field during the past 20 years so, it has also led to significant changes in both the techniques of stamp production and in the way in which mail is sorted and conveyed to its destination.

Leaving mail handling for the time being, let us consider some of the ways in which the 'quality' of the stamps themselves have changed over the years, commencing with a fairly simple aspect of this — gum.

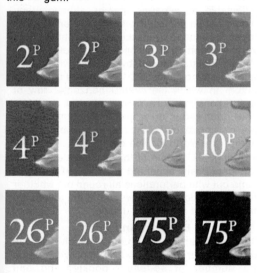

Several values exist with the numerals shown in different styles, in each case the left hand value is the first type while the right hand is type II.

Gum Types

There have been three types of gum used in the production of decimal 'Machins'; Gum Arabic, Poly Vinyl Alcohol and Poly Vinyl Alcohol Dextrin.

(i) Gum Arabic ('GA') a clear shiny gum which shows up quite obviously when a light is shone across the back of the stamp.

(ii) Poly Vinyl Alcohol ('PVA') a matt white or slightly cream coloured gum sometimes mottled in appearance — almost invisible when a light is shone across it. At one time it seemed that PVA had become a thing of the past but in recent years it has appeared on certain Litho printings and also on Enschedé photogravure stamps.

(iii) Polyvinyl Alcohol, Dextrin ('PVAD' or 'Dex') as PVA in general appearance except that a greenish blue tint has been added to the gum in order to make it more visible — the strength of this tint does tend to vary somewhat and in the case of some of the litho printings has been omitted altogether although, we are assured, the gum technically remained PVAD.

Changes to the Design and Paper

Initially, with a top value of 9p there was no difficulty in accommodating reasonably broad numerals in the lower left corner of the stamp. However a value such as 20½p could not easily be fitted into the same area. For this reason the numerals were redrawn in a narrower style. The 2p, 3p magenta, 4p greenish blue, 10p light orange, 26p red and 75p all exist with both styles as does the 1p although this is, not surprisingly, rather more difficult to identify. These changes (apart from the 1p) are not listed in *Collect British Stamps* but full details may be found in the Stanley Gibbons *Great Britain Concise Catalogue*.

Another field which has been the subject of 'improvement' is paper. Basically there are two types; phosphorised and non-phosphorised. With only a couple of exceptions, stamps with phosphor bands were all printed on non-phosphorised paper — this in turn can split into three further types which are most easily differentiated using an ultraviolet lamp.

The first decimal Machins were printed on what is known as Original Coated Paper ('OCP'), a low fluorescence paper which appears slightly greyish under the lamp with the phosphor bands appearing dark grey. Only the original twelve values up to the 9p orange and black exist on

'OCP' because later the same year we saw the introduction of a new paper, generally known as 'FCP'.

Fluorescent Coated Paper ('FCP') first appeared in September 1971. FCP is pure white under the lamp with the phosphor bands again appearing grey. This paper was used for all

Stamps with trimmed perfs (left) should be classed as damaged while those with true imperf margins (right) are collectable.

stamps on which phosphor bands were printed from 1971 to 1991 when a new printing of the 18p bright green produced by the Dutch firm of Enschedé was issued on a new non-fluorescent paper which appears dark under the lamp (although the phosphor band, as will be mentioned later, *is* fluorescent). Since then other stamps have appeared on non-fluorescent paper, including subsequent Enschedé printings, NVI stamps from booklets and the stamps in the Beatrix Potter prestige booklet.

Stamps with Imperforate Edges

One field which is not covered by this catalogue but which is relatively easy to identify and is therefore popular with some collectors is that of stamps with one or two sides imperforate from booklet panes.

From the time the first British stamp booklets appeared in 1904, the stamps contained within them were printed in large reels, perforated, made up with interleaving sheets' and covers, stitched and finally guillotined into the little

booklets sold in Post Offices. Stitched booklets began to be phased out in the late 1970's being replaced by 'folder' types but once again multiple booklets were made up and then guillotined. Ideally, when the booklets were guillotined, the cuts coincided exactly with the centre of the rows of perforation holes. In practice however this was very difficult to achieve with the result that the perforations were frequently cut off the stamps producing the dreaded 'trimmed perfs' or 'straight edges' so despised by collectors. In response to complaints from collectors, Royal Mail came up with the solution, adopted long ago in countries like Canada, of not pre-perforating the stamps. where they were going to be guillotined anyway.

Thus the outer edges of the pane (or in some cases the 'long' edges of the pane only) were intentionally imperforate producing stamps deliberately issued with either one or two edges without perforations. These are quite collectable as separate stamps although they should not be confused with the earlier 'straight edges', produced by inaccurate guillotining. It is worth mentioning at this point a batch of 1st class NVI booklets produced by Walsall which contained 4-stamp panes (SG 1516) imperf at top and bottom in which the central horizontal row of perforations measure 13 instead of 14. As these were produced in error they are not included in this catalogue but complete panes and single stamps are worth looking out for.

During 1993, some of the NVI booklets which had previously appeared with imperf margins came out with perforations all round but whether this is an indication that we are about to see the end of imperf margins is unclear.

Booklets and Coils

One last aspect of change which can be attributed purely to 'product improvement' is the number of *se-tenant* booklet and coil combinations. To be sure, these originated in the pre-decimal era but as postage rates have increased the number of combinations required in order to provide a quantity of first and second class postage stamps, dispensed in a handy package for a single coin, has led to a rapid increase in the number of such panes and coils. Very collectable in their own right of course, it is these which provide some of the gems of the standard Machin collection. It is well worth while therefore keeping an eye on Royal Mail's booklet issues to ensure that you do not miss anything. Such information can of course be readily gleaned from *Gibbons Stamp Monthly* in which specialist Machin dealer John Deering keeps you up to date with all the latest news.

Technical Improvements

Let us now turn our attention to the ways in which improved (i.e. faster) mail handling techniques have affected the stamps which we collect. Basically this comes down to one word — Phosphor.

Stamps on phosphor printed paper (left) have a blotchy appearance when compared with phosphorised paper issues (right).

Phosphor

The twelve stamps ranging in value from ½p to 9p, issued on 15 February 1971 were all printed on ordinary coated paper and overprinted with phosphor bands, one band on the 2½p, the then 2nd class postage rate, and two bands on the other values. Since that time there have been a number of developments which have affected the phosphor on British stamps but basically they can be split into two types — phosphor printed on to the surface of the paper and phosphor which is actually incorporated into the paper coating — prior to the stamps being printed.

Taking the printed phosphor first, this is nowadays reserved for stamps covering the 2nd class postage rate plus some values which are included in booklet panes which cannot be printed on phosphorised paper. Except in error all phosphors used in the production of British stamps are 'short wave', i.e. they can only be activated by short wave ultraviolet light. This remained largely unchanged right through until the late 1980s when Harrisons developed a new phosphor ink known as 'A' phosphor or 'new' phosphor which is less obvious to the naked eye (it had been felt that the old phosphor bands detracted from the appearance of the stamps) and also appears paler under the ultraviolet lamp. In late 1991 a printing of the 18p, green made by Enschedé incorporated a fluorescent component in the phosphor band which, while it does not show up to the eye, gives a bright yellow-green reaction under the lamp.

Further stamps have now appeared with these fluorescent phosphor bands.

All Over Phosphor

This affects only the 1p, 2p and 10p stamps and results from an experiment in which the phosphor was *printed* on to the paper before the stamp image. The three stamps concerned (SG X846, X850 and X887) have a matt surface when held up to the light in order to show a reflection and are frequently rather blotchy in appearance. Under ultraviolet light they show no phosphor bands and are uniformly dark in appearance.

'All over phosphor' is sometimes used to describe a situation whereby, either intentionally or by accident, a thin coating of phosphor covers the entire surface of the stamp in addition to the phosphor bands. These are difficult to detect with the naked eye although, when reflected against the light, the area of the stamp between the phosphor bands is frequently somewhat darker than is normal. Such variations are of considerable interest to specialists but fall outside the scope of this catalogue. Details may be found in the *Stanley Gibbons Great Britain Specialised Catalogue*.

Phosphorised Paper

This is often referred to as Phosphor Coated Paper ('PCP') or (in the case of more recent issues) Advanced Coated Paper ('ACP') but, as far as *Collect British Stamps* is concerned, all variants are covered by the term 'phosphorised paper'.

On these stamps the phosphor is incorporated into the coating of the paper and is not itself printed on the stamps at all. This method was used first for a printing of the 1s.6d. pre-decimal Machin (743c) followed by the recess printed 10p of 1970 (829). The 4½p Machin (X865) exists on phosphorised paper but this also had phosphor bands printed on top and is therefore difficult to distinguish from a normal 4½p without the phosphorised coating.

This was followed by the 8½p issued in 1976 (X938) which had a phosphorised coating without phosphor bands and from 1979/80 all new definitives from sheets and coils below the 50p value have been issued on phosphorised paper; the only values still being printed with phosphor bands being the current second class mail stamps or stamps from certain booklet panes.

Specialists differentiate between varying grades of phosphorised paper but from 1984 a more significant change over to a brighter, more fluorescent, paper was made. This is generally known as Advanced Coated Paper ('ACP') which shows up much more brightly under the ultra-violet lamp — even brighter than FCP and with a stronger afterglow.

Latest Developments — Elliptical Perforations

Large oval perforation holes, the length of three normal perforations, first appeared on the redesigned 'Castle' high values in 1992 as a security measure. They have also been used in the 1993 'Gift Giving' Greetings stamps and for the £10 'Britannia' stamp.

Their first appearance on Machins was on the NVI stamp booklets issued on 6 April 1993. These are listed in this edition of *Collect British Stamps* as 1664/6 and comprise the 1st class stamp, photogravure printed by Harrisons and litho printed by Walsall and the 2nd class stamp, litho printed by both Questa and Walsall. This last stamp is listed under a single number (1665) in the catalogue but interested collectors can differentiate between the two printings using the method already described (see illustration above).

Questa (Top) and Walsall printings of the 2nd class NVI stamp showing the greater detail in the crown and hair of the Walsall version.

Sheet stamps with elliptical perforations first appeared on 27 April when a 6p value printed by Joh Enschedé en Zonen was issued; this has since been followed by 1p, 5p, 10p, 30p and 35p values. These are listed as a completely separate set in this and other Stanley Gibbons catalogues starting with Y1667.

Self-Adhesive Machins

Two countries, Sierra Leone and Tonga were prominent in the early development of self-adhesive stamps. Sierra Leone issued the first such stamps in 1964 in a shape of a map of the country and continued to use them in a variety of shapes and sizes until 1972 when they returned to more conventional stamp formats. Tonga's first self-adhesive were issued in 1969 and they continued to use this type of stamp until 1985 although from 1980 onwards they abandoned the 'free form' styles for stamps which were, at least, conventional in shape.

Other countries including Gibraltar, Montserrat, Mauritius and Norfolk Island utilised self-adhesives for special issues but the only large country to experiment with them was the USA one of whose 1974 Christmas stamps was self-adhesive. The experiment was considered a failure and it has not been until the last few years that self-adhesives have started to be used again with Australia, France, Germany, Ireland, New Zealand and others issuing them. Postal users apparently find them very convenient to use and, in those countries which have them, the proportion of self-adhesives used on normal mail has increased rapidly.

In October 1993 Royal Mail issued self-adhesive stamps for the first time in books of 20 stamps. The stamps are the normal low-value Machin shape and size but in a horizontal rather than vertical format with the Queen's head reduced in size accordingly.

Initially they have appeared as '1st' class NVI stamps only and the 'perforations', although die-cut, are designed to look as much like normal perforations as possible. 'Elliptical' perforations appear at either side.

Both self adhesives and the elliptical perforation Machins described above represent new developments in British stamps and, perhaps, offer an opportunity to those who have not considered specialising in any aspect of Machins to start a new collection 'on the ground floor'.

Warning

I hope that this article has set out some of the factors which make the decimal Machins such an interesting field to collect and study and gives some assistance in identifying the stamps concerned. If, as a beginner, the field seems complex and impossibly large, do not worry — set your own boundaries before you start. Make the decision that you will ignore any of the factors which you are not happy about and, for example, concentrate your attentions upon those variations which are plainly visible to the naked eye. It is possible however that after a few months you could be actively seeking what at present seem the most obscure varieties, phosphor screens, head types, print directions, perforator changes and any number of other features of these fascinating stamps — you have been warned!

Hugh Jefferies